TRACY McGRATH & JACK

*T*wo *Feathers*

A TRUE STORY OF THE
UNBREAKABLE BOND
OF A MOTHER AND SON

First Edition, 2020
KDP ISBN: 9798657592917

Art Direction by Tracy McGrath

Designed by Joana Nunes
Cover Illustration copyright © 2020 by Joana Nunes

Published by Two Feathers Publishing
twofeatherspublishing@gmail.com

For Jennifer, who has stayed the course with me and gently healed my broken mind around the edges of the gaping hole that is grief.

For Jack, I may have given you life, however it is you who has breathed life back into me, and when I listen closely I hear your footsteps dancing across my heart.

'Mumsie it's you and me....and Teddy'

CONTENTS

PROLOGUE

MY LIFE, MY LOVE, MY SON

I love you son, you have loved me with every ounce of honesty and truth. You are my best friend, my life, my soul, my spirit. It was only you who gave me the strength I needed to face those early, very dark days eleven years ago now. I clearly recall your gentle pat on my back when I softly cried, wondering where would we live? How would we survive? I recall sleeping with you next to me as you clutched your little rosary, gazing at your sweet innocent seven-year-old face, and wondering why we were chosen to take this journey together.

Just this week I visited you in circumstances no mother should have to. I chose your clothing, brushed your hair, and prepared you for your final journey to that soft pink cloud we spoke of. I kissed your brow, stroked each finger, and tickled you softly under your chin, your soft downy chin, a sign of your eighteen years. I felt a compelling need to lay on the floor beside you. As I lay on my side I imagined myself with you one day, and as you had done eleven years before, and many times in between, you comforted me. I lay there next to you curled on my side, with my cheek resting on my hands, silently asking you to please show me a sign that you were with me; that you hadn't left me completely. Seconds later the lights flickered, then dimmed and brightened, and I felt a gentle tap on the bottom of my left foot. Oh, Jack, I thanked you then, and I thank you again today for providing me with such comfort and peace.

My Jack, you are still now and will always be my champion, my warrior, my defender, my protector, my son. As I lay beside you, with you comforting me, I recalled those early days of your life when we bonded together as mother and son. Middle of the night bottles were so intimate and special. It was as if we were the only two humans awake in the whole world. Your beautiful blue-grey eyes gazing up at me, eyelids drooping as you became drunk on milk. I gently rocked you, patting your little back, softly singing Annie's Song by John Denver, which always soothed you, as you gently drifted to a soft and secure slumber in my arms.

As you lay beside me this week, I honour you, my quirky, beautiful, selfless, kind, deeply sensitive son Jack, with our private treasured memory. My photo gallery of my Baby Jack accompanied by your lullaby, *Annie's Song*.

I

BABY BOY, OH BOY

Outstretched scrubbed arms, beyond the blue veil, and the words, 'You have a beautiful boy,' as I see my son for the first time. A caesarean section, after a forty hour labour with my baby far too snug and cosy to want to enter this world … perhaps he knew his fate. I recall the nurse bringing my boy to me late into the night, wedging him into my left side, telling me to hold him like an American football, leaving us to bond. Oh how I cherished our first meeting, the silence so comforting, inexplicably so. My swaddled boy, so sweet, so perfectly perfect. I promised to honour, love, defend, protect and cherish you. But then I broke my promise … or did I? A question that haunts my consciousness, like the sting of a stick slapping my back as I run as fast as I can from who is hitting me. Life hurts. When I do muster the courage to slow my pace, and look over my shoulder to confront who could possibly want to inflict such continuous pain, I see me.

Leaving the hospital and driving the hour-long journey home with my boy nestled in his funky, jungle-themed car seat, reversed of course, I proudly gazed in wonder, and that protective force felt a hundred miles wide. All the proud mum clichés were there; my boy would eat vegetables, my boy wouldn't dare cry out for a dummy (the nurses had used one in the hospital, grrrr!) Fifteen minutes into the car drive my boy exercised his lungs, forty-five minutes later two dummies were purchased and only fifteen minutes from home.

I named my boy Jack, a strong British name, a reminder for him of his heritage. Having been born in the United States, I felt he truly was blessed to have the best of two worlds. The rites of passage we all go through as new mums were present in the Small Years. I recall from day one Jack would sleep with his fingers all curled in, except for his index fingers on both hands that remained pointed. One night I snapped a photo of my precious boy, and again at oh, around eight, his hand peeking out from his duvet with one finger outstretched, a priceless mummy moment. I saw it again on my eighteen-year-old, shrouded in a purple and gold brocade velvet cloak, on identification day.

The baby book upkeep; first tooth, first steps, first normal poop. Life truly was utterly idyllic, a comfortable, loving, warm and fuzzy time. A minor tongue tie snip surgery sent this emotional, sensitive mummy to the chapel at the hospital. The lazy eye diagnosis and prescription eyewear, thank goodness for Harry Potter, making glasses cool again. The resulting surgery to correct the lazy eye at twenty-two months, and the ensuing fever and trickles of bloody tears in the first forty-eight hours post op. Here I was, doing as I promised at our first meeting, the swell of protection, as I swaddled my boy, his bloody tears a sign I knew of healing, sitting all night not letting go, until sleep took hold of both of us. Shirley McLaine in *Terms of Endearment* ain't got nothing on this mother lioness. That scene where her character is literally trying to get into the crib and lay with her girl, that was me, when Jack was eighteen – only it was a casket, and the floor had to do.

The beautiful, so in love with my baby boy early days were hypnotic. I loved being a mummy. My heart couldn't possibly have been more full. I had an activity bouncy seat for him with a bar attached with brightly coloured bits and bobs, and he used to sit flicking the same little butterfly over and over. So chilled and content. Jack had been gifted a beautiful white padded suit for the colder months and I was so excited when finally, at twelve months, it fit, and the two of us went shopping at a lovely indoor mall in readiness for the pending holiday season. Pushing him along, his cheeky face peeking out from the padded hood, curious at the world and all its majesty. Popping into a rather posh department store searching for gifts in the men's department and nothing particularly catching my eye, we left and headed toward Santa's Grotto. Looking down at my boy, and there he was quietly playing with a host of wallets, pairs of socks, and key chains he had somehow swiped from said posh shop. Now I giggle, but back then I was mortified, hightailing it back to the shop and managing to quickly return everything to its appropriate spot.

A career move for my husband brought about a geographical change and we moved from chilly in the winter, humid in the summer Chicago, to bright and sunny Orlando. A pretty home selected in a newly built community with a private playground and lovely pool, would have been an idyllic lifestyle for many people. I wasn't overly keen on the whole cookie cutter neighbourhood though, it wasn't exactly my thing, as I tended to err away from anything too conventional but it made sense for us as a family. I recognised that it had the potential to be a great community to raise Jack in. However, I quickly learned that the garage doors went up and went down, swallowing people into their homes and they didn't interact very much at all.

The isolation of living in a gated community for me wasn't ideal. While people hankered for this type of 'vacation lifestyle' I desperately wanted to feel part of a community. One where walking to the local shop was an option, and not a car ride to the local mall or superstore. I knew that Jack would probably be an only child and being from England originally, I did miss the intimacy of that environment and had a rosy glow around my thinking. Why shouldn't I want that white picket fence ideal where neighbours chatted to each other, and Jack would have some local friends rather than just arranging play dates with parents and car pooling left, right and centre?

Jack's baptism at the local Catholic church remains a perfect memory, and took place just after his first birthday, a delay from the norm because I really wanted him to know and recognise his own name. It was a lovely time, with both sets of grandparents and godparents visiting, the warm sunshine, and a pretty Spanish style church at the end of a lovely brick street lined with charming shops.

Jack was just two when I decided to enrol him in a much sought after preschool programme at our local church. After the expected settling in period of a week or two one of the teachers expressed concern about Jack pushing other children, seemingly for attention, and generally not sitting still. A parent had complained. I did not take this development well. Who was this teacher to portray my son in these terms? He was only two after all. That uppity school, with its SUV driving parents could seriously do one. My son belonged, I surmised, with 'real' children from 'working' families. After all, introducing him to the 'real' world was the right thing to do.

But again, two weeks into attending the local Kinder Care programme, a teacher asked to see me to discuss Jack's lack of concentration and emotions that she described as being out of line with other children his age. Well, my boy is unique, I thought to myself. He's perfect to me and at only two and a half, I couldn't help wondering if everyone had gone mad in the pre-school system. Isn't it normal for a child to not always be on task? At home he played endlessly with his Brio trains, he sat still watching his beloved *Thomas the Tank Engine* videos and he curled up while I read him all sorts of books. I just didn't get it.

I did some research on different types of pre-schools and decided my boy should attend an alternative kind of school known as Montessori. The premise at Montessori was to mix ages together in the same classroom, allowing students to learn at their own individual pace. They could lie on the floor and do their work if they so chose, they learned through cognitive development. Independent learning was encouraged.

The director of the local chapter was very welcoming, along with her two assistant teachers, and the school, while nothing special to look at, seemed to have a beautiful heartbeat. I felt hopeful that we could get through the first two weeks this time around. Sadly, we couldn't. However this time Mrs Merris, the director, offered constructive examples of how Jack interacted at her school. She explained that the Fire Marshall had come to the school to show the children his uniform and equipment etc. which, as you can imagine, was all very exciting and mesmerising for most three to five-year-olds. Jack however wasn't able to sit still and wandered around the class, staring out of the window, not engaged at all with the Fire Marshall.

In the early years class at Montessori School children learn to develop concentration skills, and one way to aid in this development was to give each child a piece of coloured paper that was secured to a cork board in front of them. The paper would have a shape drawn on it – in Jack's case it was a circle – and the children would use a push pin to punch out the shape. Obviously this requires a lot of concentration as they slowly work their way around the shape on their board. Mrs Merris showed me Jack's efforts, which had around one inch of correct hole punching and then a mass of pin dots all over the board, inside and outside of the circle. She gently asked me to consider an evaluation for ADHD (Attention Deficit Hyperactivity Disorder). I couldn't ignore this, not this time. I had to face this possibility.

Jack's father had ADHD and had been diagnosed as a young boy of six or seven. In fact, he was a guinea pig in the testing of a drug called Ritalin. Researched showed me that there was only a 25% chance of inheriting ADHD so hey, there was a 75% chance that Jack didn't have it. The school prepared some forms and I completed an in-depth questionnaire, then I took my son to visit a specialist in ADHD. After observing Jack and reading the reports from physicians, the school, and my own observations, the physician concluded that Jack did in fact have ADHD. His hyperactivity level was not off the chart and more middling but his sensitivity when mixing with his peers and inability to stay on task on simple things like getting his shoes or coat or lunch box showed a legitimate concern. I'm simplifying things here, all of us parents have difficulty getting our children to put their shoes and coat on, and fetch their lunch box, but the issue with Jack was it happened all of the time. He constantly forgot simple requests, whereas by three, most children are able to stay on task at least half the time.

Tears rolled down my cheeks as the specialist explained that Jack would only be helped so much by taking medication and that ADHD did not have a cure, it was a lifelong 'disorder' (oh how over the years I grew to hate that word) that he would learn to manage. It was a family diagnosis, the specialist said, affecting everyone. He explained in simple terms how people with ADHD struggle with focusing and likened it to going to a concert and as the theatre darkens, a spotlight appears on the stage where the singer is standing. At that moment a torrent of cameras flashes are unleashed as people take pictures. This is what is happening within the brain of someone with ADHD but taking the medication would settle all the flashing and enable my precious little boy to have more control. The specialist explained that I would see a marked difference in Jack and he would appear to be drugged but that was because I was used to seeing him with more hyperactivity. The reality was, with his meds, he would be able to fit in much better with his peers and life would be calmer at home. The clearest example of the medicine working was on the Monday after Jack visited the specialist, having only had two days of meds. When I picked him up from school Mrs Merris greeted me, grinning from ear to ear as she showed me the perfectly punched out circle. We hugged and cried together and it was so lovely for Jack, he was so proud of himself.

I don't really want to go on too much about the role of medication as there are arguments for and against, however I will say that unless you are a parent with a child struggling with ADHD, you simply cannot comprehend how difficult it is for them, and their family members. The medication seemed to be the answer and over the years, along with counselling and regular doctor visits and tweaking of his prescription, Jack seemed to be able to cope better.

I had left my job when Jack was born, and set up my own business from home, so I made the decision to make that choice permanent so I could always be there for my boy after school. When Jack's father was terminated from his employment, we made a decision to move to a more community-based environment. I was watching a show featuring bed and breakfasts one day, and one of them was based in what appeared to be a charming, quaint island. It was called Amelia Island and situated on the north eastern tip of Florida. We took a couple of trips there and fell in love with it instantly. Amelia is a barrier island two miles by nine with a beautiful coastline and the sweetest, most idyllic town. The streets are paved in red brick and the houses a throwback to colonial times. While still being in Florida, the community felt very 'olde Southern', a smaller, cuter version of Atlanta or Charleston. With a fishing port at the foot of the charming main street and stunning sunset views we felt so much at home that it was an easy decision to make the move. Jacksonville, where Jack's father had found a new job, was only a forty-five minute drive away and there was a beautiful Montessori school on the island. All in all, we were so happy to make this move.

Life on the island was a bit like living inside a long running soap opera and we eased into it very well. It really was the most fun of times. Easter, with its beautiful egg hunts on the lawns of the local beachfront hotel. The Summer Shrimp Festival, with market stalls selling shrimp in every imaginable style; lemon shrimp, coconut shrimp, barbecue shrimp, jerk shrimp, blackened shrimp. The Harvesting of the Beaujolais wine, as planes flew over and parachuted newly harvested wine onto the lawns for all to enjoy. And of course, Halloween, which was such a treat for Jack as he loved all of the different costumes. Over the years he was Pumpkin baby, Bananas in their Pyjamas, Tickle me Elmo – bobbing for apples with such aplomb – Robin Hood, King Arthur, Batman, and so on. He was cheeky and giggled like crazy. When the Spiderman movie came out there he was, in the corner at the foot of the stairs literally balancing on the moulding, so cute. I remember finding him inside the fireplace on Christmas Eve with the dust buster, cleaning feverishly. When I asked him what he was up to, he replied, 'I'm cleaning out the soot so Santa's boots don't get dirty tomorrow.' What a sweetie pie. One time, when his school had a talent show, that cheeky chappy of mine was Hula Hoopin' Elvis. Dressed in leather jacket and shades, sliding onto the stage on his knees and hula hooping with six hoops to *Hound Dog*. Everyone cheered and stamped their feet. Oh what a moment for him, for both of us. We had such a lovely time together picking the music, doing the choreography, buying the hair gel. On non-uniform school days Jack's unique sense of style revealed itself. He loved to wear his bow tie with a t shirt. His Easter hat was a white baseball cap with mini bunnies and eggs stuck all over it. He wasn't the least embarrassed. On All Saints Day there he was in my brown tunic with a piece of rope tied round his waist. Bunny rabbit and bird ('stuffies' as he called his menagerie of cuddly toys) tucked under his arm. 'Mummy Saint Francis has a hole on his head,' he told me. So we cut out a circle and dotted it with a brown marker and stuck it on the top of his head to replicate the bald spot.

Christmas in our pretty, colonial style home was picture postcard perfect, with a lovely long front porch, swing seat, flower-filled window boxes and yes, a picket fence. Fires crackled in each room, and we had a real tree with a lovely angel on the top. On Christmas Eve we would exchange a tree ornament and the local horse and carriage picked us up for a trot around the island, gazing at all the amazing twinkling lights adorning the homes. Living in a holiday destination area came with the benefit of plentiful restaurants, lovely vistas, and so many things to do. We sat on our front porch so very happy, this was where we would send our son off to college from one day. This was our home.

At three years old, interviewed and enrolled at a lovely Montessori school, a handful of little mates, and nonstop beach get togethers with other young families, life was utterly dreamy. Jack was handling his medication well, and I tried to arrange play dates etc before the buzzy, Tiggerish, emotional boy resumed. Observing Jack by sitting behind the one way mirror in the observation room at school, watching my little chap as he prepared as the other children did, for the day. Taking off his shoes and switching to Tickle Me Elmo slippers. Sitting in front of the Pink Block Tower a wonderful hands on block building activity that while appearing to be such a basic tool, but because of the Montessori style of teaching, being very hands on, I realised that this block tower was already putting in place the concept of times tables and cubism. Here I am all bathed in 'proud mummy mode', watching Jack as he pulled one of his Dad's socks out from under his polo shirt along with a piece of static cling fabric, Oh noooooo, then mortifyingly he reached down the leg of his sweats to retrieve a pair of my knickers. The two teachers sitting on their stools silently giggling as Jack with care and thoughtfulness folded my knickers along with Dad's sock, and popped them into his back pack, and returned to the Tower. To this very day I giggle when recollecting this Salad Day moment. Jack seemed so in control, and viewing him with all of his classmates with ages ranging from 3 to 5, I could see for myself that he fit in so well. The medication held in his impulsivity and kept him on task, I literally was bursting with pride. A precious few early years that only drew this boy of mine even closer to my heart. If I could have figured out a way to tuck him away inside of my chest nestled against my heart I would have.

But while everything was idyllic on the surface, I had a growing sinking feeling that Jack was more sensitive than his peer group. His sensitivity really was off the chart, and the slightest thing would send him into floods of tears. He would be really upset when I had to empty out his pockets from all the bits and bobs five year olds collect. He even found it hard to part with something like a sweet wrapper or lollipop stick, which belonged in the bin. He loved birds and had so many fluffy toy birds, each with their own sound. One day he found a blackbird in the gutter outside our house and begged me to take him and 'Blackie' to the local bird sanctuary. While I was inside getting a plastic tub to transport Blackie, a car pulled up and ran the bird over. Oh my goodness, the tears, the burial, the readings from Jack's little prayer book that ensued. It was so moving to see him say goodbye to this bird with such reverence and respect, at such a tender age.

Moving on from Montessori school was a difficult decision but with the school only progressing to age eleven, we decided to move Jack to the newly restored private Catholic school located right next to the church. It was sooner than I would have liked but the reality was if we kept him at Montessori, the chances of securing him a place at the school were slim to none, and the option of the local senior school was not a good idea for a child with his level of sensitivity. While we had never been regular church-goers, we did now have a kindergartner so more effort was duly made to attend. As well as the obvious religious element, church in this area was also a social event. Sunday brunch after church at one of the local dining establishments was a regular occurrence, it literally was life out of *Ideal Home* magazine.

The tragedy of 9/11 affected everyone, and not to take away from other communities, the USA was rocked by this event and it was a terribly sad time for months. The day the planes hit, the school arranged an evening mass and Jack was selected to take up the wine during the service. His head teacher, Sister Elizabeth, recognised that Jack would handle this role. In spite of having ADHD, his sensitivity served him well on this day. A few weeks later Sister Elizabeth asked to see me and told me that Jack had visited her in her office to tell her that he had written a letter to the parents who had died on 9/11, to let them know that their children were being taken care of and not to worry as they were all safe. Jack had asked if he could burn the letter in a candle flame so that the smoke would send the message up to the mummies and daddies. All of this was in his consciousness, at only six years old.

II

CROSSING THE ROCKY POND

When Jack was nine years old our *Ideal Home* life came to an end when his father and I divorced. We'd settled in the States because Jack's dad was American but once we'd parted, I really wanted to go home. My boy and I had endless conversations about this, and I used to lay in the bathtub every evening after tucking him in thinking and thinking about this monumental decision. I needed to go back where I belonged, plus I really felt and still do, that raising Jack in England was the best decision for him also. So, with his father's agreement, we made the move.

I'm sure some of you are questioning what role Jack's father played in all of this but this is an area I'm choosing to leave somewhat untouched. I find myself in an impossible situation. If I include my thoughts, my truth, regarding his father and his role in the break-up of our marriage, I will be damning myself, and if I chose to not include his role, again I'm damning myself. When I think about what Jack would say about this delicate subject, I find myself feeling his thoughts. He often said, 'It's you and me, Mumsie, I like it this way.' This is our story, mine and Jack's and while later in the book there will be references to his father, it is out of necessity to share what Jack, I feel, would want me to.

My close friends and a counsellor I sought advice from advised that Jack would be fine making the move at his young age, and it was far preferable to making it after Senior School had begun. With my parents and family members assuring me of their support upon my return, I made the leap and flew with my precious nine-year-old cargo to England. I have to stop here and reflect on how incredibly brave Jack was during this emotionally charged time. As I imagine most children of his tender years do, he hung on my every word. I shared pictures from a school that I had provisionally selected for him and told him we would visit there first, then choose a home together. Sitting on the plane before take-off, I held him tight, but he was holding me too. We both cried tears as this little lad of mine quietly said he would never be able to pledge allegiance to the flag of the United States again before school. Talk about out of the mouths of babes, that one stung and good. It had been a beautiful sight to see Jack, hand on heart, looking up to the flag, along with the rest of the school. I told him that of course he would be able to keep pledging allegiance and he was so lucky to have two countries that loved him.

Initially, we lived with my parents but quickly moved into our first English home. I settled on a lovely period flat in Salisbury, compromising in my mind the tranquillity of the countryside, and the stillness and peace that I really desperately needed, to help appease my parents, and enrolled Jack in the chosen school in the city. I went shopping for furnishings and made a really lovely home for the two of us that I miss to this very day. We had a cute little balcony looking out over the Wiltshire countryside, a pretty bay window with stained glass. It really was so lovely. Our bedrooms were next to each other and he still came hurtling into my room in the mornings for cuddles before school.

But in spite of our lovely new home, I was crumbling at the seams. Here I was, forty-two years old and a single mum back in a country that had changed greatly since I left it nineteen years earlier. My friends in the USA had told me to go home and breathe and watch the grass grow for six months, take it slow, acclimatise. Focus on settling Jack and settling my mind. But I found the transition more difficult than I had expected. It was tough being a single mum in Wiltshire. During the junior school years parents play a vital role it seems in socialising outside of school, and being a single mum was a lonely start. I desperately wanted to do as my friends had suggested and relax and watch the grass grow, however my parents had other ideas. Although they were wonderfully supportive during the move back, once we arrived the perception seemed to be that I was to do as I was told. I had to buy the car my father wanted me to have and live where they wanted me to live. I literally had no say at all. When I did try to speak up for myself it was obvious that my choices were not theirs and they would not support me if I didn't go along with what they thought was right. In total fairness to them, I think they were in so much shock at the divorce and my return back to the UK. Their daughter was broken, desperately trying to figure out how on earth she was going to do this all by herself. I think it was easier for my parents if they knew I was close by. They felt better to be able to respond if I needed them, being close to hand. Their hearts were in the right place, however it was obvious that Jack and I were a burden.

For Jack, the practical side of school lessons and the overall rhythm of school life basically mirrored the USA. While Jack was taking his ADHD medicine he could stay on task at school, and the teachers recognised how bright he was. He noticed what others didn't. His point of view was original, and I loved him for that. However, I recall Jack coming home from his first day at school saying how much he had heard the F-word flying around and there was a lot of disruption in the classroom environment. Oh dear. Coming from an idyllic private Catholic school run by nuns to albeit a Catholic school in England, well, the similarities seemed to end right there. We try so hard as parents to protect our children and to give them the very best education we can and to keep them safe, but when the bubble bursts in our own personal lives, the trickledown effect on them can be devastatingly difficult. Here was my adorable little boy, hanging on my every word that I would make sure he would be in a nice school and have his lovely Nana and Papa to watch over him, when the reality was just not that simple. After a few short weeks I had a very frank conversation with Jack's teacher, a lovely man who very honestly told me he felt Jack would be better off in another school. He explained that a very high percentage of the students there were basically too street smart and their edges needed polishing. This, plus the very large class sizes meant it was unlikely Jack would receive any extra attention. He felt that Jack would be better suited to a smaller, village style school. The final straw for this mother lioness was when I was informed that Jack could not have peanut butter sandwiches at school as there was a child there with a severe nut allergy. What about my child, who never ate anything other than peanut butter sandwiches? My child with an ADHD diagnosis? How were they going to help him? The child with the nut allergy wasn't even in his year or classes, surely there had to be a solution that worked for everyone? But no, there was no compromising at all. Now, on reflection, I imagine the constraints of the school in regards to the care of a child who could have had anaphylactic shock had to take precedence. It was just so darn frustrating for me as I wanted so much to settle my precious child into his new reality.

Depression began slowly taking over, without me really being aware of it. Dark thoughts were permeating my mind and what friends I did have didn't want to 'deal' with me. My emotions were so raw. I can recall sitting in the movies with Jack and allowing the tears to stream down my face in the darkness. A lovely doctor helped, prescribing me some antidepressants and various ones were tried, however I didn't seem to improve. I tried to manage the best that I could, which involved a lot of sweetness with Jack, plenty of tears behind closed doors, and sadly for Jack, sometimes not.

I was determined however to find the right school for my precious charge, so a meeting with the head teacher of a village school a twenty minute drive from our home was arranged. She explained to me that the local community was made up of a large percentage of farmers and it was a real community school. It seemed on paper to be charming and quaint. More importantly, peanut butter for lunch was not an issue. Jack was introduced to his male teacher, who involved him in sport, including football and tennis. Jack had always been a little star in 'soccer' as they called it in the USA, as well as basketball, golf and cross country running. Using up his excess energy in this manner was a help for all concerned. The trouble was, the comments from the schoolboys were so painful for Jack to manage, and me too if I'm perfectly honest. See, even in these Small Years we were two sensitive souls on this eye opening adventure together. A much more painful adventure than I had prepared myself or Jack for. All I had was what had come before. Yes, Jack was a sensitive boy, yes, at times his classmates hurt his feelings, however there seemed to be more consequences for the actions of others in America. The parental involvement was high and as we all lived on a small barrier island together, a true effort was always made at the school to keep falling out to a minimum, and resolving issues a maximum.

In the Wiltshire country school this just wasn't the case. Whether they were ill equipped, or just in their safe little bubble I don't really know, but my goodness did Jack ever suffer there. I recall one day Jack running into my arms in tears after a boy at school had told him to, 'Go home American pig'. Of course I addressed this with the school immediately, and the head teacher did intercede and speak to the boy in question. No one would have been aware of Jack having started his life in America apart from a slight accent and some word differences, i.e. cookies vs. biscuits, and eraser vs. rubber. I certainly never thought that hiding where my child was born would have been a better start to school life. It was 2004 and the UK's tolerance of all things American was waning with the Afghanistan problem, as a result of 9/11. The head teacher pointed out that this particular child's parents were quite outspoken and he had probably picked up the usual dinner chatter about news events.

I had tried to keep a nice blend of British and American traditions alive for Jack as we transitioned back into English life, and even hosted a Thanksgiving dinner for our family members at a local pub, who kindly went all out to present a beautiful meal complete with pumpkins and decorations befitting this event. A tradition we had in our American home was to go around the table and each person would light a candle that floated in water in representation for someone who was not present, whether through geography or having passed away. Our family came together for us that evening and embraced this tradition for Jack. It remains a very sweet, happy memory.

It's so painful to write this now, because recent years have bitterly divided us as a family, as you will learn, and to recall such a sweet memory, a rare memory, where we all were together with no intent other than to celebrate for Jack, deeply saddens me. My parents had offered to have Jack on a Friday after school until noon on the Saturday in order that I may have an opportunity to see old friends or just a bit of me time. They had set up a TV in his room at their house so everyone had their space. However, within a few short months my mother appeared at my home to tell me that it was too much for them having Jack and they were not prepared to commit to any kind of care and I needed to make my own plans. Mum conceded it wasn't Jack, it was my father, who she felt needed her so much that she couldn't manage both. The awful sting of rejection is still with me to this very day. My lovely little boy played with his army soldiers very gently, had his dinner, and spent the evenings in his room at their house playing on his Game Cube or watching television. I saw so many grandparents with their grandchildren in Salisbury, taking care of them, helping their children. Why oh why did my parents have to push us away? I felt like they were punishing me for living my own life and not always conforming to their expectations. They would drive by my flat and leave messages to tell me I had left a window open. It was a horribly unsettling time. I had realised in my early years in America that my parents were a sort of Ronald and Nancy Reagan. Very into each other, to the exclusion of others at times. Having lived a life apart from them through my twenties and thirties, it was a relearning time for all of us. Their comforting words on the phone to me during the divorce and assurances that they would take care of me were what I needed to hear, but the reality of having me, their youngest daughter, home with their grandson was obviously too much. When I reflect on this I feel terribly conflicted. My parents did do the best that they could. They were both quite sensitive, and that side of them is definitely an inherited gene. I recall when I moved into the flat they gave me a card with the well-known *Footprints in the Sand* quote inside. I cried so much for my love for them as I read it. They weren't religious but they knew that I had raised Jack with a sense of faith and felt that I would relate to the words of the poem. I guess we all have layers of emotions when thinking of our parents, and I'm no different.

This for me, was the beginning of a downward spiral. I found myself desperately lonely and scared. I was clinging onto any man I could to try and re-establish the old life I once had. One where I grocery shopped for three, not two. One where there would be a man who would kick a ball around with Jack, and lay next to me at night.

There was Paul, who lasted about a year but returned to his wife who he had been separated from. We both comforted each other through a difficult time, and while he didn't live with us, we saw him a couple of times a week. He did however, greatly improve my smashed self-esteem. He made me see that I was a viable, attractive woman with 30 plus more years of living to do. I saw him mostly without Jack. I arranged for sitters etc, which seemed to suit Jack. As long as he had his Game Cube and PSP, his peanut butter and jam sandwiches, a glass of chocolate milk and me, his 'Mumsie', as he began to call me, he was happy.

My wonderful doctor in Salisbury got me out of the blues and finally onto the correct anti-depressant, and I began to build a resolve. A resolve to look after my son first, and myself second. Although I freely admit there were times when maybe I did put myself first ... see there I go again, hitting myself with that stick.

I moved us away from Salisbury and prying critical eyes to Southsea. We spent 18 months there, where I have to say we were so very happy. The only bump during this transition was Paul returning to his estranged wife, which was a painful rejection, but I can now see clearly that he was the 'band aid boyfriend'; one that many of us newly separated or divorced mums choose.

We had visited Gunwharf Quays in the Southsea area one Sunday before moving and Jack had said that it reminded him of 'home.' The bobbing boats in the harbour and happy, shiny holidaymakers made for a really lovely, fun-filled time and were reminiscent of our life on the barrier island off Florida. So how could I make this work? Luckily, I found a pretty flat for us there, enrolled Jack at the local junior school that had a very good reputation, and decided I would find myself a job at a school so I could continue to still be there for Jack during non-school hours. I also was thinking about where he should go for senior school, as there was only 18 months or so to make that selection, so I gained a position as a Cover Supervisor at the local Catholic senior school. I thought this was the perfect way for me to see how senior school life was in the area. Knowing my son's sensitivity, I was keen to ensure I selected the correct choice.

Oh dear, that was a rude awakening. Living on the fringes of a big city I could see that the city schools would not be the right choice for Jack. He was far too sensitive, he still did not have any close friends. I used to dread picking him up from school, as the mothers just did not engage with me. It is such a rites of passage, single mum and junior school, particularly in a middle class environment. I could hardly wait for senior school to begin, where I sensed parental involvement would be shut down. Picking him up from birthday parties was always a pit in my stomach time. What would get said this time? There always seemed to be something and it was always to do with Jack's emotions. Hurt feelings that did not match up with his peers. No amount of ADHD medicine was going to be able to help so I enlisted a lovely young man who worked for CAMS, a group who worked with children with emotional challenges, who came to our home weekly to visit with Jack. He would chat with Jack about his week and offer advice on how to deal with his feelings. He taught him the phrase 'I'm sorry you feel that way', which Jack could use in a variety of scenarios. It simply shut down the negativity among the 10/11 year olds who didn't have the maturity to know how to respond back. I use that line myself, as it works for adults too.

It was such a yin and yang time. Our home life was for the most part, very special. Having all the stimuli of Gunwharf at our fingertips was such a treat. Jack would say 'Gunwharf is our backyard, Mum.' And indeed it was. Hot dogs from the red and white striped cart, ketchup for Jack, steaming onions for Mumsie, watching the yachts in the harbour. Jack leading the way through the maze of shops, avoiding Ted Baker at his peril, 'Muuuuummmmmm, nooooooo!' Such cute times. I recall taking him to see *Star Wars Revenge of the Sith* on a Saturday afternoon, munching popcorn, loving that movie together. I'd never really been a Star Wars fan but watching that film through Jack's eyes was just the best feeling ever. The next day we were reminiscing over how great the film was, and wished we could see it again, so we did. We just trotted back over there, another popcorn bowl and candy striped sweet bag and we landed right back into The Force.

We would take the train to London and visit galleries, shop a little, lunch, and home. One such trip was to the Tate Modern, and it was a bit of a shock to see an exhibit of magpies with one of them speared! I quickly ushered Jack away by redirecting him to the stairs and up to the Pop Art exhibit to see Marilyn and the Campbell's Soup tin I had been chattering about to him on the journey there. He knew I loved Marilyn, and that Christmas I opened a present from him, to discover a calendar of Madonna, who he thought was Marilyn. I let him think that, gorgeous boy. Anyway, back to the Tate.... we left there and lunched at St Christopher's Place. Sitting outside in the beautiful sunshine we demolished Steak frites (Jack), and Duck a l'Orange (me), looked at our empty plates and ordered the same again. Oh I love that memory. My lovely boy in his blazer with his yin/yang pin from the museum shop, his beautiful open face and having such a great day out together.

Another planned day out was for his 11th birthday, a trip to see Mary Poppins in London. Train tickets all sorted, we awoke on the day to discover the trains were not operating. His crestfallen face was just too much. I didn't have the confidence to drive to the city, as I wasn't sure about parking. But I couldn't possibly let my boy down, so I booked a return taxi. We had a lovely lunch at Café Boheme, right across the street from the Prince Edward Theatre, saw the show, purchased the parrot-topped umbrella and met our driver, who carried us safely back home for a whopping £185 round trip. We lived on peanut butter and jam sandwiches for the entire next week but we didn't care. Peanut butter was Jack's fave food so I presented it in a variety of ways. Triple decker PB&J, grilled flour tortilla PB&J, toasted sandwich PB&J, cut out animal shaped PB&J. That familiar, much loved food has not crossed my lips these long six years since Jack's leaving.

While working in my Cover Supervisor role in Portsmouth, I met a lady who lived in the Liss/Liphook area who invited us to her home for the weekend. I remember driving into the village of Liphook and immediately feeling such a welcoming, comfortable vibe. I decided to research schools in the area and through the Ofsted system I came across Bohunt School, with its wonderful report and great test scores. I contacted the school and was told that unfortunately, Year 7 was already filled. I felt this sinking feeling and we chatted for a few minutes about adding Jack to the waiting list. During our conversation, the secretary checked her email and voila – there was a family who literally had just messaged to say they were moving and a space had indeed become open. I hopped in my car and drove the 30 minutes to the school, and as I turned the corner, there, four houses from the school entrance, was the sweetest little house for rent. Kismet. Meant to be. House rented, school signed up, my son was going to experience English village life. Walk to school. No fear that he would leave his bag on the bus, let alone miss the bus. I would forgo the social life that living near a city affords, and spend the next however long tending to and loving my son.

I took Jack to visit the house, number 17 (which, in some horrible kind of foreshadowing, ended up being the date that he left) and he darted around the house with delight. He loved it, expressing how small and cute and safe it felt. He didn't seem bothered about moving as he knew I had found him such a great school and all kids leaving junior schools were going through similar transitions. This was a turning point for Jack and I. Our little family of two was safe. This village would be our home.

III

MOTHER LIONESS

Jack and I loved our sweet little house. A literal hop, skip and jump to his school, but Jack being Jack still found a way to take an even shorter cut, over the school fence into the bushes behind our home. A rip here, a tear there. Ha, such a boy. Every school day afternoon the gate clinked and my boy appeared at the back door. I know it's just a simple everyday thing but I love that memory. Dumping the backpack at the foot of the stairs, and giving me a lovely hug and a 'Hey, Mumsie', to which I would reply, 'Hey, Jammie Dodger,' my lifelong nickname for him. Sometimes, the back gate clinked at some random, earlier time, and he would come hurtling into the house, up to his room, and whizzing back past me with PE shorts in his hand!

We had our rituals, our little routine in place. I'm not exactly the most organised person but when it came to Jack I was all over him like white on rice with his homework assignments and school diary. I used to notice the medicine begin to wear off around 5pm and Tigger emerge, bouncing and racing up and down the stairs for this, that and the other. Suddenly ravenous and full of chatter and playfulness.

One such afternoon, Jack came bounding in as usual and I had asked him to pop up to the local shop to grab the newspaper, as I was now job hunting for something that would fit in with school hours. Well, of course that meant a treat or two, so off he bopped out the back door. My heart aches a little as I recall what happened next. Fifteen or so minutes later he came flying through the back door and into my arms, as I sat on the sofa, transferring wet globby patches from his school shirt onto me. 'Mummy, a boy spat on me and called me an American c**t.' After a few deep breaths and holding onto my boy, he explained that on his way to the shop, literally 50 metres from our house, there were two or three boys sitting on the electricity box and they'd attempted to stop Jack from walking up the path to the shop by blocking his way. He told me they were swearing and unkind but he had managed to dodge and dart his way round and had purchased the paper and sweets at the shop. On his way back he spied they were still sitting there, so he wisely chose to cross the street and walk on the other pavement. He had to cross back to get to our house, at which point they ran to block him from walking to our back gate, and one boy in particular spat on Jack (hence the wet splodges on his shirt and now me) and repeated the insult. Jack bolted for the back gate and the safety of home. I was mortified for him.

We sat there together wondering how to approach this situation, and I naively thought that a little mediation was possibly the best way forward. I left the house to find two boys matching Jack's description of them, one chunkier boy sitting atop the electricity box and the other scrawny kid, you know the all bark and no bite type, standing close to him. I approached and told them who I was and said that what had taken place was appalling and the best way forward for all involved, including Jack, was an apology, and to move on. To own what their roles were and that would be it. I asked for their last names also. Well, the torrent of language hurled at me, and the larger boy hocking and spitting all around me was intimidating to say the least. But I stood my ground and stated again that we could clear this up. I explained that Jack was sensitive, and sometimes he knee jerk reacted. He had told me he'd yelled back at them, 'Fuck off, leave me alone.' I explained I was trying to resolve this without involving the authorities, however in the event that we couldn't resolve this with apologies all around, I would in fact contact the local police. 'Go on then you fat cow,' came the response. That one stung me, so imagine how my eleven-year-old son would have felt, trying to adjust to life in this new country. Desperate to fit in and feel that he belonged, only to be spoken to and assaulted in that disgusting manner. I walked away and explained our options to Jack. Do nothing and hope the bullying doesn't continue. Call the school to advise of the incident, however as this had happened off of school property I already knew that nothing would be done. Then there was the option of calling the police, having told the boys that would be my next step. Surprisingly, Jack opted for the police route. I say surprisingly because I guess the potential fallout at school could have been difficult and I worried about possible comeback from the boys' parents. But Jack felt sure this was the right path, and I agreed it really was. The alternative of worrying that he would be picked on again at school was not an option and calling him that name prefaced with the word American was, as the police pointed out, a racist remark, not to mention the transference of bodily fluids. They knew from our description who the boys were. One in particular had in fact been excluded permanently from the school and did not live in the village but often waited for his mate to get out of school. They had a list of complaints against him, however no one had pursued them any further, which as they said, left them in a powerless position. They told us that the older boy had caused a lot of grief within our community and should we decide to file a formal complaint, we would be sending a clear message. Jack showed such maturity and wisdom in one so young and bouncy. When something really mattered to him he could maintain concentration very well.

Up to that point in his eleven years, I had never seen the brave young man who walked into court a few months later and sat behind the curtain set up for witnesses, so they don't have to face those accused. He stood so strong in his questioning by the defence lawyer. Later that day, a phone call from the Prosecutor to advise said 'plonker' was found guilty and had to remain at home after school for three months and was instructed to undergo counselling for anti-social behaviour. A couple of weeks later, a phone call came in from the Social Services to say the boy did not harbour bad feelings toward Jack at all, and was becoming aware of how his actions would have been traumatic for both myself and Jack. I wonder if he knows about what happened to Jack... I wonder if he sleeps well at night.

Sheepishly though, I do recall myself as a thirteen-year-old walking home from school, taking the easy option and siding with the local tough girls as they pushed and intimidated a girl two years below. Peer pressure, ugh. Going from child to tween, to teen, to young adult is a treacherous mental path. Teens don't want to leave their childhood behind, they don't want the responsibilities of adulthood, but they also don't want to leave this earth, so they move forward with a little kick here, a nudge or two there, and a fair amount of head fucking, to eventually arrive at adulthood. I get it, the actions of a fifteen-year-old boy does not shapeth the man.

Jack was making friends at school and, spending most of my time at home, I feel I was more accessible to my son and his friends, as they knew they had a place to come to and chill out. It's a club only single parents get to be a member of. Knowing his sensitivity and his total inability to allow barbs and jibes to roll off his back, the way that some kids can, while others may bottle them up, Jack's emotions welled easily and he would flee the classroom in tears on several occasions. The school student support counsellor supplied Jack with a yellow card that he could show the teacher who would allow him to leave a situation in class if he felt it was too much for him. This was a helpful tool, however as is the case with school life, once you are seen to be sensitive it unfortunately sticks with you, and those teens who delight in bullying and teasing, take on their roles also, and the horrible cycle of emotional abuse continues. While the teasing and sarcastic nasty comments Jack endured during school life, for the most part are what many children endure, it's how they are able to cope, and the role of the school in putting a halt to such mean slights that can ease the tender hearts of those more sensitive among us.

In Year 7 Jack had a great budding friendship with a lad called Leo. He felt Leo understood him and they supported and protected each other from the jibes of a particular boy who had a cutting way with words. Jack and Leo lived a twenty minute drive from each other so in a way, their friendship bloomed as a result of his mother and myself doing the car pooling. Trips to the local swimming pool, the outdoor one in particular was a firm favourite. They were two really lovely lads and it was so nice to see how well they got along together.

On one of mine and Jack's mini trips away I took him to the Cotswolds, to an idyllic village called Bourton on the Water. A quaint and charming place with pretty bridges crossing the river. I sat outside our little hotel watching my precious charge racing up and down the river, feeding the ducks and ducklings, playing Pooh sticks, a proper little Tiggerish chap. There was a Birdland in the village and Jack was in his absolute element, and loved the precious little fluffy birds of all shapes, sizes and colours. He came across a penguin called Leo, so of course a cheeky photo was snapped of Jack with the said penguin, all ready to show his mate at school on Monday. It truly was such a beautiful weekend, my son at only eleven young enough to drink in every sense around him, and me his Mumsie, falling more in love with my sweet darling son. The little hotel we stayed in had a scrabble board so we sat playing together and that little rascal managed to beat me, so of course we took a picture of the board, to share with his Papa, both of us it seems eager to please him.

It was during this time, and Jack's frequent visits to Leo's house, that I learned about the chores Leo had at home. I'd never really enforced too much in that area, and realised I probably should put a couple of chores in place also. So, keeping in mind Jack's ADHD, he had the bins to put out and bring in once a week and to help me with food shopping, bringing in the bags from the car. I had tried to educate Jack from quite an early age, to be perfectly frank, out of the blinding worrying fear that I'm sure every parent of one child has about their own mortality, and how our children would manage without us. While living in Salisbury, driving right up to the entrance of the large Tesco's, and sending Jack in at 9 years old to buy maybe a loaf of bread, a comic, a chocolate bar, or some green top milk. Giving him the money. Seeing if he could accomplish these little tasks. Trying to show him that he could do these types of errands, of course keeping a watchful eye at the door. Things that two parent families don't necessarily think so much about. Something as simple as going to use the bathroom, as a boy, when he reached that age where taking him in with me was not really a viable option. I would usually watch for another adult with his son heading to the toilet, and gently asking if it was ok if Jack accompanied them. I found people to be very kind, and it was being outgoing enough to ask that was important.

As Year 8 began, Jack's friendship with Leo shifted. To this day I really don't understand why. He would come home and share with me that the gentle boy he knew had beens replaced with someone who now seemed to revel in Jack's sensitivity, and I can only imagine it was the natural progression of peer pressure and Leo being sensitive himself, finding a coping mechanism that sadly didn't work for Jack. We didn't see Leo at all for the rest of school life, and it wasn't until Year 11, when we were at a parent / teacher day that we ran into him with his mum, and you know us mums, we chatted about this and that, while our two sons stood awkwardly next to each other. Leo's mum was very lovely. During some leaner times when Jack had lost his backpack she very generously presented him with one that he could keep. A very kind gesture.

During Year 8, Jack soldiered along, my brave steadfast boy. There was an after school games club that he enjoyed participating in, however it only took one lad, just one lad who I suspected also had ADHD, to unravel Jack, and vice versa. Two lads one medicated and one not, trying to cope in the sadly one dimensional life of a comprehensive school. Over time, friendships did form, with two or three mates, all of whom gravitated toward him, and it seems to me, for a variety of reasons. As we lived just the two of us, while certain ground rules were in place, such as farting outside and no swearing, the boys were welcome and generally appeared on a Saturday night. Joe, Louis, and Jack, on the sofa with me watching X Factor, munching on a buffet of Chinese or Indian take out. Louis, Joe's cousin, who lived with a relative, had moved south from Scotland and was visibly insecure and painfully quiet. When the boys darted upstairs to play games, Louis would sit for ten minutes or so and tell me little stories about life at school and life at home. It seemed I was a warm soft place for these boys. I took comfort in these visits myself, however always my thoughts were on Jack and how could I help keep him safe and happy. He delighted in us treating his friends to a spin to McDonalds with the top down on the car, Joe's hair standing up like a giant ginger toilet brush. Joe was such a sweet and also sensitive lad, but somehow able to laugh at himself. So laid back practically horizontal in fact, but easily able to embrace and connect to Jack's sensitive soul.

Joe was part of a lovely family called the Taylors. Walking into their home was like receiving a warm hug. Jack loved being there, as did I, both of us felt a part of the family. There was Dad Mike, plus four children, Josie the eldest, Joe came next, Sally and Sam. Sadly, Joe's mother had passed away when he was ten years old so I feel on some level, not to take away for a minute the loving support he received from his aunties and grandparents and dad, juggling work, four kids, an attempt at a private life, and of course, the grief and loss of his beloved wife, Joe sought some solace and quiet time at our home. Not to mention the treats of food, Monster drinks, hoodies, and the occasional dinner out . See, there I go again, as I'm writing this I can see how I self deprecate, how I feel and have felt for many years this feeling of not being liked just for me, and by going above and beyond for others it would mean I wouldn't be left again. A single mum spilling her own fears into the world that was Jack's. Any reason to be perfectly frank, to keep things cool for Jack, and if that meant a little chat or a 6 pack of coke and a bags of chip shop chips and sausages delivered to the Bomb Pits where they would ride their bikes, then I was more than happy to treat. Just to see Jack's face, his wide open beautiful face, the acceptance it seemed for him, that his friends approved, and their voices as I pulled away saying, 'Your mum's a legend,' unaware that this Mumsie was beaming also as I left them to their afternoon antics. As in life, friends change and evolve and one lad in particular, George, was young at heart however large in stature. He looked out for Jack at school, and Jack for George as George was a diabetic and occasionally fainted. Jack would defend him and keep him safe until help arrived, yelling at on lookers to stay away from his mate. Jack would tell me how George kept bullies at bay and protected him. George was loyal, of this I have no doubt. They were such good mates, rough housing, and generally playing silly buggers. George had a younger brother James and again I feel Jack enjoyed the company of George's family, including Mum Morgan, her partner, two boys and a dog. They were very laidback and chilled people and again a real family that, while Jack often said he loved it being just the two of us, of course he would enjoy the vibe of being part of a larger family even if it was the occasional sleepover or visit.

A quote from a favourite poem of mine by William Wordsworth:

What thought about the radiance, which was once so bright
Be now forever, taken from my sight
Though nothing can bring back the hour of splendour in the grass
of glory in the flower, we will grieve not,
rather find strength, in what remains behind.

How poignant those words are, in the light of what was to come. Never forget the gloriousness of idealistic youth.

IV

SENSITIVITY AT OUR CORE

Sensitivity in a boy has to be so difficult to live with. I feel an ache in the pit of my stomach for my Jack and what he had to endure. It's such a tough trait to have to learn how to manage. I know what it feels like to be a girl and sensitive, but at least a girl welling up or bolting out of the classroom in tears was for the most part accepted by all as part of her DNA. Girlfriends rally round each other, have that commonality of heightened emotions related to their time of the month, issues with friends, family gripes etc, all completely acceptable reasons for a girl to exhibit emotion. But what was a boy supposed to do with feeling so deeply sensitive? I tried the whole keep your enemies closer tactic, contacting the mother of the boy who appeared to enjoy tearing at Jack's self esteem any chance he could. We took them swimming together, they seemed to get along ok, as is the ilk when put in a contrived situation, away from any peers, however as soon as school resumed the next day, there were the barbs, the sarcastic comments, and the undertone of fear back in my boy's eyes.

I had encouraged Jack to pursue acting at school as he had such a funny, alternative point of view, and coordination, (Hula Hooping Hound Dog no less.) I thought it would be a helpful class to instil confidence in Jack, public speaking and role playing through drama, rather than real life situations. He auditioned for Bugsy Malone and was cast as Ritzy, one of Fat Sam's gang. Proud Mumsie, was I ever?! Rehearsals were difficult for him to deal with, bossy diva-like kids and their comments brought him close to bailing, but we would chat it out at home and run through the dance routine and off he'd go with a little more vim and vigour. Let me tell you, Jack was a standout dancer with the most energy and enthusiasm. It was so great to see him on stage rolling his homburg down his arm and back onto his head, the smallest of the group with a suit two sizes too big but a smile and a razzle dazzle that took over the entire stage, well to this Mumsie at least. Jack's smile was infectious and warming and just utterly gorgeous. In spite of how confident he was at that performance my mind casts back to arriving at the school for the show with George and his mother. We spied Jack at the entrance handing out programmes, in costume already, hair greased down in a centre parting as per the era and George laughed at him and made a snarky comment about Hitler. It was horrible to see Jack's crestfallen face, the hurt in his eyes. George was just being a teenager but for Pete's sake, that one throw-away comment stung me and dreadfully pained Jack. Worst of all, I sort of laughed with George but then, seeing Jack's face, I hugged him and reassured him how fantastic he looked and how proud I was of him.

Jack, as you now know, loved birds and I was making a little money working a couple of days a week for a wedding dress designer in London, so I was able to save for a very special holiday. I discovered that the island of Tobago had the only preserved natural rainforest, abundant with tropical birds and foliage. For me, relaxing at the private sandy cove was paramount and for Jack, the rainforest beckoned. As suited my boy, this hotel was boutique in size and we visited over New Year so kids were mainly back to school and Jack was the only teen there, which for him was ideal. The staff treated him to the use of the boogie board and would sit and chat with him in their laidback Caribbean fashion. We made a holiday friendship with a young American couple and it was sweet to see Jack flushed as this blonde, angel type young woman splashed around in the waves with him. Thanks to her fiancée for sharing.

A couple of nights we dined on our terrace and played our Black Eyed Peas and Seal CDs, having delicious jerk seasoned food, cool drinks, and dishes of creamy chocolate ice cream. This for me was the most beautiful, soul soaring, perfectly gorgeous week with my lad, it was it seems on reflection a closing to those 'splendour' years that Wordsworth talked about in his poem.

A small sign or two of Jack's sensitivity appeared as one of the island chaps, Charles, who hung out with Jack, was at times a bit on the flirty side with me. I engaged in conversation with him simply because I loved seeing Jack enjoying the company of someone other than me. It was lovely to watch him running out in the water and coming back in on his boogie board, his beautiful smile lighting up his milky skin, his entire soul ablaze with the many pleasures of this island paradise.

One afternoon we were having a little rest in our room, as you do on hols, and a tap at our patio door revealed Charles. Jack leapt off the bed, his mate was here, but I had the uncomfortable feeling that he was visiting more to speak to me. I held myself in check somewhat and when Charles left Jack was very quiet. He blurted out that I had taken his friend away from him and that Charles really wasn't his friend he was only using Jack to get to me and burst into floods of angry tears. Just writing this, the knot in my stomach transports me back. I held him close, I comforted him and I tried to explain that these young men sometimes could be distracted by a woman, however Charles was his friend not mine and I was desperately sad for him. I sought out Charles the next day and requested he put things right, and turn his amorous hormones off pronto. I explained Jack's sensitivity and for the rest of the trip the focus was directed at Jack. It felt contrived inside though and I began to feel a surge of protection again, as truly I didn't want anyone hanging out with Jack unless it was authentic. Fake I couldn't bear, neither could Jack. It's odd because with both of us being sensitive people, you would think that frivolity was a soothing agent but not so. It just made me question myself more. I was never really someone who enjoyed interacting with groups of girls or women. I found it so uncomfortable. I much prefer and always have, the intimacy of a one on one best friend and a couple of friends beyond that. I never felt as if I fit into the world of Tupperware parties and baby showers etc, while raising Jack. I really can't explain why, other than my soul, the core of who I am was too deep, and frivolity, light hearted banter that really had no meaning, I just didn't relate to. It seems in many ways Jack was similar.

Our journey back home was tense as the flight was delayed several hours, and the plane suffered the worst turbulence. My ongoing problem with DVT returned to my legs, quite seriously, as flight attendants came to my aid, providing limitless water and a stool to rest my leg upon. It was quite frightening and Jack shut himself off from me, focusing on the games on board, and not outwardly acknowledging my distress. I now understand that this was a form of protection to himself. I was all he had in the world and if I was poorly then the fear masked itself with brusque words to leave him alone. Once safely home, the mood shifted and within a day or two the effects of travel had dissipated, and we settled back to our family of two routine.

A few months after returning home, attending Jack's GCSE Drama performance and seeing his beautiful open expression as he and his group performed their scripted piece was memorable. In spite of my natural adoration of my son I did always try to keep things real. I thought he did ok, but there wasn't necessarily a natural talent for acting, he did have to work for it. When he asked me what I thought of everyone's performances I did tell the truth. I tried to gently say some of the other groups had great scenes, and within his group I thought he did well. The hurt behind his eyes when I said that causes me to slap myself with that stick over and over. I was really just trying to be completely honest. Of course I championed my Jack, I recognized his strengths and encouraged them, and this was the very first time I had decided I probably should speak with more honesty about where his strengths and perceived weaknesses were. Oh boy, I saw clearly how even a slight criticism would hurt him. He got quite cross with me over that and his words were cold and quite hurtful. He was sixteen, I wanted so much to help him but I also had the responsibility to present the world to him in all its shades. It wasn't fair to always say he was the best at everything, and it was OK to not be the best. I was playing the role of father, while living the role of sensitive, protective mother. The impending reality of college life and that broad step toward adulthood was nearing and I really felt I would be doing Jack a disservice if I painted everything in glitter and didn't keep things as real as possible. At home, Jack and I would sit together and role-play situations that may occur with his peers, however Jack found it too difficult to hear me in the 'bully' role. I was his Mumsie and he loved me so much it was evident on his face, and in his actions. I was trying anything I could to help build a resolve, build a protective layer around him. How on earth could I accomplish this when I myself lived with the same sensitivity? I would contact family members asking if they would occasionally call Jack for a chat, man to man kind of stuff, but no one ever did. Best laid plans and all that. I'm not naming and shaming, it's just I want so much to tell the absolute truth, and the absolute truth is that I asked for help from some family members and sadly did not receive it.

Unless you are in my situation, you cannot possibly understand what it is like to raise a child by yourself. Being labelled by a sibling as overly emotional, dramatic and sensitive, they probably thought I was to be taken with a pinch of salt. I just can't see why they wouldn't have stepped in more to help me. They weren't mean people, everyone has busy lives, everyone has their own truth, their own private issues. It was just me and Jack, and the sadness I felt, and the tears I cried over that very fact, when now I would bare my soul to the devil incarnate to bring back our Splendour in the Grass, our Glory in the Flower.

Jack would tell me so many times that he loved the fact that it was the two of us. He didn't have to 'deal,' he could be real with me. If we wanted to have upside down meal days we did; dinner for breakfast, dessert for lunch, breakfast for dinner. If we wanted to camp out in my bedroom all day with games and movies and pb&j sandwiches, chocolate milk, we did. With no one to judge us, they really were lovely, gentle, fun, cheeky moments. I recall one school day when I knew that Jack had a not particularly stimulating afternoon of lessons, calling the school to advise he had a medical appointment. I pulled up and Jack hopped in, expecting a trip to the dentist or something equally ugh, but no, we were pulling a sicky. Quick change into jeans and hoodie and we drove to Gunwharf, went bowling, the movies and a treat or two at HMV. And to any do-gooders tut-tutting, don't even attempt to take that afternoon away from me.

My parents would call Jack and try to guide him, however getting advice from grandparents is tough for any teen lad to take in. They bought him things, they did all that they could do for him, but it just wasn't the right kind of help. As I'm writing this I'm a few days away from burying my mother (Dad passed three months ago) and it's so easy to canonise those who have passed over, however I am compelled to keep everything I can as real as possible here, in this ode to my love and relationship with my beautiful son.

It is no one's fault. Here we were, two sensitive, delicate, feathery souls flitting from one emotion to the next, often daily, as we navigated our way through life together. My parents oddly pushed me aside to do things for Jack. Is this a natural grandparent role? I'm not sure. With comments like 'we will do anything for Jack', the emphasis on Jack, not you both. When referring to Jack's father, I recall Jack telling me that Nana had told him that just because his mum and dad were divorced, it didn't mean they loved his dad any less and cared for him just the same as they did me and that it was both our faults equally as to why we were now not married, which upset Jack immensely. He saw, he knew, he didn't need his nana, or even me for that matter, telling him how life was. He lived it, he knew, and he told his nana to stop telling him that, and it was unfair to his Mumsie for Nana to try to play both sides. It was hurtful, and my boy's protectiveness of me, of us, our new little family of two was on full display that day.

We, or I should say I, tried to do nice things for them, but it was difficult. Mum seemed unsettled when I would offer to take them out for the day. A lunch here and there was OK but anything more than that she wasn't comfortable with. Her reasoning was always their medical appointments or she was unsure of how they would be feeling, but Dad for the most part was chatty and interested in Jack. Yes, there were times when his acerbic tongue lashed out, but he was my dad, I was aware of his quiet love for me, and it was confusing but I wanted to do things for him. One trip I did manage to pull off was when Jack was only 12. Mum and Dad were both in better health, so we took a memorable trip with Dad to London, in particular the Imperial War Museum. With Dad's historical knowledge and Jack's love of history it felt like a good choice, and afterwards we had a lovely dinner that I had saved for. Dad had taken Jack to a few historical museums, Bovington Tank for one, and The Spitfire Museum, but he did seem frustrated with Jack's Tiggerish nature. Why is it that I worried more about what a couple of family members thought of Jack, and tried to get him to conform to their way of thinking, rather than telling them to do one, and living my life with my son in the way that was best for him? If that meant not seeing anyone who could hurt him I wish so much that I had. I was so torn between being too protective of my son and the conventions of these few. I knew that it wasn't in keeping with the real world to coddle him, but he had this intense sensitivity, a diagnosed medical fact. A tut tut or a stern word wasn't the answer. Anyone with a mental health situation, which let's face it most of us will have at some point, is at a disadvantage as their plight is not visible. Those with a black and white point of view were critical, it was so unfair on Jack. Having said that, the visit to the Imperial War Museum was legendary. Dad was a walking historian, giving Jack such an amazing tour of this fascinating place. Interestingly, one of the exhibits was the Kinder Transport, which was so moving and relatable for Jack and Dad as we read letters home from those children who were evacuated to England and like Dad, evacuated to Wales from his hometown of Liverpool. We took Dad to the renowned Oxo Tower restaurant for a beautiful early dinner, to which he pulled out a wad of cash that apparently Mum had given him to pay for our lunch. In the weeks that followed the author of *Goodnight Mister Tom*, the much heralded book about the relationship between a mature gentleman and an evacuee, was appearing at our local book shop so we visited for the event, met the author who wrote a beautiful note to Dad and we gifted this book to him for Christmas that year. Sadly, it didn't materialise to me during the clear out of my parents' home after they both passed within three months of each other. I have to remember that it's just 'stuff' and the event happened, and the memory is there, for me, Jack and Dad.

Later on, when Jack was 16, we discovered that War Horse was coming to the West End. With Jack having visited Nethercot Farm, which was featured in War Horse, he was excited to go. Dad very much wanted to go, however Mum didn't want to. She was reticent about allowing us to take Dad as he had difficulty with walking. I explained we would obtain a wheelchair and or walker if he needed that after arriving at Waterloo for the brief walk to a taxi which would take us straight to the theatre, and she appeared to have relented. Tickets were bought in an easily accessible row just a few back from the stage and exit door, and a taxi arranged to transport all three of us direct to London, avoiding the trains altogether. Then I received a call from Mum to advise that Dad had tripped in the garden and she wasn't comfortable with him travelling anywhere. Insisting on speaking to Dad, he told me he did want to come but had to do what Mum thought best. I realised then that I was losing the battle for a multitude of reasons. Parents now 78 and 80 years old and naturally less interested in the external world, and Mum with her routine in place, and on top of that the worrying that would consume her while we were at the theatre took precedence. It wasn't a nice feeling for either of us. Jack commented that 'Nana is holding Papa hostage', causing us both to giggle. Suffice it to say, we attended War Horse, and when asked at the box office if we wanted to sell them back our third ticket we turned and looked at each other, then back to the cashier with a resounding 'NO THANK YOU'. We watched the show with Dad's seat right there with us, and my goodness that was such an exceptional production. We purchased the full programme for Papa and his grandson rose to his feet, the very first to give a standing ovation with respectful appreciation.

I realised that I was losing the opportunity to treat my parents. I resorted to sending food gifts, and flowers at their 50th wedding anniversary were placed in Salisbury Cathedral from us as a surprise. Dad was a guide there, and they often went to services so it was a lovely moment to receive a call from them both saying tears had rolled as they heard our names mentioned as donating the Cathedral flowers in celebration of their 50 years. In the role of youngest child, they thought of me as more fragile in some ways than their other children, and of course realised my cup runneth over as a single mum. I think Mum felt I didn't possess the practicality that they needed in their twilight years. I did, she just never realised that beneath my bubbly, risk-taking, emotion driven personality, I cared deeply for their well-being, but the door continued to close on me in their latter years.

My parents and particularly my mother wanted everything to be equal all the time. No one was ever to be seen as favoured by them, and they would make this statement out loud in a group setting. However, in the privacy of our conversations, it was Jack they expressed as their favourite grandchild, and I was my Dad's favourite by a country mile. I used to think they were saying exactly the same thing to whoever was in their presence at the time. It was, and still to this day is, such a dysfunctional way to live. It's OK at times to favour one child over another, depending on the individual circumstance. I sat with my parents many times in recent years, discussing this very subject. Their stance on treating us three kids the same as being very important, and yes on balance, it does make sense, however I would point out that as children, if one of us did wrong against another, we would be sent to our room, or receive the dreaded, 'wait til your father gets home' comment, and in our adult years there could still be times when one of us may have needed more support over another. I feel when I reflect back that they put the three of us in separate boxes, treated us all very nicely, but never joined us together as a family in a natural, organic way.

It's no one's fault, I can only write how I feel, and how I know Jack felt. He recounted an incident when we were staying with my parents for a night and awoke in the morning and Nana said to Jack, right in front of me, 'What would you like for breakfast, Jack? I'll make yours but not your mum's, she can get her own'. When typed out these words don't seem to have quite the impact that they did in person. There I was sitting right next to my son on the little two-seater sofa and my mother was unwittingly hurting him terribly. Pushing his precious Mumsie to the side. As if I expected my mother to make me breakfast. As if I could ever get near the kitchen to attempt to take care of my own meal in her home anyway.

When we would visit, she would stop us outside the front door to remind Jack not to forget to say hello to Papa and give him a hug. Jack was under 10 years old, he was a little boy who wanted to run inside and get to his army soldiers, and of course he was a lovely, well-mannered lad, who occasionally would forget the formalities, but my goodness we would pay for it if we didn't remember to thank everyone 500 times for inviting us over etc.

I recall one trip in the car on the way to my half-sister Jane's home for Christmas when I was saying to Jack, 'Please, please don't forget to offer to help with dinner or cleaning up after.' There I was repeating a pattern from the past, worrying as Mum did to be honest, out of pure fear myself, trying to set things up ahead of time to avoid the critical eye of my half-sister, or stony silence, or overcompensating for her own immediate family members in front of me. Horrid unnecessary admonishments from said sister toward Jack and myself, such as, 'Jack stop wriggling,' 'Jack sit still,' 'your son has just left and run past us without saying thank you for having me.' Jack at 11 was scratched by her son's large dog and it was very upsetting of course, however there was literally not a single word of an apology to Jack, it was, 'Oh, did you startle him? and 'he's just being playful.' There was an awful lot of tut tutting around me and Jack. Why me? Have I answered that question here? Should I have been stronger from day one, or was it just not in my nature, at that time. That cold hard stick has left some permanent damage it seems.

On that Christmas Day journey home the tears began to roll from Jack's eyes and I pulled the car over to the side of the road and we both held each other and cried together. Our sensitivity was crippling, the unnecessary snarky comments were hurtful. Neither of us had wanted to go and I promised him that very day that we would never ever go there for Christmas again. We didn't, and at least he is safe now, safe from a hurtful scold or cutting remark, safe from naysayers, safe from me at times, from anyone and everyone. Everything hurt my son.

When I was 11 my parents told my brother and I that our sister Jane, who was eight years older than me, was actually our half-sister biologically, but their daughter in every way. We were told our mother had been previously married, and if we ever had any questions to go ahead and ask them. At the same time, we were told not to tell anyone, not to even tell our sister, and it was all a bit of a shameful family secret. Quite frankly, I can understand on some level why my sister would be cold and aloof toward me in particular. I was the pretty little blondie daughter, with masses of emotion on full display, open affection at the centre, whereas she was aloof, reserved, and it wasn't in her DNA to show emotion. Very practical and sensible it appeared. I felt sorry for her, I really truly did. I shed tears over her that day as I walked to school after being told this shameful secret.

Over the years, I reached out to her. One memorable time was her 50th birthday. I was living in the USA, and I sent her the Lladro sisters figurine, to try to bridge the gap between us, placed not by her or me, but by the circumstance of her birth. I recall visiting her home a year later, and looking for that figurine, only to spy it on a book shelf in the family office, not proudly out on display as were her other Lladro pieces. Never a photo of my son or me anywhere in her home. Photos of everyone else in the family, but not us. It did hurt, it really did. Maybe she felt annoyed or oddly jealous of me. Maybe my parents displayed more affection toward me? I don't really know. Blending a family is not just about providing food, clothing and shelter, it's about open communication, about being able to share and talk about the 'elephant in the room'. That elephant reappeared many times through our lives, and our parents never addressed it. If they had, I wonder how things may have been different in our overall family life. Our inherited characteristics are one thing, but if we had been able to openly talk about and ask questions about Jane's family members, things may have been easier and therefore easier on Jack. I used to try. Usually at Christmas or Jane's birthday, a card would appear from her birth grandmother but if I asked 'Who's Nanny Knight?' the room would fall silent, and the subject swiftly changed. While I was living in the USA dating Jack's father, we talked about family and he asked about whether my sister's father was alive, so as Dad had always said if I ever had a question I could ask, I called my parents and asked about the circumstances. My goodness was I ever admonished and shot down in flames by my father, who in no uncertain terms told me that he was dead and that was all I needed to know and he was her father and that was that. End of.

I learned more recently, directly from my mother that while she loved her first husband, she struggled with respect for him. They lived at his mother's home and he did not keep jobs for very long, and over time she chose to leave with her little girl, and during this break, he gassed himself in his mother's kitchen using the oven. Tragic yes, but not something to harbour and pretend as if he had never existed. What about my sister? No wonder she held herself in check around me, she wasn't able to openly talk about her birth father and relatives. I have since learned that she and Mum secretly visited her Nanny

Knight from time to time, without Dad's knowledge. I'm glad they had those visits, however I wish so much my mother hadn't been afraid to reveal the truth of the situation. I do respect her personal reasons, but it never is a good idea to keep things hidden and not share your thoughts and feelings. Those decisions put in place before I was born, impacted on me and on my son. My elder sister's aloofness unwittingly hurt me and in turn, hurt my precious sensitive boy.

Sensitivity had its reward for this Mumsie though. For my birthday and Mother's Days etc, gifts of jewellery was the running theme. The lady in the posh frock and accessories shop in the village told me Jack would pop in and rummage through his pockets, dumping coins and notes and bits of tree bark and chewing gum onto her shiny countertop. I received a lovely triple strand, multi coloured necklace with mother of pearl and crystals, and the prettiest triple strand illusion necklace with lilac crystal beads as a Christmas gift. A darling Murano glass heart necklace. Twinkly drop earrings. All loving treats from my Jammie Dodger.

On a trip to Stratford Upon Avon when Jack was just shy of 12, we discovered Lush, the lovely bath goodies shop, and Jack picked out a bright pink and purple twinkly bath ball, which we discovered was called Sex Bomb. Oh my goodness he would treat me many times to that pink and purple glitter fest that when submerged in water, fizzed glitter and pretty little flowers would float to the surface. I in turn, treated him to the Under the Sea bomb, and in fact recently, chose to buy myself that very bomb and had a ceremonial bath with seaweed and all sorts emitting through the fizz, for Jack, for those precious memories.

That trip to Stratford was just a really beautiful time. A very last minute bank holiday event. We travelled to the Dogs Trust in the area to visit Leo, a Lurcher that I had adopted for Jack. We sadly had to leave our precious Westie, Winnie, behind in America, with promises from Jack's father to send her to us once we were settled, however that was not to be. His father chose to send our girl to a family in Tennessee with promises to Jack that he would take him to see her when he next visited. This sadly did not happen, and I recall sitting in my car on the side of the road, as my son's father called me from the USA saying Jack refused to come out of the bathroom and was in a terrible emotional state to learn his father was not taking him to visit Winnie. Apparently, he could not afford the petrol for the journey. Anyway, back to our lovely Stratford mini break. We spent a love filled morning visiting beautiful Leo, who had pounced on a Westie, yes a Westie, who was off its lead, and sadly had passed away. With Dogs Trust stepping in, Leo lived a lovely life in a very large cage, with plentiful walks, albeit muzzled while out of his cage. Jack's loving heart was evident that day as he gently petted Leo through the bars of his cage, and talked softly to him.

We arrived and settled into our hotel, in the centre of the action, and enjoyed an enthralling matinee of Julius Caesar. At a wonderful book shop, I had found a cartoon version of some of Shakespeare's Plays and we read Julius Caesar before the live production, to help Jack understand the overall gist of the play. It helped me too! We had only been back in the UK a little over a year, so this mini break with Jack was just so perfect. Here I was, sitting in the Globe Theatre with my 11 year old son, watching Julius Caesar by William Shakespeare. I was introducing him to another point of view. An historical viewpoint, helping my boy settle, aiding him in rooting himself in a very British life, and what better way than the words of the great Bard himself, albeit all a bit gory. Jack loved the play, he couldn't wait to get down to the stage and touch the fake blood and meet with the actors. I recall tucking him into his hotel bed that night and taking a photo of him as he slept. I often snapped sleeping photos of my perfect, innocent, sleeping boy.

The middle years included a couple of historical school trips. Jack's interest in history served him well, and I embraced this subject along with him, watching many documentaries and films recounting the tragic loss to life in WWI and the atrocities at the hands of the Nazis in WWII. One such trip was a quick one day visit to the Ypres Salient. Jack came back and recounted the sea of graves and I could feel and see he had taken this trip seriously, and displayed an enormous amount of respect and appropriate behaviour on such a visit.

While living in the United States their equivalent to our Remembrance Day was called Memorial Day. On the small island where we lived the veterans would gather at the cenotaph for a service. Jack understood the importance of this day, particularly the mental anguish resulting in those who participated in the Vietnam War. I encouraged Jack to find a veteran, approach them, extend his hand, and thank them for fighting to keep us all safe.

At 15, Jack was part of a school trip to Poland, (the Auschwitz trip). This I personally found difficult because I had made a promise to myself when I felt Jack was old enough I would take him to Auschwitz and experience that homage with him. I grumbled for a day or two, and then let go of my own personal feelings, allowing my boy to take this trip, funded partly by Nana and Papa. Jack returned with the fluffiest Ugg-type slippers and a stunning azure blue crystal heart for me, and his own little souvenirs, salt from the salt mines and postcards symbolising the atrocities. Teen-like behaviour was present too though. He recalled they were let free one evening so they ventured to a local bar and the waitress had asked if they were old enough and did they have ID, to which one of the girls piped up, 'Uh no we don't but we are old enough, our teachers have our passports.' Exit stage left. They came across the yellow arches of McDonalds and sat on a bench in a local park munching on Maccy Ds, chatting about their parents and what to tell them was their favourite part, and they agreed on going to Auschwitz, and the Seder dinner etc. but secretly the McDonalds on the bench was the highlight. No disrespect intended, as Jack also recounted with detail the ghostlike, stark atmosphere, as he and his classmates walked in the footsteps of so many of their same age condemned to death. Jack's beloved teddy accompanied him on that trip, and Jack's recollection of the first night as the lights went out in the hotel room was of boys rustling through their bags grabbing their various blankies, woolies, and bears. Clearly these boys to men were still in need of reminders of home. Actually, Teddy deserves his own cute, adorable, teddy sized chapter.

V

TEDDY

A friend and colleague of mine gave Jack a small plaid teddy bear at just 6 weeks old, in the lead up to Christmas. It was the type with little furry paws that could be squeezed open and shut. A darling little soft beige face, and a red and green plaid cotton body. Jack had three or four cuddly toys and I would rotate them around his crib to see which he would grab for when he was able, and always it was the plaid bear, later named by Jack of course as ta da!... Teddy. During the first few years that little rubber nose was the prime comfort for teething, eventually being replaced with an artfully stitched black cotton one by yours truly.

Teddy went everywhere with Jack. I'm sure many parents can recall similar comforts, such as blankies, favourite books, and squishy toys. Always present in the car seat on the way to and from school, loyal Teddy was there to listen and chill with, to be drooled on, and sweated on during sick days. Teddy's sweet little face nestled close to my innocent little boy napping in his car seat, and cosy at bedtime. I recall snapping a photo as the two of them slept at eleven years old, as I clicked open Jack's door for my nightly last check. And then, finally, ceremoniously pinned by me to eighteen-year-old Jack's t shirt, nestled under his chin as my boy lay sleeping, permanently this time.

Oh Teddy, you weathered on like the Steadfast Tin Soldier through many an operation of blanket stitch sewing, your plaid little body eventually wasting away to a bean bag with legs, but still your sweet face endured. Teddy was lost on more than one occasion resulting in a two hour return car trip to a restaurant, the beach, a variety of car parks, and the shopping trolley hanging by one leg. The bike rides at 7 years old with his mate Ian, swooping back and forth from driveway to driveway on our quiet tree lined street ....this time never to return home. Other bears were purchased in an attempt to replace as we do, however the bubble of warm cosy love, and loyalty was burst, they were not Teddy. I called everywhere looking for a replica of Jack's beloved Teddy, and went so far as commissioning one to be made in his reflection however the plaid didn't match, and 'that's not my Teddy' was the final acceptance.

Teddy had represented those wonder years, and life was changing in so many unknown ways. Several months had passed since Teddy had disappeared, and Jack's father, who had left us by then, in an attempt to repair broken trust came home. On his first day of going to work since returning, he was sent to a woman's shelter to inspect their security system. While there he had to work more closely on the electrical panel and was lead by staff to a room housing donations of toys. The centre of the room was overflowing with a massive floor to ceiling mountain of cuddly toys, and as his dad worked he spied a sweet little face peeking out from the furry mountain....on closer inspection he reached in, to pull out ..... Teddy! While being an EXACT replica of Teddy, down to the little pinched paws, black rubber nose, and green satin bow he wasnt THE Teddy, however my goodness, what a sign I felt. Dad is home, and his first day to work, a validation of things eventually coming full circle, and working themselves out and the patience needed to live in this world was evident, in Teddy.

We sat on the sofa with Jack and told him what had happened, and while he was aware that physically, this bear was a refreshed version of the bear given to him at 6 weeks old, we all felt this was Teddy, restored, reincarnated, and how wonderful for Jack to be able to enjoy seeing his bear, Teddy in his newest form. This loyal loving friend was back ready for talks, cuddles, smelly back packs and toilet seat tops during bath times. On a holiday cruise Jack was given one of those little throw away cameras to use to capture his own memories of our holiday, so when home and film developed we delighted in a reel of photos of Teddy. Teddy the pirate, Teddy at dinner, Teddy by the pool, Teddy gazing at the downy white swan made of a towel by our cabin steward. Yay for Teddy, who adventured with Jack on school trips to Nethercot Farm, Ypres Salient, and Auschwitz... Mumsie and Jack hols to Egypt, Italy, Tobago, various UK mini breaks, and Rome for his eighteenth birthday.

Thank you Teddy, I'm eternally grateful to you as the keeper of Jack's secrets, and for remaining his most loyal companion both here in this world and now across the veil in the next.

VI

IN AND OUT OF THE NEST

School life during Years 10 and 11 slightly improved. Mature beyond his years on many levels, but less street smart than his peers, at the rebellious age when many parents are tearing their hair out, we were in the midst of the greatest mother and son love fest. Jack's rebellion surfaced much later sadly, but it was short lived.

In many ways Jack was a typical teenager, just with a more emotional and sensitive core. The messy room, loads of time in the bathroom, hours on his PlayStation. I encouraged him to embrace his individuality. We used to go online looking at clothes and I loved treating him to outfits for his skater style wardrobe, which featured heavily during his last year at senior school. He used to sneak his black hoodie on underneath his school blazer, and was always getting his knuckles rapped for wearing Converse to school. But if that was the extent of his rebelliousness then what the heck did I have to worry about? As we lived right by the school I would sometimes see him walking home and he now stood taller than most of the other kids. It was so great to see. You don't notice these things so much within the confines of a family of two, apart from the several pairs of school trousers at flood level, needing replacing. Suddenly there he was, this tall, beautiful boy with long wavy hair and beautiful blue grey eyes. I was smitten completely.

Jack really couldn't wait for senior school life to end, and for the label he'd carried all the way from the first couple of years of school, of being overly sensitive and easy to wind up, to be erased. During the last year of school, he came home so angry and upset over a boy who sadly seemed to take pleasure in needling him. I remember Jack bursting in through the back door saying he was going to get his golf club and go back to school and smash this boy to pieces. I understood that he was venting, lashing out, but I was so fed up with the school who put these band aids on things but never really seemed to solve any problems. I called the school and spoke to his year head and relayed what was being said at home, and that if they weren't going to act beyond a slapped wrist I was going to involve the police. Why is it that terrible things have to happen before real change occurs? That threat on my part worked and a whopping one day exclusion was placed on the boy leading into the weekend. I'm not laying blame here, I'm truly not. I'm sure this particular lad has had to face how maybe he could have handled things differently. People develop in different ways. Maybe he had older siblings and never had a voice at home, and used school to exert himself. Maybe peers around him played a role. I certainly hold no flame to anyone's toes.

Jack and I began discussing which college he would attend once he'd finished school. I could see that Jack was settling a little more with his friends in the village, but seeing how distressed he became over comments from not only students, but staff at his school was really awful. I have a very distressing and painful memory of Jack recounting to me that he wasn't sure about the new Head of the school and his nature. I gently explained that the poor man was dealing with a very large role in the school and had many duties to take on and maybe he appeared a bit standoffish as a result. I suggested that maybe Jack, upon encountering the Head, should introduce himself and welcome him to the school. Sadly, when he did what I advised, stopping to say hello to the Head, extending his hand, and asking how he was settling in, he was met with a blank stare, no return handshake and a turn of his back. That was absolutely it for me, I was beyond livid. I emailed said Head Teacher, and the next day the Deputy Head appeared at my door and did his level best to diffuse my ire.

What to do? My mothering instincts on high alert, I began to think that maybe Jack wasn't quite ready for college life and for mixing with new people, and maybe I wasn't ready to muster what he may need to support him through the young adult years. I found myself thinking of where I could 'hide' my boy away until his emotions settled. I thought of the time we had spent in the Cotswolds. I had some conversations with the Head of the grammar school, which just so happened to be in the same pretty community we had enjoyed so much on our Pooh sticks adventure. He had a very supportive vibe, and explained that the number of kids who stayed on for Years 12 and 13 was around fifty and in that close knit environment there was no room for bullying or anti-social behaviour. I discussed it with Jack and he agreed and seemed uplifted by the idea of living in the lovely village we had visited, and the possibility of a part time job at the bird sanctuary there. So, on it right away, I began perusing homes to rent, and the type of work I may be able to find, with Cheltenham the closest large city.

With plans to visit the school in place, I was met with Jack's anxiety about moving again, as he felt things had settled and he didn't want to leave his established mates. He said he felt like he belonged there and he was not going to allow one boy to cause him to lose his core of mates and our sweet little home. It created a bit of a laboured exhale on my part, as it seemed like the immediate panic and pain from each incident, for me at least, was agony to hear and see, and I just wanted to keep my boy safe. He assured me that he wanted to go to the local college to do his A levels. So we had another big chat, lots of hugs and l agreed to stay put, to give him his couple of college years, and then we would re-evaluate things.

During this time Jack had a little 'as and when' job at the local Chinese restaurant. They thought he was very polite and while having a regular girl in the take-out part of the business, Jack acted as an on-call employee when they were short staffed. He was called in probably around eight or ten times but I could sense he was more stressed out than happy with making some extra money for himself. The first few times he was fine, and happily came home with his pay and chicken chow mein. Gradually came the revelation that he felt out of his depth and that they hadn't trained him properly for the job, as he was expected to serve drinks and bus tables at only fifteen. The last couple of times they called he said he was busy. I wasn't really sure what to make of it, but decided to trust in what he was saying and how he felt. He was never a lazy lad, not in the slightest, it just seemed that he preferred to be cocooned away.

During this same time I noticed a change in his command of the English language. As the kids played on their PlayStations with microphones I could hear parts of conversations, which included quite a large amount of the f-word, and the dreaded ugly four letter c-word. While he wasn't talking to me like that, I did find it strangely abusive. It was like living next door to a noisy neighbour you can't seem to get away from. Over time it begins to wear you down. I discussed this with Jack's Cams doctor, who we visited every six months. During our visit, as school was winding down, he had a chat with Jack about respect and suggested that when he was out with his mates, it was OK to drop the f-bomb, but within earshot of Mum, perhaps he should keep his bedroom door closed or speak softly. The doctor encouraged Jack to strongly consider getting a different part-time job. He seemed quite good with Jack and they gelled, so while Jack did not want to get a job as he felt scared about it, the doctor explained to him, as I had already tried to, that it was part of growing from a boy to a young man, and from this part-time job he would gain people skills, and make new friends, and begin to gain a little independence as he earned some money for himself. We three agreed that during the summer before college he would find part-time work, and I agreed not to bring it up until then.

Jack didn't seem particularly stressed out about taking his GCSEs. Probably no more or less than most teenagers. A fun element of the final year of senior school was the upcoming prom. We had such a great day out shopping for what Jack would wear. I thought for sure he would want to wear a suit, skinny tie a la Vivienne Westwood, and some hair gel and pomade, but oh no, he wanted to wear a top hat and tails. The protective mother lioness to her cub was 'No! Why put yourself in the firing line to get teased?' But he dug his heels in, as this was the look he wanted. From the sound of the dance moves thudding through the ceiling leading up to prom, I could tell this would be a watershed moment for Jack. We shopped for a slick black tails with all the trimmings, down to the cane and white gloves. It was such a lovely day out with my boy. We decided to trim his top hat and selected a purple ribbon to wrap around with a green feather to add a little shazzam. He shared with me that he was going to ask a girl to prom. I tried to figure out where she ranked socially, worrying if he might be punching too high, or not high enough. While of course to me Jack was, is and always will be utterly perfect, reality could bite, especially in the form of a turn down for such an event. He received a bit of a, 'Oh, I'm not sure, can I let you know?' answer. In other words, a no. But Jack handled it very well, as I gently explained to him that beauty was completely in the eye of the beholder, and combined with peer pressure, exams pressure, and girls changing their minds every fifteen seconds, going to prom with a group of mates was a far better option.

He looked so incredibly handsome on prom day. Taller than most of his friends, and with that beautiful open smile painted across his milky face, my heart soared with pride. I will never forget the limo arriving at the hotel and as Jack stepped out, a couple of girls squealing, 'Oh wow look at Jack!' He shared with me the next day that it was the very best night he had had ever. He said he broke out his dance moves and the kids all cleared the floor and watched him, cheering and clapping. He knew his boundaries and he crossed them when he was ready, and I just delighted in him. If my heart could sing it would have. It was as if the bird with the clipped wings was finally free to express himself, to be who he was born to be.

The only down side was when he told me that they didn't have a place set for him at any of the tables, but that one of the teachers sorted it out for him. He was on enough of a high to not let it interfere with his happiness, but my goodness I felt so sick inside. Wouldn't any mum have the same feeling? Or would they be able to have a laugh and brush it off? Was I projecting my own insecurities and worries onto my precious boy? Life would have been so much easier to bear if I didn't feel on such an intense level.

I recall seeing a counsellor during my divorce, and her telling me, 'Tracy you feel life with all of its rainbow of colours, the bright neon pinks, the rich poppy reds, the cool blues, the muddled grey, and the dense black. You are living your life fully, you are feeling everything, and that is a blessing.' I reluctantly think she is probably right, but my goodness when the grey mixes with the black it's such a dark and painful way to live. If this is how it feels as an adult woman, goodness knows how my sweet sixteen-year-old son managed. I remember him telling me that sometimes he wished he could take his brain out of his head and give it a good shake, and put it back in.

I came upon this poem, by Andrea Chesterman-Smith and oh how I wish I had been able to read it during those teen years. It's not as if I didn't already have clarity on ADHD, it's just that when living my life alongside my boy, and our worlds intertwining, me being the Mum, Dad, and everything to him, and with my own insecurities, sadness, trying so hard to conform myself to society, did I miss something? I'm so conflicted inside to this very day. I was Jack, Jack was me, I tried my very best I really truly did.

ADHD

Take my hand and come with me,
I want to teach you about ADHD.
I need you to know, I want to explain,
I have a very different brain.
Sights, sounds, and thoughts collide.
What to do first? I can't decide.
Please understand I'm not to blame,
I just can't process things the same.
Take my hand and walk with me,
Let me show you about ADHD.
I try to behave, I want to be good,
But I sometimes forget to do as I should.
Walk with me and wear my shoes,
You'll see its not the way I'd choose.
I do know what I'm supposed to do,
But my brain is slow getting the message through.

IN AND OUT OF THE NEST

Take my hand and talk with me,
I want to tell you about ADHD.
I rarely think before I talk,
I often run when I should walk.
It's hard to get my school work done,
My thoughts are outside having fun.
I never know just where to start,
I think with my feelings and see with my heart.
Take my hand and stand by me,
I need you to know about ADHD.
It's hard to explain but I want you to know,
I can't help letting my feelings show.
Sometimes I'm angry, jealous, or sad.
I feel overwhelmed, frustrated, and mad.
I can't concentrate and I lose all my stuff.
I try really hard but it's never enough.
Take my hand and learn with me,
We need to know more about ADHD.
I worry a lot about getting things wrong,
Everything I do takes twice as long.
Everyday is exhausting for me,
Looking through the fog of ADHD.
I'm often so misunderstood,
I would change in a heartbeat if I could.
Take my hand and listen to me,
I want to share a secret about ADHD.
I want you to know there is more to me.
I'm not defined by it, you see.
I'm sensitive, kind and lots of fun.
I'm blamed for things I haven't done.
I'm the loyalist friend you'll ever know,
I just need a chance to let it show.
Take my hand and look at me
Just forget about the ADHD.

I have real feelings just like you.
The love in my heart is just as true.
I may have a brain that can never rest,
But please understand I'm trying my best.
I want you to know, I need you to see,
I'm more than the label, I am still me.

The summer before college was such a great summer for us both and we spent much of it hanging out at Jack's friend Joe's house. Jack loved hanging out at Joe's as for him, it was a vibrant, 'real' family. Joe's sister 'crushing' on Jack was so lovely to experience, with her flushed cheeks and his million watt smile. The Taylor's felt safe, and we belonged. They truly were a complete delight and their door always open to us.

With the conclusion of senior school the kids were planning a bit of a rave at the Bombpits, where they would hang out back in the day. With Joe's dad's permission some cans of beer were purchased for the lads to take to the party. They were absolutely thrilled to bits with this and left with a carrier bag of loot. When they returned several hours later, they recounted being stopped by the local community police who took all the beer and left them with one can each. Oh well, they were only sixteen after all, and it is a rite of passage, for us parents and younglings.

Upon finishing senior school Jack announced that he no longer wanted to take his ADHD medication. He felt strongly about this, and we had several conversations about this decision and how it may or may not impact life for him at college as well as at home. During the summer before college life was marching along with no particular structure per se. It was hard to gauge whether there was a pressing need for Jack to take medication. Beginning college would tell the tale. That son of mine became the boy he was born to be that summer. He was back to being Tigger; cheeky, funny, edgy, affectionate, just about the most utterly perfect young man.

Exam result day arrived and living next to the school had its blessings as Jack bolted down there first thing and came home pretty happy with his lot. Passes in all but two, only one point from a C in Maths and an epic fail in Technology, oddly epic for pretty much every student apparently, as they all received much lower grades than had been expected. These results confirmed a place at a very good local college. The college had a day for students to visit with their results, and to discuss what subjects to take and basically go through the entry process. Jack felt confident to do this himself, as parents at this point weren't involved in student life, and I encouraged him to be independent. It was just a meeting with the college careers person to look at his results and place him appropriately. Later into the day I answered my phone to my son in tears and terribly emotional. He told me the careers lady had told him he wasn't able to attend the college as he hadn't received a pass in English Language. He told me he had tried to explain to her that he had taken his English Language exam the year before and passed it, and that's why the result was not on the list. He felt terribly panicked and understandably upset and to hear him sobbing in the boys' toilets at the college was more than I could bear. I got straight on the phone with the college and I was on my way. I remember the road was blocked off and I had to weave all over the place to get to him. Jack met me outside the college as I pulled up and we had a long hug. We made our way to the room where the various heads were meeting with students, and after some conversation and an email from Jack's senior school all was sorted. But my goodness, it was so upsetting. A clerical error, a small harmless slight, causing gigantic harm to my son on what was supposed to be such a happy, grown-up day. The staff very kindly arranged Jack's subjects with me sitting protectively by him. A decision was made to follow his interest in History, English Literature, and Film, as well as a retake of his Maths GCSE. Jack had a genuine interest in History, English Literature made sense as he had a creative energy and flair for the dramatic. Film was a little nudge from me I guess, as we spent our Sundays together sharing many films and roast dinners. It seemed a great research opportunity and a cheeky way for me to stay involved in Jack's emerging new life.

I had always had a hankering toward classic movies. As a teenager my bedroom walls were covered in posters of Lauren Bacall, James Dean and

Marilyn Monroe and my Sundays would be spent curled up on the sofa with Mum and Dad as they introduced me to classics like *From Here to Eternity, Splendour in the Grass, Giant, The Great Escape, Ben Hur* and so on. We would delight in Mum's yummy roast dinners, then settle on the sofa with a chocolate bar each and step back in time.

Bringing that tradition into our little family unit of two led to an agreement that Sunday was our day, a day spent at home. Jack's friends knew this and respected his space. I would hear him occasionally reminding them Sunday was his day with Mumsie. He never said it in a tortured teen way, just that's how it was. We would sleep in and Jack would chill in his room on his games, or we worked on homework projects. We would always have a lovely Sunday lunch, whether we went out, ordered in, cooked, or just laid a table filled with nibbles. Then we would indulge in my childhood tradition of a movie, but took it in turn choosing, so it would go something like this, me: *Dr Zhivago, A Place in the Sun,* Jack: *Troy, Sausage Party* (yikes!) both of us: *Schindler's List, Stalingrad,* episode upon episode of *Only Fools and Horses.* Sometimes we would have a game of chess, chequers or scrabble, creating a lovely mental scrapbook of Sunday afternoon memories. Then of course, he retreated back to his nest, his beloved games and convos with Joe, Ben and other friends, brought together from all over the country through technology. My boy was becoming a college bound young man, but it seemed he still needed me along for the ride.

VII

DECISIONS DECISIONS

As I reflect back I realise that, at the time when decisions are made, they seem like the right thing to do, even if hindsight might prove differently. With our decision made to stay put in Liphook, and for Jack to attend the local college, it was time for me to figure out how I was going to live my life aside from loving and supporting Jack. I had spent the past few years in the bridal industry. As Jack became a teenager and the rules changed regarding the benefits available to single parents, I decided to find work. This time however, I wanted to work in a more frivolous environment. My career thus far had been that of business sales in the uniform and education marketplaces, and a natural gift for selling seemed evident. I still very much wanted to be on hand for Jack, so I landed a position in London working for a bridal designer two days a week, one of them being a Saturday. Therefore I was still very much there for Jack upon his return home. I loved that job so much, the adrenaline rush was intense selling dresses in the £3,000 price range. Sadly, one day while carrying a heavy wedding dress downstairs to dress a future bride, who requested not to be viewed through the shop window, I tripped and snapped a bone in my foot. An ugly end to an otherwise delightful six months ensued, with the shop owner accepting no culpability, and no offer for me to return to work once healed. So I was left to figure out another source of income, while healing a broken foot and all the while the horrible system nipping at my heels as to why I wasn't working. I managed to work from home doing some sales for a wholesale florist but I felt the vice-like grip of the system pinching my resolve. I knew I loved the buzz of working with brides and it was for the most part a happy environment, so I studied local trade magazines searching for a similar role. An opportunity presented itself working as a Regional Manager for a wholesale company selling dresses direct to shops, and I found a natural ability to form relationships with those shop owners, which therefore led to some sizable dress orders. The company I worked for were new and I was their golden girl. My schedule was perfect as I worked from home, still allowing me the flexibility to be completely invested in Jack as he prepared for college. However the behind the scenes machinations of the company I worked for were questionable at best, and upon delivery of the gowns I had sold, it became clear that the production side was not supplying the same quality of garment that was demonstrated with my set of samples. I found this to be unconscionable. Here I was out on the road, selling to up and coming shops, one in particular had purchased their entire inventory from me, only to discover that when they reordered a dress it did not arrive made to the specifications of their shop-owned sample. I took my job very seriously, and felt terribly embarrassed. So I made the decision to end my job with said company, who within twelve months of my resignation, closed their doors.

All was not an epic fail however. Out of that time, I gained the dearest friend. Hope and her daughter Simone were opening a shop in Ashford, Kent and I had arranged to meet them at Hope's home. Upon entering her sweet little flat, to a welcome of sandwiches and tea, I felt awash with comfort and affection toward Lesley and I am told it was mutual. Her two daughters were working with Hope to open their dream shop and they fell in love with our dresses, placing two very healthy orders. After the dreadful customer service revealed itself, I felt a responsibility of sorts to be there and try to help Hope and Simone as much as I could. I participated in two or three events for them and while we shared compensation, for me it was more about seeing this young mother raising two children by herself succeed in an ever changing, competitive industry. Over that first year a true friendship developed, and to this very day I count Hope and Simone as older and younger 'sisters'. Their friendship saved me, quite literally, as you will learn later. I now found myself with some experience of both sides of the business but very few pennies in the bank. I was aware of an evening dress/prom shop in a town just fifteen minutes from our home and, while they weren't advertising for staff, I decided to give them a call and after detailing my experience and success in sales, the shop owner invited me for a visit. It turned out that she had, as she put it, brought me there 'under false pretences'. She was actually looking for a buyer. She had only been there for a year, and with my research showing no other wedding dress shops in the area and a small loan from a business friend, on December 12th 2011 I became a Proprietor. I had nothing to support myself or Jack with, however our benefits and the government ordered maintenance from his father were just enough to keep us afloat as I went about rebranding the business. Jack and I were beyond happy, it was such a great time. We talked about the possibility of one day being able to own the house we had privately rented those past seven years and we both felt like we were finally home. Mumsie busy with her shop and her precious seventeen-year-old Jammie Dodger was settling into college.

My dreaded 50th birthday arrived, and that darling boy bought me a book of Shakespeare's Sonnets. He knew I loved the film *Sense and Sensibility*, he watched it with me a couple of times, bless him. In the film there's a lovely scene where Willoughby, the dashing rogue, presents a pocket-size book of the sonnets to the heroine Marianne. I would find myself completely swept away with that film. It actually captured Jack too, who after an initial hurrumph, would become transfixed and fully invested in the characters. A card accompanied his perfect gift, showing three teddy bears holding the letters M U M, followed by my son's written words:

You are the most amazing Mum I could of ever wished for.
You now have your beautiful shop and things are finally working in your favour.
No matter what happens, I will always be there for you to comfort you, or watch
Dr. Zhivago with you because I love you and you are everything I have.

lots of love
Jack
XXXXX XXXXX OOOOO OOOOO
♥♥♥♥♥♥♥♥

With Jack's steadfast decision to not take any more ADHD medication when he began college I was very concerned about his concentration and ability to stay on task. But he felt he would be able to manage, so we decided a wait and see approach was a fair compromise. To see my boy go from a chrysalis to a butterfly was just the most beautiful feeling. He was bouncy like Tigger, but so happy. The biggest smiles ever across his cheeky beautiful boy-to-man face, as stubble appeared and his voice deepened. Through those physical changes, the beating heart of my precious son, the mood board of his soul, now devoid of mood-altering medication, was evident for all to embrace. He now stood just shy of six foot, all of his confidence on full display.

Jack embraced the individuality of college. He loved that he could wear his funky cool clothes, and blend right into the college dynamic. He used to come into my room before college with his pot of gel asking me to style his hair for him. Me half asleep gelling up this emo-esque layered confection. Even, once in a while, a dab of eyeliner. I loved seeing him display his individuality. He was making new friends at college, and it seemed the ones he related to the most, and vice versa, were of a somewhat creative and intellectual variety. The debaters, the photographers, the artists, the historians. A boy called Matt, a very good looking lad and overly confident, who I learned was not particularly popular with his peers, attached himself to Jack and they became fast friends. I surmised that having a friend who oozed confidence could only be a good thing for Jack and he appeared to be super happy with his life. Matt often popped over and referred to us as his family away from home, and that Jack was just the best friend ever. I guess it was terribly flattering for Jack, however I recognised in Matt a deep insecurity and I thought there was a pretty good match between the two of them. Matt with his million and one ideas and ambition, which intrigued Jack, and Jack's sensitivity and caring nature, softening Matt's tough shell.

Recognising that Jack was 'happy busy' between college, his new pals and his core local mates, allowed me the time to devote to my shop. It was an incredibly risky move and an enormous amount of pressure as I went from rebranding the shop from its grungy decor and prom dresses only to a stylish new interior and name, launching it as a vintage-inspired bridal boutique. I managed this transformation by offering my stock of prom dresses at only £99 each. I was working towards accumulating the funds to be able to purchase my bridal stock. Jack was there at the launch, preferring to be in the background, washing dishes and glasses in the kitchen area as various guests popped in for a snowball, Babycham, or cherry brandy, in keeping with the vintage 1950s vibe. We left the shop that day laden down with left over vintage sweet treats from the local candy shop. Upon reaching our home Jack spied a mate called Harry, so we pulled over and shelled sweet treats all over him. I was stunned to hear from Jack that this was one of the boys present during the spitting incident five years previously. And yet now here he was, one of Jack's local village mates.

During this time my niece Jill and her fiancé Stu announced their wedding plans to marry in Thailand. The wedding was actually during the half term break in February, so Jack would only miss two days of college. As is the norm with me, I dived in and used the funds I'd saved to buy my bridal stock to take Jack with me to my delightful niece's wedding. Being in the bridal industry, and loving my niece so much, I couldn't help but treat her maids to their dresses and upon our arrival in Thailand, Jack and I hosted a cocktail party in our splendid oceanfront rooms. Jill's maids and friends who attended the wedding were a complete delight. They welcomed and included Jack, and it was lovely to see. At the same time I had to leave the shop and was carrying a pressure cooker of stress as to how I was going to fund my opening stock of wedding gowns. The supplier was OK with a net 60 terms however, this had never been my intention, it had always been to pay for everything up front. But I felt that taking Jack to my niece's wedding would help to secure and bond him with the few family members we had.

Oddly, it was during this time that I noticed a shift in Jack. I can't really pinpoint it to a precise event. The best way I can describe it was that, at seventeen, an impatient, huffy Jack appeared. It felt very similar to how his friends had acted around their parents at age fifteen or sixteen. Us both being super sensitive, it was difficult to experience this mood shift and I felt hurt and rejected, but I would try to rationalize it as normal teen stuff, just happening a year or two later than his peers. One minute he was Mister Independent, the next curling up beside me for affection and guidance.

During our Thailand stay we spent a couple of days relaxing on the beach while the wedding party attended to planned events. We would sit at the ocean's edge and allow the breeze to cool us and chatter to other guests. One such guest was a pretty, edgy looking girl from Germany, someone I could see was Jack's type. They would smile at each other and spent a couple of hours chatting to each other in the ocean. Her English was good enough to cross the language barrier and I sat back on my lounger watching with delight as Jack interacted with her. Jack and I chattered about her that evening when we went to dinner, and how nice it was for him, and it was wonderful to see his face so bright and happy. Of course the next day we were back on the same spot on the beach in anticipation for this budding friendship to continue. This time however, she seemed slightly guarded and the conversation did not flow and the crestfallen pain behind my precious son's eyes was excruciating to bear witness to.

Later, we sat in our room and he laid on the bed and the tears rolled and the deep sadness he was experiencing was so evident. It was so terribly sad to see the rejection he felt, and I felt too. This is where our sameness began to reveal itself slightly. As a mum I was there to raise my child, provide him with food, shelter, love, affection, all of which were in abundance, but now there was this additional layer of managing his expectations with other people. Our bubble of love was snagging and tearing as the real world encroached. I tried to ease his angst by explaining that we just don't know how other people act and why, and that whatever they say and do is always about them and has nothing to do with us or in this case, him. I tried to make him see that we didn't know anything about the girl, or her family. We didn't know if her father possibly didn't want his daughter talking to a boy, or maybe the family wanted a day just for them. There were so many 'what ifs' and I tried so hard to ease his sorrow and to talk about how painful sensitivity can be. It truly is the very best and the very worst of traits that we were both deigned to have.

The wedding itself was just lovely, the food delicious, the drinks plentiful, a really special day. I have treasured memories of my amazing son asking some of the ladies present to dance, and seeing their faces swept up in his sweet gesture. And I received a slew of compliments for what a polite, lovely, charming young man I had raised. I watched my gorgeous boy approach the prettiest young woman there, ten years his senior, for a romantic slow dance. I sat with the other maids gazing in wonder as my boy protectively held her and they danced his very first and as it turned out, only slow dance, to Aerosmith's, *I Don't Want To Miss A Thing*. Tears rolled down my cheeks, tears of pride, of love, of release, of knowing that my son was moving from boy to man right in front of me. One maid handed me her bouquet as a parting gift, which touched me so very deeply. It was such a lovely personal moment.

I had asked my niece Jill about maybe having a dinner with her and her new husband on one of the evenings after the wedding, but it was never accepted, instead a lunch with them was arranged during the day. The night time they wouldn't give up, this is how we felt. This was the level of our sensitivity, the presence of Jane always brought an uncomfortable, conformist vibe. It's not her fault, it's no one's fault, it's just a blended family that in my opinion never blended, as I've mentioned previously. No one seemed to understand Jack's ADHD. His fear to try new foods. His bouncy Tiggerish nature. Meal times were so incredibly tense when dining with others, and this lunch was no exception. I felt the pressure to be more mainstream with Jack. To make him try new things when he wasn't ready, to fit in with everyone better, and never was that more evident than in the company of Jane. Jack barely ate at that meal, the choices were not for him. We returned to our room for an afternoon chill, and I spent the next hour trying to order some nice food for later in the evening that would suit him better, and myself. I felt myself boiling over inside, frustrated and upset that he couldn't just fit in for one bloody meal, and we both ended up in tears in our room. My anxiety over Jane so much in the forefront, and with Jack as my companion, friend, and son, the recipient of my angst.

We spent the remaining couple of days chilling on our large lanai or watching TV. I treated myself to a fantastic Thai massage, a personal highlight of the trip, and fell in love with the Laying Buddha sculpture on display in the Spa and with some gentle negotiating, became the owner of said Buddha. The distance between us was still underlying as we both 'survived' the remaining couple of days before we could get out of Thailand and back home, to our little nest, mother and baby duckie all safe again.

VIII

CHRYSALIS TO BUTTERFLY BOY

With Jack seemingly settled into college and with his blessing, I contacted the restaurant manager at a local country club, with a view to finding Jack a part-time job there. The manager recognised Jack's polite, well-spoken manner, and his exceptional table manners, and agreed to take him on. Jack settled on a job in the kitchen washing dishes. He wanted to be hidden away where no one could hurt him. He refused point blank to work in the restaurant, and even when the manager cajoled him with the offer of a higher pay level, Jack wouldn't budge. He didn't want to put himself in any situation that he might perceive himself as 'failing' in, or the possibility of hurt feelings. He wasn't ready, he told me, he just wanted to do what he did and for everyone to back off and let him. He liked his kitchen mates, and appeared comfortable in that role. I loved seeing him propped up at a little bistro set we had in the living room in his checked trousers and blue, chef-style top, chattering about the shenanigans of life in the kitchen of such a busy hotel. Jack and his closest workmate, Santino, had identified a corner of the kitchen out of sight to the security cameras and would dance and goof about there, during less busy times. Jack really liked Santino, and explained to me that he was Spanish and waiting to begin his vet training. When I met Santino I picked up on his gentle nature and could see why Jack felt comfortable around him. There was no side, and with Santino being five or six years older, he became a sort of older brother to Jack.

I let Jack be, preparing for adult life on his own schedule. The kitchen porter hours were not as intense or late as a waiter's, so he was usually home at a reasonable hour. And I was thrilled when he received his first pay cheque and treated me to some Lush bath products. He knew I loved them and it was such a treat to be handed a bag containing sweet-smelling bath bombs. He was such a generous young man. And seeing how happy and settled he was, both with college and work, I saw our decision to stay put as definitely being the right one.

I could see that Jack was trying his best at college. He often took the late bus home in order to complete assignments within the college environment. He felt he was coping and staying on task if work was completed there, rather than at home, with the distractions of TV, me, gaming, and mates. His affable Tiggerish nature was on full display, and it was such a thrilling day when he came home excited to tell me that he'd been told that a girl called Leila – "not LAYLA, Mumsie!" – liked him. I got right on board with this revelation, and he showed me her Facebook page and images. She was a lovely looking, edgy girl from a very nice area. After a few group dates, and plenty of chatter at college, Jack made plans for a movie date with Leila. It wasn't near pay day so I provided the cash and explained to him that it would be important to make sure that she was safely on her train home before he left for his train, after the date. I remember him coming home from the date so happy and telling me all about it. He had purchased tickets for the movie *War Horse* and it turned out that Leila was horse crazy, having one of her own, so it was the perfect first date. We giggled like mad when Jack said they got the tickets early then went to get some food and a drink as they had an hour or so to kill, and in typical Tiggerish fashion, he lost the tickets! He said they still managed to get into the movie as the chap who sold them the tickets recognised them. How could he not? They must have been hands down the cutest couple ever to grace his ticket window!

Jack recounted making sure Leila was on her train, and was beside himself with thanks to me for the suggestion, because there was about forty-five minutes before the train departed, so he sat with her and they established that they were officially dating, and shared a soft kiss. Then he quickly hightailed it up to his room to message said shiny new girlfriend. I love that memory, it's one of those firsts us mums the world over are never likely to forget.

The words in Jack's written hand on Mother's Day during this loving beautiful time resonate:

Dear Mumsie,
Thank you for being here for me every waking moment in life.
I couldn't have had a girlfriend without your loving support, and nobody could ever
try and tamper with that special bond which we share.

All the love in the world
Jack
XXXXXXXXXX XXXXXXXXX
OOOOOOOOOO OOOOOOOOOO
♥ ♥ ♥

I was working in my shop on this particular Mother's Day and I returned home to a beautiful roast dinner all cooked by my lovely son, and a bouquet of pretty white roses. We sat side by side enjoying such a thoughtful dinner, with lots of hugs and of course, a repeat viewing of *Sense and Sensibility*. It was Mother's Day after all.

My emotions were swept away with Jack's. He just adored Leila and she, from what he told me, felt the same also. He used to carry her books for her and they'd spend their lunch breaks together. He recounted how sensitive and tender she was, and they seemed to really understand each other, chatting online into the wee hours and sending a plethora of texts. On one occasion, when a cronie of the main bully at his high school shouted a nasty comment about Jack across the college field, Leila took his hand and gently told him to ignore him as she immediately sensed his hurt feelings. Why, why, why did my boy have to feel things on such an emotional level?

Jack's mood seemed to rise and fall depending on how he perceived Leila to be on any given day. It was such a rollercoaster time for him. His first girlfriend, and all the emotions that come with that. I explained to him on countless occasions that teenage girls can be all over the place hormonally, as can boys for that matter, and that he mustn't take her mood shifts personally, things would be OK and to just coast with it. Initially, there would be beaming smiles when he came in from college, then a couple of downcast ones, then very quickly the smiles became less as my unravelling, panicked boy was unsure of how to deal with what he perceived to be her aloofness. Not allowing him to carry her books, saying she had other things to do, and not having the time for him that she initially did.

It was during one of these weeks of more lows than highs that the two of us sat and talked. As I'm sure most mums would do, I explained to Jack how good looking he was, and such a fantastic human, he didn't have to settle if things didn't feel right. These were his college years and he needed to realise that there were a boat load of other lovely girls out there, and if this one was too moody and aloof, then perhaps it would be better to cool it. The next day he came home distressed again, feeling horribly rejected and decided right then and there that he didn't want to see her anymore and he was going to message her to tell her. I told him he needed to do that face to face, but he refused, ran upstairs, grabbed his laptop and sat half way down the stairs, composing a message basically saying he didn't feel good in her company and was moving on. In my life I have often made knee jerk decisions and found myself regretting them an hour later, and I so didn't want this to happen to my boy. However, the minute he clicked the send button it was as if the weight of the world lifted from him, and that beautiful open smile reappeared as he bounded to his room to regroup with his online mates for some battles.

The next day he returned from college having had to deal with the fall out of the email break-up from Leila's mates. Poor Jack, it stung so much to be rebuked, and my goodness I felt the rebuke right along with him. Instant regret was evident and after a few days he messaged her with my help, in an attempt to apologise for how he had ended things and to try and put a friendship in place but no reply came. A week or so later, a crestfallen boy came home to my arms and recounted how one of his mates, Eric, was now dating her. All of his other mates rallied round Jack in solidarity with the old 'bros before hoes' edict but Jack struggled terribly with what had happened. We had many lengthy conversations over Jack feeling so betrayed. With the wisdom of life experience I understood the teen angst element of feeling betrayed, and explained as best I could that while maybe Jack felt the boy code was super important, not everyone would feel that way. It was a bit shitty, but at the same time, I thought that logically relationships were bound to overlap in a college environment, and also in the real world.

With summer approaching and plans to go clubbing and working at the country club, along with Matt now driving, Jack was in full seventeen-year-old mode. He contributed greatly during that summer as I navigated my shop and the rebranding into the bridal boutique. Money was very tight but this beautiful boy of mine willingly gave me as much as half of his pay at times to help out.

With extra working hours during the summer, Jack was happily blending work life and social time with a bit of Sunday Mumsie time. Shopping was fun for Jack and he would come home with new clothes, always super stylish, he was so far ahead of the game on looking cool. I'll take a titch of credit for that, from day one that boy of mine was a mini fashionisto. I loved treating him when I could to clothes, and we would sit and scour on the laptop together, him dropping hints about his fave stuff, and me ordering them secretly the next day. Skinny jeans in royal blue, purple, red and black striped, and most memorable of all, a skull belt studded with purple swarovskis. My edgy boy was not afraid to express himself, gaining confidence as he let go of the emotions connected to his first love. He loved to go to the club foam parties that were popular for the under 18s. He came home from his first one flying high as he described dancing and the floor being cleared while everyone watched him showing off his moves to LMFAO's *Party Rock* Anthem. His sensitivity was still evident though, when his mate let him down not once but twice with plans they had to go clubbing.

One such let down was particularly crushing as they were scheduled to go to a foam party when Jack was let down. He was so disappointed and I sat with him and we had a great talk about how he absolutely could still go clubbing and he didn't have to go with anyone. I explained to him how, when we came back to England, I would go to the local club by myself for the odd night out. I suggested he give it a chance and reassured him I would be here to pick him up if he wasn't comfortable when he got there. So my boy took the train to Gunwharf Quays to the bar where the under 18 foam party was taking place. I sat at home on the sofa hoping so much that he would have a great night. When he got there he sent me a text saying, 'Mumsie I'm in the queue but it's like 2 miles long, not sure I'll get in.' I replied 'um I don't think it's quite 2 miles sweetie just hold on you will be fine.' Then he sent a crestfallen message saying that he didn't think he was going to make it in. I was grabbing my bag to go and pick him up when another message arrived: 'Mumsieeeee, guess what? The doorman came out and pointed at me and this other boy and let us in.' I asked him why they'd been chosen and when I received Jack's reply; 'the doorman said that there weren't enough good looking Emos inside!' my heart just soared with love and excitement for him. Things went quiet for a few hours then he texted to say he was on the train back. That boy of mine came bounding into my bedroom covered in orange foam, saying he'd had the best night ever. Girls were swarming, and he danced the night away, even enjoying a cheeky kiss or two. Beaming, he thanked me for giving him the confidence to go, and bopped off to his bedroom to no doubt get online to chat with those teens he had spent the 'best night of his life' with.

The next time Jack was let down by his friend when they were supposed to go clubbing I talked to him about the need to expand his friendship group, telling him that he could have friends for different reasons. I reminded him of his sensitivity and that plans do change, but heck I felt the same way he did – hurt and disappointed that he had been let down again. It was time to diversify. Jack mentioned a boy he really liked called Dylan and with some encouragement, he messaged him and it turned out he was really up for a clubbing night out. I remember driving home from work and seeing them heading toward the station, so I stopped and gave them a lift. Dylan was staying the night so off they went, with a promise of bacon bagels in the morning. Dylan was such a gentle soul and a great match for Jack. While they didn't live too close to each other they did interact at college and Jack felt confident in his growing group of mates. I was recently kindly invited to Dylan's wedding, and his sweet bride and maids did all their shopping at my shop. It was an honour and a privilege. This young man, with all that he had on his mind on his wedding day, as he walked back down the aisle with his new wife, spied me and reached out to hug and kiss me. Later that evening he blew me away as he toasted Jack. It was so meaningful that five years on, this lad still cared.

During that summer Jack found himself invited to an 18th birthday celebrity costume party, so he and his all-time bestie, Joe, got ready together at our home for inspiration. Joe with his ginger locks, some messy jelled hair and Jack's skinny-legged suit was the perfect Ed Sheeran, and Jack in skinny jeans, leather jacket, scarf, Ray Ban sunglasses, and a reminder from me that this was the one and only time a cigarette (unlit) would droop from his lips, was Liam Gallagher from Oasis. It was such a hoot and the two of them had the best time. This was an awesome friendship, with both lads being sensitive in differing ways, forgetful, and general plonkers, but I love them both to pieces.

Jack happily returned to Year 2 of college, with the usual morning wake up call for me to gel his hair, and as always a compliment or two on his clothing choices. He came home a week or so into college in a fluster about the queue of girls on either side of the sofa in the college shop, where the students less comfortable in the Refectory, the meeting place of the 'normals' in their separate cliques, would congregate. The Rejectory, so named by the Refectory cliques, all merged together in one massive, all-encompassing clique, accepting of each other, wanting to have a cuddle or a chat. What was he to do? 'Enjoy every second' was my cheery retort. I think for Jack, college represented a social environment away from the reminders of senior school, as I imagine many other young adults feel. He seemed to enjoy his courses and had achieved AS levels of 2 Bs and a C, which was brilliant. He had maturely decided during exam season to take his ADHD meds, and had told me it had helped keep him focused. So on balance, my Tiggerish, forgetful boy seemed to be holding his own.

One day he bounded through the door with the news that there was a new gal in tow. Allie was her name and he described her as being very unique and in an 'open relationship' with a girl. Now, how's a mum supposed to process this one? Rejectory comes to mind… Oh dear, does that make me a Refectory as middle age takes over? Heck no! This was the beginning of the whole pan sexual revolution at the college level but I didn't even know what it meant. Turns out I wasn't as on the pulse as I thought I was! Even so, my natural reaction was, 'Of all the girls in college, this is the one you fall for?' He explained that Allie was from Croatia and her parents didn't speak very good English but he'd been invited to stay over there. It's difficult as a parent when your child is 17, approaching 18, but still 17. Should I call the mum to make sure it was OK with her? What to do? Surprisingly, Jack willingly obtained Allie's mum's number and she had no issue with Allie having friends stay over. I learned from Refectory Matt that Allie was 'a nutter' and wandered round school carrying dolls dressed as girls even though their bits were boys. He said she was whacked and other mates at college couldn't understand what the heck Jack was doing with her. I took their comments on board and I was concerned with his choice, although not necessarily worried, more a 'hmm, this is odd'. I sat with Jack and talked about it and discovered that he felt very close to Allie because of how she spoke to him, and the kinds of words she used to express herself. She never ever said a mean word to him, she was gentle with her words and described to him how she loved the curve of his spine, and his soul-filled eyes. OK, I got it. Here was an edgy, alternative girl, which seemed to be Jack's 'type', as Leila also had a unique beauty. So I became on board with it, and offered that Allie could visit our home also. She lived a short train ride from college so again, not someone who could pop in, but a relationship that was formed and acted out at college.

IX

SALAD DAYS WITH VINEGAR DRESSING

With Jack's 18th birthday upon him, life was so full of promise. I suggested a fun shopping spree in London and said he could bring a friend with him. Matt was his choice. Unknown to the two lads, I had arranged for a Hummer with driver to transport us to London, firstly to eclectic Camden Market and a much anticipated visit to the amazing Cyberdog, where funky clothes and even apparently an X-rated room on the lower ground floor beckoned. I knew my place, I sat in the car with the driver, who had brought along some Pimms, and the lads darted out to shop. It was great to see them return with various items. Memorable to me was a cool t-shirt in red black and white puffy paint. On the trip from Camden to central London, Jack's phone rang and he diverted the call. It rang again and again he diverted. I asked him who it was but was met with a stony face. My phone now started ringing and seeing it was his father, and with it being our son's 18th birthday I took the call. He had sent £185 to cover the cost of a ring Jack was excited to buy that he had been admiring on Vivienne Westwood's website – the Armour ring. So there we were, in the Hummer on Oxford Street, probably fifteen minutes from visiting Vivienne Westwood's store and there was Dad on the phone, complaining about Jack choosing that ring. Apparently he had decided to Google the item, and wasn't pleased that it was not gold. Inside I was livid that his dad was adding doom and gloom to what had been a superb day. I recall saying something along the lines of, 'Well, if you would like to put a 1 in front of the 185 I'm sure we can find Jack a gold ring.' Sarcasm, of course. I turned to look at my boy and he just had such a dead look in his face. I ended the call with a basic, here we go again retort.

We arrived at Dame Viv's boutique and awkwardly entered the shop. We gazed at the various pieces of jewellery but Jack was so quiet. The phone call had hurt him very much. I took him to the side and we went over all the money we had in total for him to spend that day, and agreed that we would use his Dad's money to pay for the lovely dinner that was coming up at our fave restaurant, and that he would use other birthday money to pay for his ring. This cheered him and settled his thinking, and from there the day continued with much frivolity, with Matt exclaiming that he could be a model as he sauntered up and down the boutique, confidence busting out as per the norm, while the sales assistant was whispering to Jack at the jewellery counter that it was he who had their look, which put a mile-wide smile across his face. An amazing Armour ring and necklace purchased, the lads headed off to do their own shopping for a few hours. Then we met up for dinner at our favourite restaurant, and the waitress there remembered us, and treated Jack to his fave, Strawberry Mojito.

A final surprise in store was a trip to Rome. I had the lads open their phone calendars and type in on November 8th, 'Rome holiday' that I had planned and paid for the three of us. Mouths dropped to the floor and there were hugs and 'thank you's all over the place. The shop was beginning to provide an income and what better way to spend some of it than on a trip to Rome? Having such a keen interest in history and movies, for Jack visiting the Coliseum with visions of Gladiators, Ben Hur and the endless history of this iconic city, was a fantastic prospect and his response was evidence of his excitement. We ended the evening with glasses of champagne and a photo or two with the cutest cocktail waitress, which was the perfect end to a fantastic and memorable day.

With my shop getting busier, the all too serious second year of A levels in full swing, and Jack's part time job, we were a busy little family of two. I would come home from work to Jack getting ready to go to work, and overall things were finally feeling like they were falling into place. Jack still enjoyed hanging out with the local lads in the evenings, playing his PS3, and appeared to be loving life.

During this time I sadly had the most awful chesty cough, and had visited the doctor several times, receiving various rounds of antibiotics and cough syrups, none of which were helping. It was at the point where if I even spoke the tickle on my chest made me cough. I was either resting in bed or on the sofa, as this condition showed no signs of dissipating. Jack and I would text each other from our bedrooms to save my voice, and my lovely lad helped me with changing bedding, as at this point the coughing was affecting my bladder and this meant changing the sheets on my bed every day or two. It truly was a bloody awful ordeal. While Jack did help me he seemed irritated with me. It reminded me of when we were flying home from Tobago and the flight was very rocky and my leg had swollen up, and he sat in the seat next to me almost alienating himself from me. Sometimes when he came in from college, he would walk by me and not even speak to me. While to most parents this would be considered normal teen behaviour when their kids were a few years younger, I didn't really know how to handle this mood change. I truly was as reliant on Jack as he was me. I understand now that when someone you love is very poorly, it can be easier to alienate yourself emotionally in order to cope, but at the time it was super hurtful and we were quite 'punchy' with each other.

He still needed me though. He flopped on the sofa one day head downcast, sad that his bestie at work, Santino, had told him he'd received his assignment and was relocating to Wales to begin training to become a vet. Of course, Jack was pleased for his friend but at the same time bummed at how things always seemed to change. We chatted about the hospitality industry, and how it was an environment where people would come and go, as he himself would upon completion of college.

With the trip to Rome only three weeks away, I had a chat with Jack about my medical situation. I truly was not so much concerned with myself, as I was with the fact that I was up coughing every night, and this would impact their sleep and the general mood. This was the trip of a lifetime and I wanted so much for it to be memorable for him. The decision was made that I would not go on the trip and after Matt discussed it with his parents, who were on board, the lads felt they could manage together. I had arranged transportation for them to and from all airports, breakfasts and a beautiful room in one of Rome's finest hotels. La Dolce Vita for my boy. All was in alignment and I desperately didn't want to spoil his birthday treat. This was Jack's trip and he was eighteen, well travelled, and I can proudly say, so very polite, so I knew he would hold his own, they both would, together.

Jack was super excited when he had the opportunity to see Allie on a Friday after college, and spend the night at hers before his trip. He was chatting about it for the whole week leading up to their date. He had explained that the girl who was in an open relationship with Allie didn't infringe on him and I began to understand it for what it was. Kids exploring, and being rebellious in whatever way they could, and so long as he was happy, which he really was, then OK, Jammie Dodger, I was on board the Allie train.

Off he went that Friday morning oh so happy, with a few quid in his pocket and a cute girl to go home with that evening. It was just so lovely to see my boy gaining more independence and confidence. I was in the middle of planning a photo-shoot for prom dresses in the shop when I saw that my phone had blown up with missed calls and messages from Matt. Upon speaking with Matt it turned out that he was super angry, referring to Jack as 'your son' and he spat out that Jack had called him a cunt and had hung the phone up on him. After calming Matt, I rang Jack, who was on the college bus on his way home. He initially said he didn't want to talk about it and his voice was quite flat. As soon as he arrived home, he explained what had taken place. Usually, on a Friday afternoon Jack and Matt played pool at the pub local to college as they both had free time. Jack told me that he'd told Matt several times that he was meeting Allie, but his words fell on deaf ears. Matt just did not engage in that part of the conversation, and with Jack's personality being less combative he didn't get his point across. After classes ended he went to meet Allie at the station. He received a flurry of text messages from Matt with the classic 'what happened to bros before hoes' and they ended up speaking by phone and both equally, it seemed, lost the plot with each other, leading to Jack uttering that horrid word and hanging up the phone. He explained that he had seen Allie at the station, but he was so terribly conflicted over who he was going to hurt that he made the decision not to see either of them, and turned and left Allie crestfallen at the station. He arrived back at college, and I have since learned that he literally fell to pieces in tears, with his mate Ben comforting him and holding him in his arms as he cried.

With the trip to Rome now less than two weeks away, I tried to be the peacemaker and arranged for Jack and Matt to meet for lunch the following day and have a man to man chat. It took some persuading on my part, with both lads meeting over a couple of drinks and some comfort food at the local pub, they both apologised and all was right in teenville again. The following Friday Jack and Allie did indeed have their night together, me naively thinking he'd be on the sofa, only to find out in a text message from him that he had done the deed and she was laying in his arms, and he was oh so proud of himself. I on the other hand, while understanding sex was a part of most seventeen and eighteen-years-old's lives, did feel disappointed that he chosen to have his first time with this girl who for all intents and purposes, was quite strange. I did tell him so the next day, but quickly regretted it when he explained again to me how gentle she was, how sweet and quirky. He showed me drawings and paintings she had made for him, and he again assured me he was so happy. As always, we really truly felt each other's emotions on every level. Being sensitive together we both understood each other, but with my son growing into this beautiful man however exhibiting teen-like behaviour and me ploughing every last thought and emotion into my shop, we both had less patience with each other.

The boys returned from Rome late on a Sunday night and rang me from the airport as they couldn't locate the taxi. Why do I remember this? Because I heard the f-word bouncing into my eardrum. I'd had four days of silence. I remember being upset on the phone, telling them to stop and it was too much and not solving anything, to which they had seemingly found the driver and promptly ended the call. I recall drifting off to sleep with the pressing feeling that my eighteen-year-old would be home in a few hours and while I was so happy that he was safe and I was sure, full of news of his trip, my head throbbed with anxiety as to my boy's mood. It was such a miserable time for me health-wise and I wanted so much to be full of bounce and energy, but while there'd been a slight improvement, I knew I wasn't going to be my usual bubbly self. It was the early hours by the time they got home and with college beckoning in the morning there were quick hugs and a promise to take them both for an Italian dinner where they could share all the news of the Eternal City.

The very next day, upon his return from college, Jack announced that he had ended things with Allie. His English Lit professor was cracking the whip and Jack announced that he was focusing fully on college, and girls could wait. As I write this I'm aware that it must read as a mature decision, however I could see the innocence behind his eyes, the same look I saw when he sent the dreaded break-up email to Leila. It seemed as if he was convincing himself that it was the right thing to do. Of course I was pleased to hear this, and we arranged to have dinner at our local pub on Wednesday and talk through plans for the future. We briefly watched an interview I had recorded for Jack featuring Psy of Gangnam fame, and Jack sat there with the most beautiful open smile on his face as we watched it together. Psy came across as such a gentle, decent chap and Jack loved seeing that side of the man behind the black shades and crack pot dance moves.

We had a brief chat about Rome but Jack was scheduled to work that evening, and informed me that the following evening he had volunteered to represent his college at his senior school open house. I was shocked by this. Jack was so sad and hurt about his school and often commented how much he'd hated it there, but here he was representing his college. It wasn't the learning for him, it was the social side, the bullying he endured and his perceived lack of support or otherwise he seemingly set aside. Anyway, we saved our chat until Wednesday. I was frantically preparing for the prom photo-shoot taking place on Friday so we were a very busy family, and I felt a tiny release of the ever present worry in my mind about how my boy would manage his life without me. It seemed to be happening and it felt lovely.

On the Wednesday we took the two minute walk to our local pub, sat as always in the bay window table and ordered our dinner – Jack's fave, the Chicken New Yorker, for two. He didn't have his usual appetite however, only eating a small amount, and he seemed a little removed somehow. He told me that at the open evening the night before he felt really good and enjoyed helping the prospective students and their parents, and shared how a couple of the mums had to redirect their daughters' attention away from the college boy with his edgy hair and skinny jeans, complete with his skull belt buckle. Oh, I loved hearing that and we reminisced a little over the geeky years, and my assurances that he would find his place in life and the girls would continue to come. Jack mentioned that his favourite teacher had been astounded by his height and good looks and had offered to take him to the pub the following week for a pint or two. My heart swelled to think that finally, there was an adult male who had extended this opportunity. Jack had cried a year or two before as he saw his two closest mates making similar plans with their dads. Jack mentioned that he had told his teacher he was considering applying to Dartmouth Naval College, and shared with me his intense hurt when his teacher laughed at this. My mother lioness was seething, who the fuck was he to laugh at my son? I expressed this to Jack but he carried on to say he could see that his teacher realised he had injured Jack and was sorry.

Jack expressed to me that after college he needed to take a break and would prefer to hide away in his room for a year before facing his next life challenge. This sent my mind all over the place. Here I was a single mum running my newly opened business, figuring out how on earth I was going to manage with my only other source of income, sadly my son, wanting to bail out of life. I brought up his job at the country club and said that he could stay there doing more hours and it was OK not to make the next big step yet, but I did need him to bring home an income and the monthly shortfall at its worst could be £800 and other months I wouldn't need anything. I reminded him that we had agreed to stay in Liphook so he could keep his friends and go to the local college but after college, moving was the next logical step. With the hope at the time of a possible naval career, Jack would be away a lot and I could move, possibly back to Gunwharf that we had both loved, and with some contribution from Jack (we had agreed on one week's wage per month) we would forge ahead together. There was a real shift right in front of me as Jack ranted about why hadn't I found a man to make life easier then he wouldn't have to help me, and he might as well move out with his mates. From there I drew on a past conversation with my father, who had outlined for me the expenses involved in leaving home. I sat and explained to Jack the expenses that I had to meet every month in order to keep not only our home moving along, but also the expenses related to the shop. Two lots of rent, gas, electricity, mobile phones, Sky TV, not to mention the car expenses and food. I was so scared of how on earth we would survive. Jack's dad was already insisting that he didn't have to pay for Jack as he was now eighteen, and refused to acknowledge the 'he's still in full time education' stipulation in our divorce decree, as in the USA kids end their high school education as seventeen year olds turning eighteen. The amount he paid was only around £200 per month on average, but to me it was significant to our lives and it was a frightening prospect to lose child benefit and a huge reduction in housing benefit as a result of having an over eighteen-year-old living with me. After explaining things clearly to Jack, and the obvious angst and worry I emoted, my boy took me in his arms and held me so tight, whispering that he had no idea of the pressure I was under and told me how proud he was of me. I realised right there we needed to make a realistic plan and Jack staying in our sweet little house where he felt safe among his friends was optimum.

We agreed together that he could have this gap year, however he did need to increase to thirty-plus hours at his job. He also had to clean the house on a Saturday morning. I wouldn't comment about his room and vice versa. Common spaces Jack would take care of. A tiny two up and one down was doable. I put a little cheat sheet on the refrigerator for cleaning. Being aware of his ADHD I tried my best to understand his forgetfulness, but it really was weighing on me. I felt sad in myself and disappointed about not selecting the right man. Those words from my son were powerful. The stick was in full swing now, more than ever. This super sensitive girl, woman, mother, feeling my own pain alongside my son's and using food to comfort myself. I'm not entirely sure if comfort is the right word, it seemed to be more of a control issue. The *only* thing I had control over was putting my hand to my mouth, feeding this excruciating loneliness inside my soul. Fighting the fight, being the mother lioness, looking out for my Jack at every turn, but sadly dumping my loneliness and tears onto him at times. It is beyond painful to write these words. I had guilt mixed up with hopes and dreams mixed up with fear and panic, topped off with dreadful self esteem. It was Jack whose tears and words back at me began to strengthen me. "Mumsie you have me, I don't want to be with anyone else Mum just you." The outburst about the lack of a man in our home was just that, a teen outburst. I'm literally only understanding that as I type this. Jack was OK with it just being me, why, why, why didn't I realise that sooner?

X

THEY CALL IT MALEVOLENCE RIGHT?

After college on Thursday we regrouped on the sofa to revisit our talk from the night before. Just a few minutes into our conversation, Jack's phone rang. It was his dad and totally out of character, he answered the call, all the while looking at me with a blank stare. It was a brief conversation and I could sense by Jack's responses that his dad was asking about the Rome trip. It was ridiculous to my thinking, after such a revealing chat the night before, and my commitment to stay in Liphook, that here I was feeling so uncomfortable in front of my son as he engaged politely with his dad. Jack's rejection of his father had become so evident over the past three or so years, which caused angst between us as the monthly payment from him being much needed and at times meant me having to cajole Jack to call his dad. He just didn't want to. He didn't want anything to do with him. I understood why on some levels, but on others I wasn't entirely convinced. Kids love their parents, even the ones that burn them with cigarettes. Why reject his father? He expressed that he felt embarrassed by him, embarrassed by his lack of integrity. He hated being compared to him, as of course I had done sometimes over the years. What parent hasn't if we are true to ourselves? Jack expressed that most of the time when he did talk to his father it was almost always negative and moody. I did try to explain that when parents divorce, and live a long distance apart, the parent not in the home will do two things. Overcompensate when they do see their child, and out of blinding fear of losing their relationship, try to parent them from afar, which of course was not realistic. Especially as to Jack, his dad was a massive kid. I felt it, and he did too. It wasn't placed in his mind by me, he had his own experiences, some during the marriage, and some after. When the odd family member enquired after his dad, Jack would ask them not to ask about him. Why were we the only two people in this family who spoke with our hearts, our souls? It was and is a trait Jack introduced to my consciousness, and to this day, I just cannot do polite conversation for the sake of it. Thank you Jack, you cheeky Jammie Dodger of mine.

Once the call was over I tried to get Jack focused back on our plans and how we were going to move through the next few years. I even suggested that I speak to our landlord in the hope that maybe once Jack was working we could buy this little house together and then he would always have a home, even when I wasn't around anymore. But he didn't seem to be listening to me and just gave 'yes' and 'uh huh' responses. Responses most parents of young adults are familiar with, but not this Mumsie. I realise now that he was withdrawing in the same way he did in that phone call with his father. In between rotten coughing fits I explained to Jack that I needed him to pick up some medicine for me after college on Friday. It was super important as I was doing a photo-shoot that day and would be leaving the house before the pharmacy opened and not returning until the early evening. I expressed how important it was and to please put a reminder in his phone. We did have a nice chat about Rome, and Jack expressed his wonder at the Vatican. He had gone with gladiators on his mind, but had come home quite animated and moved by Vatican City in all its splendour. He described with such intelligence the tour he had taken and the thought expressed to others in the group to tip the tour guide at the end, to which they'd retorted that they had paid 50 euros each for the privilege; he had joined on to an existing group completely unaware. I loved that cheeky reference from Jack, the Tiggerish ADHD cutie pie that he was without medication.

He told me that Matt refused to go into the Vatican, and it really wound him up as he felt that Matt wasn't respecting him as Jack often found himself going along with things to please others. While being empathetic as usual, I did try to explain that Jack had seen a lot of the world and appreciated some of the culture in a way that maybe Matt didn't, as he hadn't had the same experiences. While being what appeared to be somewhat testy with Matt, he also was very protective of his mate, sharing talks they had in Rome, when Matt had advised him regarding girls and awkward situations. He recounted how Matt who the morning they left to go to Rome had encouraged Jack as he waivered on the staircase to ,yeah bring Teddy,' which turned out to be fortuitous as the boys not following my instructions to get straight into a private taxi, decided to take the cheaper option and take a coach that made stops to hotels along the route. When arriving at their hotel, the last on the route, the boys discovered that the last remaining backpack was not Jack's, sooooo off they went with the coach driver back to various hotels to thankfully arrive at one where they spied a lady standing holding Jack's backpack with Teddy's head peering out from the top, as she realised she too had the wrong bag! Without Teddy uh well I dread to think how they would have managed as he revealed his passport and money was also in the back pack! Big props to Matt and Teddy that day.

I sensed more than in past talks with me that Jack was very conflicted about so much; college life, managing mates, the issues I was facing, his future and not wanting to engage beyond the right now. Inspite of all that teen angst, he had brought me home the most beautiful rosary of lavender beads. I had purchased a rosary when I was au pairing in Italy many moons ago, and had lost it and my lovely lad had remembered and presented me with a pretty box containing a shimmering replica.

Friday arrived and Jack was up and off to college with the usual stop at my door for a quick hair gel. I gave him a reminder about my prescription then turned my focus to the day ahead. It literally flew by with my three models, a hair and makeup team and multiple dress changes, a great photographer, and me art directing. By the time I arrived home and checked in with Jack, he had again forgotten to get my prescription. Luckily, I was home just before six so I was able to fill it. Feeling shattered I ordered Chinese to be picked up and messaged Jack, who was at Joe's. He did as I asked and returned home with our usual takeout. We sat side by side as we often did, and I asked my usual, 'How were the girls today?' But this time Jack, with his head lowered, told me that he really just wanted his Leila back, and hoped so much that if she and Eric did part ways, this would happen, as he would feel so much better if he had her. He told me that he really regretted ending things so abruptly, and wished so much he could undo that. Pushing his food around his plate, he said that he'd had a pot noodle and some pizza at Joe's and wasn't that hungry. Jack wasn't a huge eater but it seemed odd that he didn't want to eat his favourite Chinese, but I was more concerned at this point with his feelings. I gently spoke of things not having to be final, and that maybe right now was not the right time for them, but to not think of it as forever. To enjoy the attention from girls, to go out on dates, to drink in their interest, and to think of Leila as just away at the moment, and that she may be back but at no exact date. This is what I would tell myself when my relationships ended, it was so much easier than the finality of something being over forever. It seemed to help me, so my hope was that my beloved son would embrace this notion. Leila hadn't gone away completely. Nothing was final. Having work the next day and after this gargantuan one, I was exhausted. Jack was in two minds as to whether stay home or go back to Joe's. He had work the next day too, but not until noon so he headed out.

Sleep overtook me and I awoke to my alarm buzzing, and a stressy work day ahead. I had two appointments booked in and was pretty anxious to convert them to sales. Jack was out of dosh, with his pay day a week away. When you are self employed there is this ongoing rollercoaster of emotion as you exalt from a dress sale then, within a day or two, your mind churns over with so many 'what if' scenarios. I had read the book *Who Moved My Cheese?* which was a bible of sorts for sales people. You only get out what you put in. After the pricey last couple of months, pennies were tight so the rollercoaster ride was in full tilt. I was getting ready in the bathroom for work when Jack appeared from his room expressing that he wanted a bath. I told him to just let me get ready for work and the bath would be his. However, I was met with impatience. He didn't have work until noon so I couldn't understand what the testiness was for. Back in my room, dressing, I thought it probably best to not keep reminding him about his chores that morning. We'd had enough conversations about it, so I left for work with a knock to the bathroom door and our usual 'bye bye love you's, and headed off to my shop.

Thankfully the work day was lucrative, with two happy brides and this shop owner gleeful. I decided to stop at M&S and get something really nice in for Sunday lunch. It felt so lovely to treat us both to some posh nosh. I was utterly exhausted however, from the intensity of the previous day's photo shoot, the pressure to achieve sales, and truly all in all it had been a bit of an emotion filled week. I was looking forward to a few snacks, a bottle of wine, and *The X Factor*. In the back of my mind I was feeling quite confident that the house would be tidy. I came in through the back door as always, and spied a crisp packet I had purposely not picked up on my way out that morning. I wanted to see with my own eyes that Jack had done his chores and that would have been the first signal that he had. I looked around the room, anguish taking over. Nothing had been done. The kitchen was the same as I had left it. No vacuuming, no rubbish removal, no sign of Jack. Is this what he thought tidy was, I asked myself. Aware of course, of his ADHD, I tried to reason this through but I couldn't.

I slumped on the sofa, head in my hands feeling utterly dejected. What could I do to make my boy see that I needed his help? I couldn't manage everything myself. And why was this happening now? He was eighteen not fourteen. Now was the time when things were supposed to get a little easier. My mind began to replay over and over the amount of times he'd forgotten to do things, his refusal to take his ADHD medicine, which affected me as well. Here I was, Mum, Dad, everything to my son, why, why, why had he again not done his chores? I felt so desperate to repair, to renew, but how? I couldn't ground him, he was eighteen. I couldn't remove his PS3, it wouldn't make a hill of beans of difference. He'd just play at his mates anyway. Why was he so sensitive? Why was I? I told myself sternly that I needed to be Mum and Dad right here, right now.

I rang my sister, who really was the perfect person to call, being so practical and sensible. I thought that if anyone was going to calm me and guide me it would be her. I explained what had happened and that I was thinking about not letting Jack stay at home that night. I thought that maybe removing him from his creature comforts was the jolt he needed. It was a fairly brief conversation and with no exact plan in place, it seemed logical to her to wait and see what happened when he came home and if the outcome was more moodiness then that maybe was the shake up Jack needed. I fired off a text message to him saying how disappointed I was and that he didn't deserve to have his creature comforts. I reminded him of our conversations and that I felt I was giving all I could and I didn't know what else to do. I lambasted him, I really did. I was super upset but I also had a steely reserve that this time I wasn't going to cave as I had so many times in the past.

I attempted to call Jack but there was no reply. I knew the signal was poor where he worked but I tried anyway. I'd thought better of the hasty message I had sent and wanted to speak to him. Every person I had ever shared my love and my feelings for my son with entered my mind, wondering what they would advise I do. I needed to do something and this was the first and hopefully last time I would banish my son from his home. I'd already surmised he would go to one of his mates in the village for the night. I had to stay strong. It was for him too. He had to help, he really had to.

When he rang me back I quickly realised that he was phoning over the missed call and not had actually read my message but he sounded aloof and I sternly told him to come home. A few minutes passed and the gate clinked and in he walked with a huffy 'What's up?' I asked if he had read my message and he said no as his phone was low on charge. I handed him my phone and he glanced at the message then threw the phone down on the sofa and walked passed me up to his room. I felt hurt, angry, sad, confused, on a bullet train hurtling along and the brakes wouldn't work, I needed to stop this *now*. I could hear the vacuum start and movement upstairs which ended after about ten minutes. My stomach in knots, I climbed the stairs to Jack's room to see him sitting on his bed, baseball cap still on, eyes blank, arms outstretched, holding his beloved Teddy. My mind was so torn. No, no, no, do not back down now, I told myself, and out came, 'Get out, you are out for the night, you don't deserve to have your things, HE (meaning Jack's dad) was a loser and so are you.' I turned and headed down the stairs and sat back on the sofa. Within a couple of minutes Jack was in front of me. He told me he'd fallen asleep in the bath, and was late to work and had to run all the way there so as not to be late. My heart sank. Oh fuck, he had a reason. But no, no, no... 'Well, if you hadn't stayed out late then you would have had enough sleep.' I remember looking at my boy, desperate for him to say, 'I'm sorry Mum,' but he didn't. He looked so aloof. 'What am I supposed to do Jack?' I asked. 'I've had all these talks with you and we had everything set but the first time you're supposed to do your chores you don't do them. What can I do to get your attention? How about I chop my hair off?' I cried, knowing how much Jack loved my hair. 'Is that what you want?' and I slapped my own face right in front of him. As he turned to the door, I cried out, 'If you do anything I'll kill myself.' He turned back to me and said, 'Say goodbye to your son.' 'Oh, *bye bye,*' was my sarcastic response. Door shut, gate clink, silence.

XI

NO WORDS

It was the only time that neither Jack or myself had backed down from each other. I had been internally begging that he show me some kind of remorse, but would I have acted any differently? This is just one of countless questions that run through my mind, that torture me, that tear at my very being. The TV was playing *The X Factor* still and I stared at the screen but my mind was not connecting. Only a few moments passed before I grabbed my phone and rang Joe but his phone was not turned on. All I could think of was putting in place an immediate safety net for Jack. I rang Joe's dad, Mike, and I told him that Jack and I had had a falling out and I'd sent him out for the night and would it be OK if Jack slept over at their home, but to not tell Jack that I had asked. I was trying to protect and punish him at the same time. Mike's response sent panic rushing through me. 'Trace, no one's home, and I'm out too.' He said he'd try to reach Joe and have him call me. Still sitting in the same spot I felt panic and regret sweeping over me, mixed with racing thoughts as I tried to rationalise; trying not to be what I perceived some to think of me, too dramatic. The only friends' numbers I had were Joe's and Matt's. I knew Matt was at work at the same country club Jack worked at. Even though I knew it was unlikely I'd reach Matt, I dialled his number but it connected straight to voice mail. I wondered if I ought to go out looking for Jack. Or should I just stay calm? I was being Mum and Dad, I reminded myself. I was trying to parent my son. And then I felt the wave of nausea that hasn't left me since. Why did I have to say those things to him? God, what the hell was I thinking? No, no, no, stop it. I was beside myself with how to manage my life, our life, I couldn't do it by myself, I'd blurted those mean words out of blind desperation. It feels so pathetic to write this now, it seems so out of proportion to tell my son he had no home for the night, over not doing his chores. For fuck's sake, it wasn't like he was a bad kid. I had to figure out a way to sort this. Maybe just the fact that I'd told him to leave would now be enough. Maybe I should go looking. No, no, no. And I'd be back full circle again. I decided to call him but his phone was switched off, or was it a bad signal? I typed out a text telling him I was sorry. I didn't want to be too forgiving though. I said that things had to change. I asked him to please reply or call me just to let me know that he was OK. He was allowed to be cross and upset but just please let me know where he was and that he was OK. I told him if he didn't want to contact me then contact Joe or Matt or someone, so at least someone could be there for him. What to do? What to do? I rang Mike again, but he hadn't been able to reach Joe but he was reassuring, telling me Jack would be OK and not to worry. He said he'd message Joe again and promised he'd call me the minute he heard anything. I left all the lights on and the back door unlocked and decided to push through this by getting into bed and before I knew it he would be back, or Matt or Joe or someone would be in touch. I went upstairs and turned toward his room. I don't really know why, I just did. His bed was made and the room was fairly tidy. Laying on his pillow, arms outstretched, was Jack's beloved Teddy. I clutched Teddy to me and climbed into my bed, keeping my door open and lights on. Heart sick and riddled with worry and now panicked as to whether to go looking for my boy. But what if he came back and I wasn't here? I rang him and rang him and rang him but no luck. His phone was off. The exhaustion of the last few days crept over me and I found myself drifting into an agonising state of sleep. Then I opened my eyes with a start, thinking, oh my god he's been hit by a train. Then, why am I thinking these thoughts? Why am I self torturing? I checked my phone but there were no messages from anyone. On and on my fear thoughts came and went, then clutching Teddy to my chest, I oddly fell asleep on my back, something I never do, exhaustion pushing me into a catatonic state.

BRRRIIIIINNNNNGGGGG. I jolted out of sleep at the sound of the front doorbell. Oh my gosh, thank God, the front door! I couldn't leave it unlocked from the inside, he's come to the front. I dashed to look out of his bedroom window that was directly above the front door, and saw a police car and flew down the stairs. At that point I was thinking that he'd been picked up by the local police and they'd brought him home. Shit, what a colossal mess. I opened the door and the words raced out of my mouth, the hopeful words, if I say the words it will be true. 'Oh hi, oh God, thank goodness you are here, me and my son had a falling out. Have you got him? He's in the car right? Right? Right?????' And then I was on the sofa. How was I on the sofa? I was there with two police officers, my back pushing into the back of the sofa, my heart jumping, mouth dry, as I listened.

'We were called to Liphook train station after an incident report and found a young man, we believe to be your son Jack and he is deceased.'

The floor. I'm on the floor. I hear blood curdling screaming. It's me. 'I killed my son! I killed my son! I killed my son!' Rolling on the floor. Rolling on the floor. Now I'm in the bathroom upstairs. Why am I here? Shock. Shock. No no no no no! A police officer at the door asking me to come out. Half way down the stairs, then back on the sofa. They're telling me I need to call someone.

'Hold me, hold me, hold me!' I begged, screaming, crying. 'Hold me, hold me, hold me.'

The second of the two officers sat next to me and awkwardly half held me.

'No no no no no!' I'm on the stairs, half way up the stairs. Mike rushing into my arms, holding me.

'Tracy, I'm so sorry. I'm so sorry.'

I cried racking sobs as I clung to him. Then back on the sofa. Matt ringing my phone. Mike's voice, 'Just come here come here, Matt, to Jack's.' Matt bursting through the door, loud voice, same as mine. Talk loud, it will drown out the truth.

'I'm going to the skate park, I'm just off work. You don't need the police I'll go find him.'

'Sit down, sit down, Matt. Sit down.'

I couldn't say the words so Mike said them for me. A boy hunched over next to me hearing his best friend's fate, his usual confidence replaced with shock and a sickening realisation. Had he spoken to Jack? No came the reply. 'Any text message?' was Mike's question. Matt's phone out, scrolling and stopping on Jack's name, seeing, 'I'VE MADE MY FINAL DECISION, MY MUM PSYCHOLOGICALLY ABUSED ME'

'Don't read that, Trace,' Mike's voice. My mind searing in an agony I simply cannot describe. Those few typed words, burned into my consciousness, punching me in the throat, my heart smashing to splinters. It's my fault. The police were saying I needed to call someone. Mike was there but even in my muddled thoughts I knew that he needed to be home for Joe and the rest of his children. I didn't know what to do. I couldn't call my parents, they were both elderly and not driving. I rang George's mum Morgan twice but there was no answer. The police were insistent that I couldn't be left by myself and they had duties to attend to so I had no choice but to call my sister, who I'd spoken to earlier that evening. Her tired voice aroused by my call and the knowledge that Jack was gone, her voice cracking as she told her husband. Stretching my hand out, an officer took over the call. Me transfixed on the sofa and people coming in and out. Then I realised that I had to call Jack's dad. Searching through my phone I rang, he answered. I asked to speak to his partner. He asked why but I kept asking for her. I couldn't tell him, he needed to hear it gently from her, not me. Her voice came on. 'Hi.' I told her what had happened. She cried out, then she told him and I heard him cry out. Click.

Jane arrived she hugged me and I remember her words, "Silly boy to have done that to you" I know she cared in her way, and who knows how to react to tragic news? My tearful, aching response was, "No, he wasn't silly, he's lovely." Never ever had I spoken back to her. Her nature being so different to mine was no one's fault. Thank goodness she was there though because her ability to take notes, organise people and go into some kind of practical mode at this awful time was, without me realising at the time, putting in place her first step toward taking over arrangements that were going to have to be made, which you will learn about later and bring the most agonising, ugly twist, the kind even the darkest of souls couldn't imagine. I recall Matt's mother, who I had never met, arriving to take care of her beloved son, and the stomach knot feeling more prevalent as without the melee, I'd have to think and I didn't want to. Jane's voice 'Go and pack your things' are the words that stung at my ears. I'm being told to go and pack a bag, and I can't even put a cohesive sentence together. I did as I was told and dragged my body up the stairs to my room and I used a carrier bag and I don't really know what I put in it. I grabbed the rosary Jack had given me and clutched his beloved teddy.

I recall words about getting a prescription filled I think. I was numb, dead, nothing, black, shock, cold. I was so cold. Blanket on me in a bed screaming, sobbing, crying non-stop, alone. I was alone in a room, a bedroom, no one came. Agonising, wailing, crying and sobbing and yet no one came. I recall this overwhelming need to be held, to be comforted. I had my phone with me so I made the god awful phone call to my best friend Carol who lived in the USA. Her comforting words washed over me. She told me she'd fly out ASAP and for me to hold on hold on, she would be there. Disconnecting from the call my phone rang again immediately. It was Jack's dad's partner. She let me know that he was medicated and sleeping and she expressed to me her deep sadness and promised that from this very minute she would make every effort to encourage calmness and peace between Brad and me. I begged her to please come with him. I'd never met her but I was afraid for him to come alone. He would need support. Don't come yet, I stressed. Not yet, not yet.

The next day was somewhat of a blur. Jane had gone to my parents. I hear non-stop wretched sobs and my voice echoing over and over, 'I killed my son, it's my fault,' hundreds, thousands of times. Voices saying, 'No, you didn't, it's not your fault' pinging back at me. My niece and her friend Carly holding me as my sobs and self-recrimination wailed throughout upstairs. Begging my niece not to leave me alone that night, pleading not to leave me alone until Carol arrived from Michigan. She promised she wouldn't but as the evening drew in she did, she left me alone again. Irrational thoughts permeating my brain mixed with the thought that the solace and comfort of her husband is what she needed. This tragedy wasn't just mine, it belonged to so many.

Mum and Dad arriving. Dad, in early dementia, shuffling into the room. I was on the sofa. I don't recall how. Mummy and Daddy holding me, laying in bed with me as we sobbed through the night. Their beloved grandson was no longer and their desperate sadness weighed in my chest as my wails again returned. 'My fault, my fault, I sent him out the door. My fault, my fault, I killed my son.' Guilt tore my brain to shreds as Mummy held me in her arms.

Carol arriving by taxi and I felt her holding me, staying quiet, allowing me to lay in her lap as she stroked my hair. Sitting in the garden to escape the voices in the house, as she took a rest after her journey. Nonstop text messages from Jack's pals as word began to spread. Morgan ringing me sobbing into the phone asking, 'Is it true? Please tell me it's not true.' The bond of our two sons evident as she expressed George's total devastation.

Brad chose to fly straight to England, however his partner was not coming, so my anxiety heightened. He was a man who tended to blame others and never took accountability for anything he said or did. This was somewhat enabled by me in the early years, as job after job failed and I stood loyal. However, with this circumstance I simply didn't know what to expect. I could barely function myself let alone be responsible for his overly early pending arrival. The setting was awkward, I felt an impostor there. It's no one's fault, it's just how I felt. My mother agreed for Brad to go to them for a night or two while I got back home and had time to attempt to think. To think something other than the ringing sentence, 'I killed my son', that had become my mantra. The funeral arrangements had to be dealt with. My family members assured me the choices would and should be mine and my parents stepped in to make the financial arrangements.

A man from the funeral directors called Colin arrived and I recall his stance, hands clasped together, head slightly lowered, dark suit. My name was entered as the client and I selected purple paint as the colour to enrobe my boy's casket. I couldn't say the other c word I couldn't even let it into my consciousness. My mind was in such a jumble that suggestions of Jack's services taking place at his college and where he worked were possibilities. They were completely unrealistic but I didn't know what to do. My mind was lost, lost forever, I didn't want it to improve. I'd start shaking my head from side to side as the shock took hold.

Brad arrived and took up residence at Jane's, as she insisted he stay there, over-ruling, as per the norm in our fractured sisterhood, my request for him to be with my parents. In our marriage Brad had no time for Jane and her family. There was zero connection and plenty of snarky comments, whereas his friendship with my father was at times as father and son, and other times adversaries, as my father's mood swings and demeanour affected both of us terribly. Two sensitive people, one with ADHD, we burned out as impatience grew. I had no energy to fight Jane's ruling, I just wanted to get away from there. It was the most suffocating, oppressive, god awful three days on a multitude of levels. Brad and I sat quietly together in his assigned room. He told me he had thought out a speech on the plane over that included many glowing references to me and he knew I was going it alone. He showed me Jack's first pair of trainers that he'd brought over with him and, mysteriously, a photo album of images of our precious son and family life that I had asked for copies of on multiple occasions, only to be told he didn't have them. I knew this to be untrue as Jack had told me he'd seen the album in the storage cupboard 'outside Dad's flat' on one of his visits to see him. But that didn't matter now. We were Jack's parents and this was a time to connect, to share, to cry together. The 'why' question was on his lips and I knew I had to tell him what I had seen of the message on Matt's phone. At the time I felt Jack's death was entirely my fault, so the prospect of telling him about the message was terrifying. I told him what I had read, the only lines I saw. His response was a bit of a 'what?' almost quizzical as, choking on my words, I tried to say I was having to handle everything myself and that maybe Jack was just venting at me. Brad agreed that 'you hurt who you love the most.' It was OK, we were two very different people those days, but with the bond of our son, we were responsible for ensuring his life was memorialised in the way we felt best. The humanist side to reflect Jack through his beautiful friends, and the graveside for whoever would like to be there, with a sonnet read from my cherished gift, and a single white dove to be released by just the two of us, as an offering to the heavens above. The dove would be symbolic of Jack's love of birds and of course the Dove of Peace painting hanging in his bedroom, his sixteenth birthday gift.

Brad and I were kind with each other when alone, however any time I entered a room Brad was in with others present he would back away from me as if in fear. This happened several times. The only time he stood strong with me was when my sister announced that she was going to identify Jack. I was in pieces but Brad stood firm and said that no, we were going to see our son. I couldn't understand why Jane was being so practical, sensible, with no filter on holding back over clinical language I couldn't bear to hear. I really can't speak for her and on reflection maybe she thought it would be fractious between me and Brad, as she was not a party to our softer, private words. I even tucked him in on his first night in England, and kissed his forehead, whispering softly that the kiss was from Jack. I managed to care for him, it was the right thing to do, and the union of the two of us with Jack bearing witness was so important. I desperately wanted the affection back just for this surreal time. But it didn't come.

I received a phone call – the coroner's assistant asking me to send him a recent photo of my boy. Why? I didn't understand. I'd been told he was found on the platform, that he was whole. So why did they need a photo? I had a sick, awful feeling. A photo was selected and emailed and a prompt reply received to say, 'We recognise your son,' which I could only interpret as meaning he wasn't disfigured, so when I visited I'd see my boy and be able to comfort him. The request to send an image had propelled me to look at images of Jack on our Facebook pages and I was then able to select four images to represent my boy at his service. A lovely photo of him as an innocent eleven-year-old, which I vividly remembered taking. I had snapped the photo as Jack had his hand slightly in his hair, and I said, 'Lick your lips, you cutie pie', which he did. This sweet precious image I had carried on my phone for seven years. Another image was Jack decked out in his newly gifted clothes one Christmas morning, at age fifteen, looking so frickin' cute. Also an image I took in our garden on prom day of Jack in his adorned top hat, with purple ribbon and green feather, tails, cane, million watt smile. Lastly, one of my absolute favourite pics of my boy, at seventeen, after a visit to have his hair cut by the director of Tony and Guy. He had been scouring pages for the right image and was nervously excited to make the train journey to Guildford for this monumental occasion. I remember picking him up from the station and as I sat in the car, watching him coming across the walkway in my rear view mirror, my heart leapt at how amazing his hair looked. Wow, my son was actually a hottie! We took a few photos as we pulled up to our house and Jack said he was going to take a walk to see which mates were out. He leaned against our high brick wall and bent one leg in as I snapped another image of his brooding face, his amazing new hair and wearing the skull belt buckle encrusted with purple rhinestones. Such a great image, such a great day. This final image, to represent my son as a young adult.

Curt, my nephew, worked for a copying company so he arranged for the images to be blown up to poster size and I requested plain Perspex covers with clips, no frames. This after all was ceremonial, not decorative. Brad approved easily, as I showed him the various images. His input was minor, by choice. I can only assume making any decision was difficult, it was for me, and knowing his limited skills in that area due sadly to his ADHD, I understood. I shared everything with him, and the answer was always the same, 'Yes, that's fine'.

Twenty-four hours on, it was identification day. Oddly, Brad rode in a separate car to me. I didn't understand why we were separated and to this day, I still don't. Was it him or Jane who thought better? Why this ongoing division of Jack's parents? If anyone should have insisted on us travelling together it should have been me, as I felt especially with our private conversations that we would stay united for Jack, and for us both. My strength to request anything just wasn't there. I recall sitting in the back of the car feeling desolate, but looking forward to seeing my son. I feel really uneasy even writing that last sentence, but I hadn't seen him, I missed him, I wanted to care for him, somehow.

Arriving I don't actually remember where, I think a hospital, my slow pace of body and heart, holding onto Carol. Entering a reception room the clerk greeted me and I remember being guided to my boy and walking into a large room with a bed of sorts, and there lay my Jack. A purple velvet blanket with gold covering him up to his neck. 'Hello my sweetheart, my Jammie.' Why do I remember this? But I really do so well. I was in protector mode, mummy mode. I approached and a chemical odour lingered and I remember seeing some tape just below his neck with a tube and wondering why it was there. I think it may have been something to do with the embalming process, I don't really know. 'My boy, my beautiful boy Mumsie is here.' I recall saying 'I love you' over and over. Chatter from the waiting room muffled my brain. This was my time with my boy, why could I hear people talking? I stepped away and asked the clerk to tell whoever it was to lower their voices. I rejoined my lad and spied his left hand peeking out from the blanket. It astounded me, here was his hand, his fingers curled in apart from his index finger pointing straight. Exactly how he had slept from a baby. I often noticed this cute unique hand position. In fact, I recall checking on my boy as I did every single night, and spying his little hand at about age thirteen and snapping a photo of it on my camera. This sight sent a flash of comfort through me. He's just sleeping. I stroked each finger and sat quietly on a little chair mustering some need to comfort my boy. As I had on so many nights when he was an infant, I softly sang the words from Annie's Song. Again, the chatter outside invaded my brain. I felt utterly disrespected. Why wasn't the clerk insisting the voices remain quiet? I sang and sang, repeating each verse several times through. I had an odd sense of protection over Jack mixed with an inexplicable euphoria as my voice chattered away to my boy. Stroking his hair, holding his hand. I brightly said to the clerk how nice it was that I could hold his hand and it was resting in a familiar position which comforted me so much, to which his retort was to not look at the other hand as they'd kept it covered for a reason. Oh God, what an unnecessary comment to say to me right as I was grasping this tiny comfort. I remember thinking and still do to this very day that he'd clearly been doing his job for too long and it had made him wholly insensitive. I think I may have even told him that, being a protective mummy to her cub and to herself. The clerk advised that Jack's father was waiting, so I parted, backing away, not turning my back. Reminded by the clerk that I would see my son again when he was with the funeral director. I don't recall the journey back to Jane's house, or much else.

XII

BITING BACK, FORGIVE MY INDULGENCE

Why are people acting differently to me in front of others? Was I losing my mind? My thoughts were insular, I can only surmise the horrific shock had me in such a state of paranoia. The same paranoia that had consumed me for the past nine years, centering around the fear of Brad and his trail of threats to withhold money, and to have his lawyer brother go to court to stop me from taking Jack to Egypt for a holiday. The accusations levied at me as the reason why Jack did not call him. It was apparently my fault Jack had nits on one trip to America to visit his Dad. Brad screamed at me down the phone that I had done it deliberately. He told me he'd had to fumigate his home and shave Jack's head, to which I was left crying in the middle of a department store at his recriminations and begging and pleading with him not to shave my boy's hair off. His girlfriend called and told me he was being too unkind and unfair and that the doctor had told him not to shave as the eggs would be in the scalp not the actual hair. Jack returned home from that trip with buzzed hair and in tears about his dad speaking unkindly of Nana and Papa and how he'd run away and hidden until eventually found an hour or so later. Of how Dad had taken him to an electronics shop and stolen a phone charger and how Dad laughed about me, saying I was fat and making pig noises. My little lad bursting into tears, telling me he laughed with Dad but he only did so because he was alone in America and didn't have me there and he was completely devastated and ashamed and in so much pain that he had laughed. He was crying all over me with regret, remorse.

Why, why, why did I do the right thing legally and send Jack to visit on the three occasions he did? Brad took no time off work and left Jack with his girlfriend. The only time he did take off was when a trip to Chicago was planned to coincide with Jack's visit. Why did my phone ring to hear Jack crying from a changing room as his father insisting he had to wear a proper shirt and beige trousers as they had a family dinner to go to for his birthday (Jack had turned 13 months earlier), and he had to look a certain way. 'Mum he's just trying to dress me up for show,' Jack said, in tears, telling me he didn't want to go. Me, calming and soothing the best I could, but inside a burning rage, acutely aware that during the five years we had been back in England no one from Brad's side of the family had sent him a single birthday or Christmas card, let alone a gift, so why now? His grandparents did occasionally send a little money but always through Brad. It became apparent that on more than one occasion, Brad had sent birthday money to Jack from him when in fact the money was from the grandparents. It was disgusting on every imaginable level. Always the hard luck story. Never ever enough money to visit Jack more than twice, and when he did visit calling me the night before his trip saying he didn't have the money for the apartment I had arranged for him and could he stay at our house.

One gift we really could have done without was when my boy came home from a visit to the US with a shiny new laptop. One day I was perplexed because I couldn't find some information from the search history. When I asked Jack about it he banged my bedroom door and stomped away, only to crawl into my bed in the early hours of the morning in absolute pieces as he shared that his dad had showed him how to look up soft porn and delete the history so I would never know, it could be their secret! I cuddled my precious little lad in my arms as he sobbed his heart out and had to have the chat with him about respect for women and that it was ok to be curious, a couple of years too early.

Brad spent forty two days with his son in the last nine years of his life. Bemoaning how he should never have 'let' me take him to England on the one hand, and on the other asking me to write job interview letters for him, which I did. Nothing had changed there, it was the same negative doom and gloom manner that had sucked the life blood out of me and brought about resentment and a complete lack of respect during the final months of our marriage. No wonder he and Jane latched on to each other, they had a commonality in discrediting me, but now the ONLY person who gets to do any discrediting is ME. I've found my voice and I'm sharing in this homage to my son the light, the shade, the whole complete truth and unless you have walked in my shoes, you do not know the mental strain I lived under. My goodness, wisdom really does come with age. Young and carefree, falling in love with this beautiful young man, many happy years, but as is the case for so many of us, we change and evolve as people and no longer see each other in the same way. Yes when asked I did tell Jack the truth about his Dad and why our marriage ended, however I also shared with my boy countless lovely memories explaining that he was born from love and the truly happiest day of both our lives when he was born. We'd laugh together about his Dad, not at him with him, Jack asking I wonder what Dad is doing today mum and replying himself,' laying on the couch, remote control in his hand watching The Who!' Ok so he did have fairly decent taste in music, that one he can have. We both changed, I became more weighed down with the responsibilities of wife, mother and business owner, and Brad just didn't seem to grow up, in fact I feel he was rebelling against it. I feel inside that I may have set things up this way where I was similarly with Jack, defending and protecting Brad from himself and some of his extremely judgemental family members, having his corner but getting worn out, and becoming more exhausted with the defending of certain behaviours he exhibited, seeing him as another child in our family and not really my husband.

When I mentioned that I wanted to write this book a few years back my father said that it should include Brad because it wouldn't be the whole truth if I didn't. My recriminations in print are out of protection and loyalty to Jack. My marriage breakdown and subsequent divorce could be its own True Movie, but doesn't fairly contribute to mine and Jack's story that I'm trying desperately to keep authentic, and muddying it with the circumstances of our marriage break down would be horribly unfair to Jack. But part of the unravelling of Jack was undoubtedly his lack of interest in his father, stemming from the above events. You've read my own words from that fateful evening, telling him he was just like his dad, the word 'loser' leaving my lips. Jack also had to face different personalities that he wasn't yet ready to deal with, as well as the pressures of adult life, girls, and saying goodbye to his bestie at work, Santino. All the things many teens face, but add ADHD and sensitivity into the mix and many a young person can sadly knee jerk react.

Plans were in place to leave my sister's and go back to my house, and Jane offered to drive us. The man I fell out of love with was evident. Going on and on about himself and how he felt and what he needed. Seeing Jane scurrying off to the shop to buy him an ongoing supply of cigarettes, memorably in fact on the day Carol and I were returning home, she kept us waiting for 30 awful agonising minutes in her hall way as she stalled us all ready with our shoes on bags in hand, because Brad needed cigarettes. Carol trapped in someone else's home, being polite, talking recipes and mind numbing conversation, alluding to the Stepford home we were in. She sat in the back with me holding my hand as Jane drove the 75 minutes home, deciding not to take the direct route to get me home, but a leisurely country drive to show Carol our part of England, which included passing by memories I wasn't yet ready to face. I tried to express that it was too much for me but my words fell on deaf ears. Eventually, close to home, we stopped at a petrol station to get milk and we bought Jane a very nice bottle of wine. I gave this to her, thanking her for all that she had done, and said at some point I'd find another way but for now it was all I could manage. I could handle things going forward. We had agreed she would return two days later to bring Brad so he and I could pick out our son's resting place and make arrangements with Colin the funeral director, while she took Carol food shopping.

When I got home I discovered it had been cleaned from top to bottom by Morgan and Jane, which was so very kind of them. Morgan had been there to greet me and took me aside to explain that against her wishes, Jane had stripped all of Jack's bedding and washed his scent away. I couldn't understand why she would have done that. It didn't matter if his sheets were overdue a wash, the smell was the connection, the only sensory memory I could have but now it was gone. Morgan was dreadfully upset and expressed that me coming back home was the healthiest decision, and while she had two sons and a partner, she would make time for me and to just ask if I needed anything. We hadn't seen or spoken to each other in about six months, so for her to step forward like this was a true gift. She had the blend of work horse along with her emotional core, she was just what I needed.

It felt as if I was dragging a 100 kilo boulder everywhere. Putting one step in front of the other was such hard work. I needed company but I couldn't bear any sound like television or radio. I was in a vacuum of desolation. Morgan managed to procure some stronger sleeping pills and on my first night home, I crept into my boy's bed. I didn't know what to feel, how to think. I was laying where I'd last seen my Jack. Drifting in and out of sleep. Wracking, awful sobbing then snatches of sleep. Text messages still flowing in, which oddly gave me something to do. There is no way to explain or truly understand what it is like to lose a child to suicide. I kept saying to myself over and over that once the services were over I'd end my life the same way as Jack. I'd say this over and over in my mind. It's such a wholly irrational head fuck, truly. I don't really recall much of those couple of days at home apart from the warm tea that Carol kept on supply, and the knowledge that Colin was coming to meet me and Brad to prepare for our son's final journey and view a possible final resting place.

Matt came in to see me one day. He was staying away from college for a couple of weeks, the shock of losing his mate, his confidant, pressing down on him. As we sat on the sofa side by side, as Jack and I did countless times, he quietly handed me a small box saying it was a gift that he had bought for me in Rome, and he had been torn between two and it was Jack who made the final decision on which to bring home for me. I opened the little box, and unwrapped the tissue to reveal a miniature of The Pieta. For those of you not familiar with this most heralded of statues in the Catholic faith, it is of Mary sitting holding her son in her arms after he's been taken down from the cross. At the time I quietly thanked Matt, however inside I was beyond heart sick, I truly felt physically ill, it was as if someone was punishing me. To see this image days after losing my son was just too much. I placed the statue back in the box and put it in a cabinet drawer in my living room.

Jane brought Brad over and the energy in the room shifted upon their arrival. Brad went into a dramatic rant about needing Jane to come with him because he needed her to make notes. This was so utterly beyond bizarre on every imaginable level. In spite of my awful feelings of loss, I knew this half-sister of mine well enough to know that this must have been her idea. She sat piously on the sofa as Brad sat spouting about his need to have her there. Somewhere deep inside of me I managed to voice that this wasn't the plan and that he had me and this was something we had to do together for our boy. But Brad kept insisting Jane come and I insisted back that no, Colin would be taking us and he would keep notes. I felt sick to my stomach at this ploy to control my own child's services and it seemed nothing short of a satirical black comedy.

Saved by the doorbell, I rushed to greet Colin, who came into the hallway. He saw the distress on my face and I asked him to please wait in the hall. I again looked at Brad, who was getting red faced and petulant. I reminded him that Jack was our son and it was up to us to honour him, to which he leapt from his seat and screamed right in my face, 'You killed him! I need Jane.'

For the first time in my life I spoke up for myself, for my son, for the respect of the situation. It went something like this; 'How disgusting for you to say that, and look at you, my supposed sister just sitting there not stepping in to support me.' I turned to Brad, 'Do you want me to go there? I don't need you here to plan this, I can do it myself. I can raise the money, and cover the expense.'

Brad retreated to the garden, and I faced this woman, this person, who for no reason I could understand held me in such a low regard. 'Jane what are you doing? I'm asking you to go upstairs and get Carol and go do what we had agreed.'

'NO,' came the reply.

'You said you would never ever do this again remember?'

'Do what?' she replied.

'Get involved with Brad after his first visit and how awful he acted. You told me you would never support him, you said he was a jerk. Jane please, please leave me to do this, I've lost my child you're making things worse, please leave'.

'No, I'm not,' she stood and screamed at me.

How to get rid of her, what was I to do? Oh God why, why, why, is she interfering in the worst time when she should be supporting me, as she along with my parents and my niece Lisa had said they would two days prior, during Colin's first visit. I knew her trigger, so I summoned it. 'Who made you mother of the year? Your son moved his family far away from you, I wonder why?' I grabbed my phone. 'Get out of my house now or I'm calling the police to remove you.' At which point, she promptly scuttled out the back door.

Never, ever had I spoken up to her like this. Little did I know at the time that, in doing so I opened a Pandora's box, the likes of which you will learn about later, in what I can only describe as a blackest of black comedy. She heard probably for the first time ever what she could not ever acknowledge herself, as the self-appointed head of our family. The one who spoke for my parents, who cleverly under the radar using pious undertones, oppressed me, squashed my innocence, tut tutted countless times over my flightiness, my spirit, my soul, crushing my child with her, as he often described her 'curt tone and abrasive manner'. Jack was scared of her, I was scared of her. And here I was, five days from losing my child. I lashed out, I slayed the metaphorical dragon, coming out swinging, for me, for Jack.

The irony of the drama Brad brought into my home that day is not lost here. I trod so gently during our hour or so. I included and requested his input on every single point, and apart from insisting he read first, at all other suggestions he repeatedly told me and Colin that he trusted me to make everything beautiful and he just wanted to go he was exhausted. Of course he was, I did understand, but I felt so awful that I had to manage all these decisions when I was also in a state of shock, in some kind of vacuous tunnel on automatic pilot. To this very day I truly feel that the sudden and unexpected loss of someone does bring a madness to the situation, everyone feeling their own guilt, confusion, shock, and we all react in differing ways. I'm simply expressing how the loss of my child affected me, and how I perceived others and their reactions.

The events of this day under the eye of Colin drew him closer to my broken soul. The funeral director was so kind and expressed his deep regret and sympathy to me for having to endure the spiteful accusation from Brad that he had overheard, the shrieking from Jane, my exhaustion. There was no one there for me in the way that I needed. Colin witnessed this and stepped in to aid my suffering.

XIII

PLEASE SUN DON'T RISE, SCORCHING REALITY

The planning of The Gathering was arranged, with music choices and readers selected. I rang and texted Brad on every step but any choice I made was OK with him. He couldn't handle the decision making. I do understand that. Shock is like being slammed in your face with a boulder but being left still walking and having to exist. Through the planning I seemed to be able to cope. It gave me something to do. Jack's friends were hugely significant during this time, with the doorbell regularly going with visits from them. I asked precious Chloe, who I will always refer to as 'the girl with the red shoes' to read and she found a beautiful poem about friendship. Joe and Matt prepared a music video presentation of images of Jack, along with a soundtrack of Eminem's *Without Me* and a speech to introduce it, both taking their part to share their thoughts on Jack. I asked Ben, the lad Jack had cried on during that day in the college when he had been so conflicted, to write something. I asked Jack's college professor to read Shakespeare's Sonnet 71 from the beloved book Jack had given me, at the graveside. My mother wanted to say a few words. I also asked Carol to contribute. George would try his best but if he couldn't manage then Morgan would step in for him. I wrote my piece in the silence of the night and selected baby pictures of Jack to show while his lullaby *Annie's Song* would play. Mike and his eldest daughter Josie sorted out the drinks for the visit at my house after the Gathering. Having drinks and conversation at my house was so important to me. Something would be going on, I would be surrounded by these lovely youngsters.

It became more apparent as the days continued that Brad had retreated into the dragon's den, my metaphorical slaying had resulted in silence from Jane, and Colin acted as a go between for Brad and I. He memorably rang to tell me that picture frames had arrived at the office to be used for Jack's photos. He described them as the cheap gilt looking ones. This was not right, not right at all. Why were they even thinking they wanted to decorate Jacks images? They were ceremonial not decorative, so Colin said he'd conveniently lose them. He knew what I was enduring. He had received several calls from Jane trying to find out about plans and he reminded her that as my name was listed as the client, all arrangements, regardless of who was actually paying, were mine, which made things easier to bear.

I felt so fiercely protective of Jack. I didn't want a single ounce of normality in his humanist service. It had to reflect him. His friends decided that his shade of purple and his colourful, funky clothes, along with his winning smile and funky dance moves, was how best to represent him. A Facebook event was opened by Josie, announcing the request to dress up for Jack. 'Wear your converse, your skinnies, dress to celebrate Jack, no black please, please no black.' I thought deeply about his friends. They were an extension of our family on various levels. Jack loved our village, it was where he belonged, and he was going to forever have a little piece of England. We had to keep this service authentic to him.

I have a vague memory that Christian, the vicar of the parish, had visited me and learned about Jack and his personality, his sensitivity, his connection to the church, albeit the catholic one, and made the arrangements for a humanist service to take place in the local church hall that Brad and I had decided upon, with the burial held by Christian in St Mary's, Bramshott. Christian would become a real source of light for me in the following year.

The house felt less painful to be in as Jack's friends popped in and planning continued for his Gathering. Joe was particularly supportive in his quiet way. We talked about Jack's personal items because I couldn't decide whether to put some of Jack's jewellery with him and Joe said, 'No, no, we can take his ring and necklace from his eighteenth and set them in a shadow box with his other favourite things'. That way they would still feel like Jack was with them. They were his friends and they mattered so much and helped me deal with some difficult decisions. I made a mental note to leave a little piece of Jack with each of his friends. How I would do that I wasn't sure but his legacy was theirs now. I recall receiving biting texts from his father asking where Jack's Vivienne Westwood ring was and I fibbed and said it was with Colin, who was going to place it with Jack. I hated lying but my inner mother lioness was in full protection mode. I recalled how only a few weeks earlier, he had deemed that ring so insignificant and how Jack had ended up buying this amazing piece of armour for himself with his birthday money, disassociating his father from it completely. I knew exactly what Brad was up to. He wanted the ring and sure enough, Colin advised me that calls had been made to their offices from Brad ranting about the ring, wanting to know where it was. On one such rant, this time directed at me, I realised it wasn't fair to involve Colin and his team, so I told Brad that the ring was being kept, with plans from his friends to create a memorial with it, so to speak. I offered to purchase another ring in its place for him, but this fell on deaf ears. I think with loss, all of those close to the situation will reflect back on themselves and their relationship with that person and remember things they had done together, happy shiny memories, a myriad of them, sad ones too, but Brad's grief had to be shockingly horrendous in the silence of his own thoughts. He managed by transferring blame to others and never being accountable. But no threats and recriminations were going to remove the armour of that ring from my life.

A day or so later my back gate clinked and I saw my niece with Brad. I sat paralysed to the sofa as he said he'd come to get the photo album he brought over from the States. He'd allowed me to bring it home so I could get copies of the photographs. I went up to my bedroom to retrieve it and he barked that he wanted to see Jack's room. I said of course he could and I pointed out to him the beginnings of a box of mementoes I had begun to assemble that I would send to him. He looked inside, moving cuddly birds, and various trophies I had placed there, showing no interest whatsoever. I knew this man, he was after one thing. The armour ring, that I had thankfully hidden safely in my room. I learned after Brad and my niece left that he had entered my bedroom, where

Carol was resting, and tried to cajole her to get it for him. Of course she did not engage with him and told me she had to ask him to leave several times. He grabbed the album from me and that was the last I ever saw of the memories encapsulated on film of our little boy pre-divorce – happy, sweet images of the three of us, cute Halloween pictures, new baby photos, holiday snaps. I had all the memories in my heart though and it was me who shared countless private moments with our son. Those memories might have been painful right then but they were mine and I resigned myself to the fact that I'd never see those images again. I learned later that the visit was a plan formulated the night before. My brother and his wife had arrived at Jane's and a decision was made to not give me any notice and hopefully the surprise element would be the best way for Brad to get his hands on Jack's ring. That really was it for me. Of course, if he wanted to visit where his son grew up, his schools etc he should, and those offers had been made by me in the previous few days, but when I'd attempt to call to see if he wanted to come, his ongoing reply was always an exhausted 'not yet.' Lisa apparently had that role. The thing that I just cannot get my head around is why did everyone rally around Brad? Yes, he was in the country at their home and would have certain needs and if he refused to accept my help then in some ways I can see why they acted as his guide, but to not advise me or let me know what they were doing caused such a divide. I knew Jane was behind all of this. It wasn't paranoia, it was her modus operandi to control everyone and every situation at all times. At the same time, in my mind I was questioning that maybe I was imagining things. Everything would be OK at the service, I tried to reassure myself. We would come together as a family should, even one that wasn't close. That's what families do after all.

Colin rang me daily with updates, and the afternoon before the Gathering I visited my boy again. This time I arrived clutching his beloved teddy bear. I had to let him have his teddy. That way I could think of Teddy comforting Jack and he wouldn't be alone in the ground. Colin supplied a safety pin and I carefully pinned this loyal sweet bear to the t shirt of his best friend, my Jack. They needed each other. It was such a beautiful sight, my Jack sleeping with the keeper of all his secrets tucked under his chin. It was incredibly personal and beautiful and quiet and calm. I knew on this visit that my Jack wasn't there now. It's odd I don't really know why, I just had this sense that this body, while still looking like Jack, was actually his shell. Jack wasn't there, but where was he? Colin stood with me as I sang Annie's Song as I backed out of the room. No, I wouldn't turn my back, I just backed away softly singing, knowing Teddy would protect my son.

With Brad refusing to take my calls the night before the service I realised that I had to represent Jack for who he was. There wasn't a fake, malicious bone in his body and I felt almost as if I was channelling my son. He wasn't fake and I wasn't going to be either. Carol and Morgan reminded me that this was a day when I had to feel that I represented Jack with dignity and respect, and I truly was afraid. I recall fear, anxiety and this ongoing numbness, with a knot in my stomach that just hadn't released since the night he'd gone. I was lucky that I had such lovely people around me. Joe's family, the Taylors, apart from organising the evening drinks at my house, handled the messages on Facebook and updated everyone with dates, times, protocol, or in this case, lack of protocol.

The unexpected arrival of younglings who were so incredibly supportive and loving to me, each had their own grief to deal with, somehow came into my life in such an intimate way to comfort me. Names, some I recognised, some I didn't, but each one with a beautiful pearl about how Jack had affected their lives. All of this beautiful commentary, the outpouring of messages, notes through the door, visits from a girl who sat and sobbed that she'd loved Jack and wished she'd told him. The teens loved the idea of a flock of doves being released, so Colin arranged for a group of Jack's closest friends to do this. His mates doing this was so special to my heart. Their readings, their thoughts, their feelings were on a higher realm to mine. I couldn't remotely begin to think of my own feelings, other than shock, shock, shock.

I chose to wear a bright pair of palazzo trousers in turquoise, white and black. Jack had loved them and this day was for him, so I'd represent his unique sense of style along with his mates, who that morning arrived all wearing purple somewhere in their outfits. My lovely hairdresser came and curled my hair for me. That might sound superficial but Jack loved my long blonde locks and I was going to present myself in the best way that I could. I even managed a little make-up. I had to, this was the last event I would plan for my son and I wasn't going to let him down. I worried incessantly about where he was, it was such a surreal time. I remember walking down the stairs into my living room and there were Matt, Joe, Chloe, Jamie, Mike. Lovely Chloe in a shiny pair of red shoes, her prom shoes she told me. My niece's husband Stu arrived as one of the pall bearers but there was no sign of Brad. We asked where he was and got no real answer, just outside somewhere. We stood in a circle and each took a sip from a blue WKD bottle, a favourite drink of Jack's. Colin appeared with the sombre news that Jack had arrived and assured me that Teddy was still securely snuggled beneath his chin. I recall the lads riding with me the two or three minute drive before realising that Brad was sitting next to the driver of our beloved son's transport. I had only glanced at the purple casket with my offering of a teddy bear, what else, with a purple bow tie, in white carnations that Sue, the florist I knew through my dress shop, had assured me would last the longest. She took care of my request with the experience and soft spoken words that came with her profession. I spied a pile of long stemmed white roses that I later found out were ordered by Brad's parents. It was so painful to see as Jack used to buy me white roses, he knew they were my favourite. It's so unexplainable how the tiniest thing could affect me. I recall arriving and standing solitary as the chosen men, they were men, they became men that day, were schooled by the professionals on how to transport Jack to the front of the hall.

Kevin, Jack's manager at the country club, had offered to walk with me behind Jack and held me steady as Aerosmith's *I Don't Want To Miss A Thing* made things all too real. I'd chosen the song to honour the memory of watching my beautiful son tenderly dancing with the prettiest girl in the room. I heard giggles mixed with sobbing as I took that walk. The giggles weren't disrespectful. We'd had the words *I'm Sexy and I Know It* by LMFAO, painted on one side of the purple casket, and on the other, a quote from Gangnam Style. Jack's headphones and snap back baseball cap sat atop the casket along with my teddy offering. Little bird stickers headed the casket and at the rear were Spongebob pics, in homage to Jack's bright yellow boxers with eyes peeping over that he often displayed, wearing his skinnies low-slung, as was the trend.

I approached my place saved at the front in between Morgan, Carol, my customer Lynn, who had quickly become a close friend and my dearest life-long friend Millie. As I turned to sit I saw the next several rows full of faces all meaningful to me and Jack. Our beloved Taylors, Jack's army of closest mates, Hope and Simone who had journeyed from Kent. This stilled my anxiety. Despite the tension between Brad and me, I wasn't alone. I was surrounded by the most beautiful sight, the faces of those Jack truly loved, and who loved him in return.

I spied Colin and there was an audible gasp as he stood wearing his top hat adorned with a purple ribbon, as Jack had done on prom day. He introduced Brad. There was silence as he stepped forward holding the little Reebok sneakers Jack had had. His voice hurt my skin. How could it be that this man all in black holding my son's shoes, this man that I loved, had estranged himself from me at this time when we needed each other the most. Maybe he coped by not looking at me or engaging with me. Or was it me estranging myself from him? I had tried, I really had. It was all too, too much. Shoes placed back on casket, he returned to his seat and loud clapping pierced my brain, from my sister and her family members, followed by an awkward ripple throughout the filled room. I felt so sick. I was so angry, I looked up at Colin and he approached them saying, 'No clapping please, no clapping.' Then he whispered to me, 'No one else will do that, sorry, so sorry.'

I don't recall the order of readers but I know my mum stood for a few minutes and talked about her precious little grandson and the peanut butter sandwiches he loved and the knicker-bocker glories she made him. Carol read a poem about birds. Jack had given her a first edition book on birds for her birthday and they'd shared their love of winged beauties so it was fitting. Chloe, my girl in the red shoes, read a gorgeous poem, voice cracking. I remember feeling so proud of her, mixed with the sickening feeling of the dreaded emptiness that the next day would bring. I forced myself to focus, stay present, telling myself my mind must not drift. Ben stepped forward and read his thoughts on his beloved mate, emotional beautiful words. He was such a brave lad, crumbling as he pushed out the last few words then fled from the podium. I turned and saw a friend comfort him, he was not alone. Then Morgan was up, speaking for George and infusing a touch of humour, recounting the sounds resonating from George's room as our two sons rough housed. The 'dick head, twat' back and forth. A momentary glimpse of happiness for Jack.

Then finally, it was my turn and the room hushed. I had to do this. I had to stand next to my son and share the words that had come to me in the middle of the night a couple of days previously. The words you read at the beginning of this book. I looked across the sea of faces who brought me such support. I was reading for Jack, pausing to capture my emotions, my dad's voice ringing out, 'Keep going, girl!' Oh my daddy, he loved me. I turned to face Jack and complete my piece as I awaited the beginning of *Annie's Song*. The screen started showing images but there was no music. Everything was out of place. What to do? What to do? Lynn rose and asked Colin to stop the video and sort out the mess. The laptop unable to play the music, Christian darted home next door, returning with a CD player. I felt heartsick, but Lynn urged me to, 'Do it again, Tracy, this is about your love for Jack'. I rose back to the podium and read again, clearer this time. Please, please all hear me, I was thinking. Please know he's still here, he didn't leave. This time as I turned to face Jack and complete my reading, I felt a compelling need to reach over and grab his snap back cap, put it on my head and drop to the floor cross-legged in front of his casket to view the video images. I sensed shuffling behind me and saw a throng of young faces had joined me. *Annie's Song* playing, the swell of tearful sobs. Pulled back to my feet. A chorus of 'love you, Tracy' fed my soul from the sweet voices of these kids.

Matt and Joe took turns to read. Joe slow and steady, Matt hurtling through jumbled words. I understood why, it just wasn't happening for him yet. Video rolling with a sea of images of my boy and his mates, with the Eminem song *Without Me* playing. It was so, so painful, beautifully so.

Then I was at the podium again, reminding my younglings of their duty now to do this for Jack, as the opening beats of Gangnam filled the air. These walking angels on their feet, filled the aisle, dancing their hearts and souls out for their friend, their Jack. I stood among them as they rocked out for Jack. This day was theirs and it was the only way to push through, to hand the day to them.

LMFAO lyrics as we left. Solitary outside the church as Colin assured me he would be back to come and get me. First he had to ensure Jack would arrive safely for his burial. A young lad approached me. I remembered him, Cory. He handed me flowers and expressed his sympathies. Jack really liked this lad. He struggled with quite severe Aspergers and I recall he was part of Jack's drama class and absolutely brilliant in his GCSE performance. He literally channelled Kramer from Seinfeld, although I'm not sure he realised he was acting. It was hard to tell with Cory! Now, here he was, head bowed, handing me these pretty blooms. I thanked him and offered a hug but he awkwardly backed away, it stung a little, but I got it. Unable to demonstrate affection, the polar opposite of Jack, but it was a cherished moment. I spied Leila coming towards me and I was pretty sure she was with Eric. Having not heard a peep from her since Jack died I wasn't sure what to think. She stepped forward and introduced herself. I blanked Eric. I couldn't help it, I was in protective mode. Leila had an orchid for me and flowers for Jack. I think I hugged her, I was confused. If I spoke to this boy would I be betraying Jack? I knew how betrayed he had felt but I also knew that this was all part of being young adults. Hurt feelings, perceived betrayals, gossip. What was I to do, he was standing right in front of me. I asked Leila who he was and she replied that he was Eric. I turned to him and said something along the lines of, 'This one's for Jack' and kicked him on his leg, then promptly threw my arms around both of them as they chimed in that they had made up with Jack a long time ago. I acknowledged this and we all hugged. I spoke briefly about Jack's intense sensitivity. At this point none of us actually knew what had taken place at the station. My thoughts were muddled. Was it an accident? What about the message though? Did he get close and then the rush of the train affected his stance? Did his jacket catch on something? No one knew so it seemed no one was really thinking in terms of why, or at least not expressing their thoughts to me.

I don't recall how I was transported to the site of the burial. I do remember walking behind my son as his mates carried him, Morgan at my side. The throng of mourners standing silently. I've never ever taken that path since, I choose an alternative route. I didn't really 'see' anyone. I felt an army behind me though as I stood with Morgan in front of this hole in the ground. The cooing of the birds helped to soothe me and Brad stepped forward to release his dove. I don't recall much about the service, apart from the respectful tones of Jerry reading the sonnet directly to Jack's casket as it now sat high, raised above the earth below. It was lovely to see these loving friends of Jack stepping forward and forming a beautiful semi-circle, each clutching a dove and releasing in unison. The flurry of doves as they circled not once but twice and the rise in emotion from my rows of steadfast tin soldiers.

I still had the robe of shock protecting me. Milling people, soldiers out of formation, a pretty, dark-haired girl approached and handed me a bright pink rose, saying, 'Hello, I'm Allie.' We held each other and I thanked her for being so kind to Jack and told her he loved the way she used her words. Then I had to leave and let the others mingle. I didn't want to see the earth cover my boy. Lovely Wayne and Jake, dear friends who we had met on a holiday in Pisa five years before, took me under their wing and I journeyed with them to the country club.

At the club images of Jack had been placed around the lounge and a screen looped the video put together by Matt and Joe. People began arriving, milling. Many respectful words coming at me. A gift made by some of the local teens, a beautiful collage of images of their memories, gifted to me. I was so moved and deeply touched by a smaller image of the Union Jack with a story of Jack in pictures made by a sweet artistic girl. I cherish those two pieces and we all shared a long emotional hug. It was such a moment in their grief to think of me, to represent Jack in such an artistic and creative way. As the room swarmed with these beautiful friends of my son and his face repeating on the screen, a sickness came over me, as the shroud of shock began to dissipate.

Several of my niece Lisa's friends from our Thailand holiday stepping forward to offer their words of comfort. How odd, not Lisa but her friends giving me, Jack's Mumsie, the respect befitting the occasion. Needing to go to the toilet but petrified Brad would approach me in a stolen moment, the college girls accompanied me.

The odd person leaving, with Colin's watchful eye always present. Kevin, the restaurant manager, approached me to say they were sending a lantern to the sky and I should join Brad. 'No' was my insistent reply as he tried to cajole me, speaking of how I would regret not doing that. I don't even know how to describe my state of mind. I felt very frightened deep inside, but I was on some kind of automatic pilot and had to stay like that. Being asked to get close to anyone who might say an unkind word was terrifying, so I did not participate, instead I stood with some of the remaining lads, all a bit boozy by then, as they wrapped their arms around me and kept me safe. They didn't realise it but for the first time that day I felt protected. I looked at the bar and saw empty spaces where Jack's pictures had been displayed. The looping video had been replaced by blank wall. Home, I needed to get home. The kids would be there. *Don't leave me alone. No one leave me alone,* pressed into my mind.

Colin drove me home, with a promise to return as he was needed to finalise matters at the hotel. A throng of young people greeted me as someone had keys, apparently. The Taylors had set up drinks aplenty and a sort of party ensued. I don't really know what else to call it. Music was playing as I passed through my little house looking at this sea of faces, the chatter, and upon seeing me, a hug, a kind word, then white noise all around me. I escaped to my room, laying on my bed petrified for what tomorrow would bring. Colin was downstairs and the house chanted his name, referring to him as a legend, the top hat had captured so many of them, and he received this compliment with grace and reverence. He had with him Jack's pictures from the day, which he placed on Jack's bed. He told me, hands clasped, that his duties were complete as far as the services went, however he would call me the next day to see how I was. I don't recall thinking how kind he was at that time, I just was so beholden to him, so reliant on him for guiding me through and steadying me. So grateful of his offer to call me.

Now back in the throng of the evening, an out of body feeling came over me. There on the sofa sat Jack, wasn't it? Who was this boy? Pale faced with dark tousled hair and shockingly pale. Who was he? I grabbed Matt, who relayed that it was Joel from college. *Get him out of here*, screamed in my brain. I couldn't bear to see another boy so like my Jack. I escaped upstairs to sit in his room to discover Joe's little sister, Sally, sitting on his bed gazing at the pictures, tears streaming. Back into comforter mode, I held her, told her he loved her. Then I left her to her time with Jack. Trying to engage with others while in my bubble, the opening bars of Gangnam began and there were shouts to me to join in. *No!* screamed in my head, so I stood and watched as this merry throng, all coping in the very best way they could, cranked up the sound and danced their pain away, replacing the refrain 'Gangnam Style' with 'Jack Wall style'. Joe and his little bro Sam not more than twelve wearing one of Jack's ties. A sea of jumping up and down as the track repeated. My eyes locked on Matt, standing, blank eyes, just like Jack's eyes the last time I saw him. This lad was hurting. Noticing the boy, Joel, eerily similar to Jack, I forced myself to speak to him and settled next to him. He revealed that it was he who Jack had borrowed his eyeliner from. He appreciated Jack's style and after my initial reaction, I was now comforted by the familiarity between them. Smiley, cheeky, chubby Harris perched on my coffee table, crack. Oops! Recriminations came flying at him, oh dear, but it was a welcome distraction. Lovely Gemma, the artist who created my Union Jack piped up that her dad would repair the table, as he was a handy man. He'd come tomorrow. Tomorrow, what did that mean? I'd go visit Jack, that's what I'd do.

XIV

ANGELS CROOKED AND OTHERWISE

I don't recall sleeping but I guess I must have as I awoke to daylight and the sense that I wasn't alone. Some of the younglings had stayed and were busy cleaning the house, and darling gentle Gemma was organising everyone. Off she went out to buy cleaner for my living room rug, that was awash with spills from a variety of concoctions. I retreated to my room while these lovely younglings cleaned and polished my little house, popping in with cups of tea and warm hugs for me.

Isn't it interesting how the human mind works? I can remember in such detail most of that day but I only recall pockets of the ensuing weeks. I learned from my mother that Brad had returned to the USA. A visit from Chloe, aka the girl with the red shoes, with swollen eyes and a downcast face as she explained that many notes and cards and flowers had been left at the station in tribute to Jack but now the notes were missing, including one she'd written to Jack herself. Chloe had discovered that Brad had taken the notes and asked if I would please contact him to request he return them. This was an uncomfortable dilemma. Chloe said that her mother would contact him if I didn't feel I could, but I wanted things handled, so I sent a message to Brad expressing how terribly upset Jack's friends were that he had taken the notes and asked if he could please return them right away. I suggested of course that if he wanted these memories then to go ahead and photocopy them but to please, please return them for Jack's friends. The response received back simply stated, 'send me the ring and I'll send the notes'. Jack's friends were sickened at this ultimatum, insisting that I should keep the ring. We then learned that the station manager himself had cleared all remaining flowers etc. as apparently it was normal to remove them after a week or two. This ultimately helped Chloe, who journeyed by train to her college, and with her birthday approaching, I sourced a pretty pink sapphire ring and gifted it to her from Jack. The first of many gifts I've bestowed here and there these past few years, as what must have been a coping mechanism in the grief tunnel, as I fumbled along, clinging on so very tight to Jack's besties. I never did respond to Brad's message. Knowing that I must protect myself, I felt there was no real good to be done by getting into a back and forth over this issue. Jack's mates were coping with this unexpected stab, so I would try to stay strong for them, as it seemed they were for me.

Colin visited me pretty much every day. I was petrified to be left alone. When I was alone a panic would ensue as an overwhelming sense of loss enveloped me and I clung to this man. I racked tears into countless shirts, and he would kindly hold my hand and allow me to sob as the realisation was permeating of how I would manage my life without my boy. I talked endlessly about going to be with Jack.

Sensing that I was in too deep, with my state of mind crumbling as the bleakest and darkest of thoughts swirled, my lovely friend Hope drove 100 miles to come and take me back to her home, her thoughts being to get me away from the sensory overload. My beautiful friend allowed me to rest my head in her lap and wail and cry and release. She bathed me, prepared small meals to nourish me, and comforted me as my own mother had done, however this time with no memory of the pain behind my parents' eyes. For those few soothing days I could put to one side the overwhelming hideous guilt and angst. Hope's daughter, Simone returned me home with the knowledge that I could return to them whenever I chose to. Friends and family, lines most certainly blurred with these two beautiful souls.

Christian visited often and was so kind. He suggested I go to a church group weekly and I did so out of fear of being alone. They were nice people, kind people. They prayed with me, they prayed for me but not for Jack. Jack was with God apparently and it was me who needed and would benefit from

ANGELS CROOKED AND OTHERWISE

their prayers. I desperately wanted to know where he was. Had the lights gone out? Was he in the dark? I couldn't stop worrying for my boy. Christian prayed deeply for me and told me that the Holy Spirit would be with me and would show me his presence. That very evening I returned home and went straight to Jack's laptop, as I did every day, checking his Facebook, checking mine, doing mind numbing searches – anything to not have to think. I was on a department store website, I needed nightwear and I came across a pack of t-shirt style night dresses. I clicked on the reviews. There in print, was the name of the top review by JAMMIE DODGER. Oh my, a sign right in front of my face. What on earth were the chances of a reviewer having Jack's nickname? It was a blue veil moment, some force was with me. I didn't understand how but I took solace. Those prayerful times with Christian were so soothing. His voice was hypnotic and I found immense comfort for a few minutes every few days as he would drop by the house with pantry food. He brought a calmness, a stillness, an intimacy. Morgan would visit some days for cuddles and hand holding. It was the evenings I feared the most. The younglings popped in in the evenings but I was still so, so lost in my head. I couldn't watch television. I could watch anything recorded but I couldn't see news or hear about life outside of my grief.

The school that Jack had attended invited me to see Jack's teacher. I lived four doors from the school but the walk was agonisingly difficult. Each step there was that weight I was dragging around with me everywhere. No one from the school had attended the Gathering and they were full of apologies as Jack's year head had called in sick that day. More white noise. They suggested a tree to be planted at the school for my boy and they said they would select something perfect for Jack and would be in touch in a couple of weeks. On the walk home, head bowed, my mind still almost dead inside, I felt arms around me. It was a young girl. To this day I have no idea who she was but she obviously recognised me. Thank you, young girl.

A visit came from a police officer, who said he was there to take a statement from me. Morgan sat next to me as I recounted the events of that fateful day. Heavy mind, heavy heart, I answered his questions and he gently informed me that he had a statement from the driver of the train. I needed to know. Up to that point there was a lot of why, why, why and wondering if it had been some kind of tragic accident. He told me the driver was travelling at his normal speed and spied someone on the platform, I don't recall if he said sitting or standing. He said as the train approached this person stepped forward and leaned, turning his head away from the train. Impact. Nothing else I needed to know, he assured me. He explained that there would be an inquest, probably in a couple months, and I'd be notified. I recall not being able to cry. I was dead inside as I heard what he said. I thought that Jack couldn't have been leaning far. I saw my son, he didn't have injuries in line with someone leaning over. It was all I had.

Unknown to me, my friend and customer, Lynn, was working to get me some professional support. I had the obligatory visit from a local NHS Counsellor but her words felt cold, generic. I was desperate for support, as in my mind I had none. I had a couple of friends and the kids but I was out of my mind with grief. I'm told that I was uncontrollably sobbing for weeks and not eating and all I talked about was going to be with Jack.

During one of Colin's visits he assured me Jack was safe. But how did he know? I didn't understand and I pleaded with him to explain. He spoke of the other side of life. In his work role he was familiar with people wanting to communicate with loved ones on the other side and he knew of someone he could take me to. My intellectual mind had red flags everywhere, but in my grief stricken pleading and heartsick droning as to where my boy was, it was all I could think of. Arrangements were made and Colin drove me to his offices, where we were to meet with a man named Edward. Colin assured me that this man had a fine reputation and I was so desperate to know my boy was safe. I recall waiting and the sickening feeling coming over me as I became aware that I was in another funeral home. Not the one I saw Jack in but the interior was similar. I couldn't bear to see the funeral brochures and the window filled with urns and carriage images. Upon Edward's arrival Colin stepped out and I saw a man slightly dishevelled, wearing a cardigan.

What I do recall from that meeting was a lot of guessing ie; 'I have a blonde haired boy here'. I had blonde hair but Jack didn't. 'Was it a car accident?' He appeared to be trying very hard to bring me some comfort and he told me there was so much emotion in him that it was almost too much to take on. The only thing he did say was he kept tasting meat and this spirit was often eating greasy meat, a kebab, he felt. That was a glimpse that maybe there was some kind of life after death here. Jack had loved kebabs, often coming home from his jaunts out around the village with a doner kebab wrap. It was all I had but it was something. The sceptic in me thought that's what most teenage boys ate, but no, no this was what Jack feasted on. Pathetic, the place I was in, pure desperation. Colin gently told me that while I was with Edward he had sensed Jack's presence. He explained it as if there was someone in the hallway standing outside the room I was in and he was sure it was Jack. It was way too much to process. During the ride home I had been notified that the police had been called by one of Jack's friends, desperately concerned for me, as she had been to my house and when I was not home panic ensued. The fall out of Jack's passing was still very much present with the younger community, and I felt the beginning of a sense of purpose to try to look after those who needed a cuddle and a chat. Colin offered to sleep on the sofa that night. Climbing the stairs to my bedroom was so incredibly difficult, there was no relief from the weight I was still dragging. I was so frightened to go to sleep, as that meant waking up and I didn't want to.

Sleeping pills taken, most nights Colin would sit in the hallway on the top step and not leave until he knew I was asleep. He would stretch his arm into my room and hold my hand in his as the pills took over. I recall on one occasion a soft kiss on my hand and an 'I love you'. Survival this must be, I recall thinking that. How grateful I was to Colin. I knew I had someone who was there for me in the evenings when everyone was with their families. We would just sit on the sofa and sip hot tea, that I found so comforting although I'd never had been that much of a tea drinker. I was clinging on with all I could to this lovely decent man. This is how I saw him. I was aware as a woman that maybe he was smitten, but being completely honest, I didn't feel anything. It was impossible to feel. I was weeks from losing my child. I was dragging myself through life minute by minute and he stepped in to help me.

The holiday season arrived and people were busy with their own lives. The phone rang less often, the core friends were still there for me but they made shorter visits and less frequently. Lost in the depths of grief with Christmas approaching I spent most days just sitting on the sofa with my warm tea in a trance of sorts. I had painful glimpses at Facebook as I saw cheeky happy comments being posted by people who had been at his services, friends of his and the like, talking about birthday plans, Christmas get togethers, the lols the hahas. It was so difficult to see how life was moving on for others but mine had stood still. I was in a vacuum. A vacuum of, 'Say goodbye to your son,' 'Bye-byeeeee,' click, gone. Over and over, this played in my mind. The blame was wholly mine, I couldn't see any other solution. The blame I levied at myself, mixed with this love, this blinding, hypnotic, protective love. My fault. I love him. My fault. Love. My fault… on and on I punished myself.

I used to endlessly scroll through Jack's Facebook page, looking up his friends. Some I didn't know, some I did. I would send out little messages hoping for a reply and always receiving one. Filling the lonely nights with little loving messages from my boy's Facebook account. One friend I came across was Santino, who Jack had worked with in the kitchen at the country club. I could see that he was now in Wales and I recalled how much Jack mentioned him and had been visibly upset when he found out his friend was moving. I sent him a message thanking him for always being such a nice friend to Jack, and received an immediate reply. He told me he had blamed himself terribly for Jack's leaving, and said that the very night that Jack left us all, he had said goodbye to his friend. It had been Santino's last day and he described how Jack hugged him for such a long time and told him how proud he was of him, and how he would visit him in Wales. In comparison to others he worked with, he sensed Jack's real pain at having to say goodbye. When he learned of Jack's passing the next day as he left for Wales he had carried this guilt that it was somehow his fault. This admission added another layer to the why? I was able to reply to Santino, advising him of other elements surrounding my loss, his loss too, and that, no, of course it wasn't his fault. Here I was, receiving comfort, giving comfort, it was an insanity of sorts. Reaching out as I did was helping me though, as I now knew that Jack had walked in the door that night tired, grumpy, downcast over Santino leaving. Not only did he have me pecking at him, he had just said goodbye to Santino, but I didn't know it.

Two lovely girls, both very attached to Jack, continued to pop in to visit me and at different times they stayed over, with their parents' approval, as they were only sixteen. They had their time in Jack's room. Remembering their first love. So sweet. One of the girls was Joe's younger sister Sally, who had such a crush on Jack. Being four years older than her, Jack was flattered but knew his place and they were great friends. The other girl, Diana I had no clue about. She arrived on my doorstep the day after the Gathering and I instantly recognised her beautiful blue eyes. This was one of the many faces who had gathered to sit behind me on the floor. I had turned to look at them all and I remember her almost beseeching face. She wanted me to know that she was here for me and that she knew Jack, who was in the year above her at college, and he was so kind to her. She told me that on her first day of college she was really nervous to board the bus along with the older crowd. She described it as uncomfortably quiet, then Jack threw his baseball cap down the bus, did a little dance jig in the aisle, and broke the ice as everyone giggled. She told me that when the bus arrived at the college, Jack immediately took her to meet his friends and showed her around. The friends she made were a direct result of Jack and she loved him and promptly burst into tears. I comforted her, and she unknowingly comforted me so, so much. To hear of my beloved son being so caring of others was the beginning of a watershed moment, as more and more sweet stories arrived in my inbox, or upon chance meetings. Darling, sweet, pure Diana told me she felt such awful guilt as she'd been getting the nerve up to tell Jack that she loved him and had decided to do it on the Friday but she noticed he seemed preoccupied somehow so decided that was not the day. She cried and expressed that if she had told him maybe he would still be here. No, no, I assured her, it wasn't her fault. I was carrying that guilt, the stick was permanently embedded in my back. I gifted both girls. One with a bracelet and the other with Jack's knitted hat, along with a purple crystal angel for Sally's eighteenth and a purple Swarovski wrap bracelet for Diana. Purple and twinkly, keepsakes of their sweet memories of their secret love, their first young love, immortalised forever at eighteen.

I wondered how on earth I was going to push through the holiday season. My eyes were closed to the shininess of it as I avoided TV completely and only watched DVDs or recorded mind-numbing programmes where I could whizz through the commercials. I had thought about going to midnight mass. It wasn't out of some sense of duty, it was pure survival. I didn't know what I believed anymore but knowing Jack was there on that freezing cold icy night I made the short drive to the church where he was buried. My boy was there, Christian was there. Diana had mentioned she was going to midnight mass with a friend, which helped ease my fear as she assured me she would save a seat for me so I didn't have to arrive super early. This young girl reached her hand across to mine, my head bowed most of the time as silent tears trickled and with Christian's soothing voice, I endured another hour or so of not being alone. He so compassionately greeted me at communion and sought me out after for words of comfort. I don't recall what he said, I just know that this man's voice was soothing, almost hypnotic. Diana was leaving and we hugged and shared a tear. My body felt so weighed down as I realised the drive home to nothing was approaching. As I started down the frost covered path as one of the last to leave, there in front of me was Colin. I must have mentioned I was going and he cared so much for my well-being he came to escort me home, driving cautiously as I followed him. Settled in for the night, me in my bed, hand held by this man from the hallway on this awful sad day was a beautiful thing. Who was this man, I didn't even know anything of him, only his incredible kindness and generosity of spirit as he lessened the burden from my parents, who could offer emotional and some financial support, but living almost a two hour drive away, and Mum caring for my dad's needs as she always had, Colin was a true gift.

Christmas Day was upon me. I had told most people not to contact me, partly out of what would they say if they did message, what would I say if they called, and also trying not to engage in the day. I felt so incredibly lonely, the silence was deafening. I recall making a cup of tea and just sitting numb, sad, dead inside. Today I would spend the day with Jack, this was the only choice that felt right. I wrapped up warm and drove the five minutes to the church. Head lowered as I drove, in a dark tunnel, just get there, don't look around, don't see children on their new bikes, don't listen to the festive chatter from the local pub.

I walked along the path and down the steps, each step so, so painful. A mound of tufted grass at the end of the row. There was a bench I imagine gifted from someone, so I managed to move it a little closer and there I sat. I'd visited a few times and cleared the flowers etc from the Gathering, and I spied a couple of cards and a small posy of flowers. The chill was biting but there I sat gazing at the mound. I wanted to get in the dirt, I just wanted to get into the dirt. I was worried he was cold. I was heartsick. It truly was the saddest day of my life. Sadder than the day he left, sadder than the Gathering. I had shock to protect me then. Today the reality was right in front of my eyes. A mound of dirt, a temporary cross, 'all part of the service.' No one there, not a single soul. They would all be tucking into their turkey by now, already visited in the morning maybe, who knows. Tears streamed down my face. I couldn't go on. Where was my boy? He's there, he's in that box in the ground. I let out a wretched wail and sobbed for I really don't know how long. I couldn't leave him, I had to stay with him. I imagined swallowing all my sleeping pills, and laying right there on top. Someone would find me and all they'd have to do is dig a hole and chuck me in and then I'd be with my boy. I imagined laying on my side as I had on that day I went to see him after he left. I imagined my cheek pressing against Jack's. As close to him as I could possibly be. I thought endlessly of Teddy comforting Jack and I thanked him countless times for taking care of my boy. I stood and sang Annie's Song many times over, feet numbing, ears cold. I couldn't leave him there. I couldn't walk away. I couldn't. *I couldn't.* Silence.

Then I glanced up and spied some figures. As they ambled closer I saw the most healing sight. Al, Harry, Kyle, holding a blue WKD drink and a lantern. Three beautiful souls, three lads, all three with bad boy reputations of varying degrees, visiting their mate Jack on this day. They greeted me jovially and we four shared the bench and a rollie, my very first. I watched these lads as they stood at my son's side. They unwrapped the lantern over Jack and attempted to light it, however the wind pulled it out of their grasp and they went hurtling across graves to recapture it. I giggled. I felt for them, I felt for Jack. All safely back in place, the bright blue lantern headed skyward as these lads stood watching. I could leave now. I wasn't leaving Jack alone. I was leaving him with his mates, as a mum should do. This was their time. So I walked away and left my son in the very best hands, this most personal of gifts to him. Thank you, Al, Harry, Kyle.

I truthfully don't recall the rest of the day, other than the taste of a cheese and tomato toastie, my sandwich toaster was the only way I ate, if I ate anything, always the same warming sensation, and soothing cups of tea.

On Boxing Day my parents visited. Colin offered to bring them to me and my father included him in our day. He brought a portable wheelchair so Dad could visit his grandson and the three of us sat in a deep embrace, Mum saying, 'You have your little piece of England now,' as tears rolled, trying to stay strong for Dad, who looked ashen. They were both there for me. It was so loving of them to journey to me, with Colin guiding them both and me through our attempt at a festive meal at the hotel where Jack had worked. Eating but no taste, swallowing without chewing. We managed the best we could. Crackers being pulled and families sharing this season was just a blur that I blocked from my mind. Colin returned us to my little house and I managed a nice warm cappuccino and a little slice of cake that Mum had brought, along with other pantry items. I gathered Jack's college work and sat reading for them both the most beautifully written piece of work by their beloved grandson, his thoughts on the writer Carol Ann Duffy. Dad expressed how so very proud he was – so proud of my boy, their boy. Then he lowered his head and from behind his handkerchief came muffled sobs, mixed with his own self recrimination. 'What did I do wrong? Why didn't he come to me, Eileen? Why, why has our grandson died? Our name has died with him.'

The three of us huddled together that afternoon, as we did the night we'd slept together, and the wave of agonising guilt still washed over me. The pain they both were in, this pain was a result of me. *It was my fault. I killed my son,* began droning in my mind. Taking on this responsibility for them. I shared with them all the cards and little notes I had received which, while not cheering them, gave them an hour of warmth, the words written by so many helping to soothe. I knew Jane would be all over where they were on this day so Mum told me not to worry and she would just say they took a taxi. Colin transported them safely home and called me to talk to me as I took my sleeping pills. He stayed on the phone with me until sleep saved me.

I always knew that Colin's help was extraordinary. But he was the only adult person I had. Without him I literally cannot fathom what my state of mind would have been. Mum and Dad were so grateful to him for helping their daughter, for helping them. I was still desperate for his support and only just beginning to realise what a selfless man he was. I learned he had a daughter in her teens and a wife, although not a happy marriage. He said that she understood his type of work and when I did question their home life situation, he assured me that she wasn't really present emotionally and their lives were not ideal. It was such a surreal time.

I'd speak to Mum most days and Morgan and Lynn checked in on me, Morgan popping in for an hour or two. Lynn sending comforting text messages. But everything was so dark in my mind. What was the point of my life now? I was in a dark tunnel of grief with no way ever, ever of feeling better. I didn't want to feel better. I sobbed down the phone to Morgan that I just wanted to get in the dirt, I couldn't bear the deafening silence. I was crying, begging for help to make this pain go away but there was no remedy. After ending my call I sat stoic I don't really know for how long. I wanted to be with Jack, this I knew without a doubt, I just needed to know he was OK. The iPad gave me the time of the next fast train passing through the village, so I slipped on my shoes and took the few steps to the back door as Jack had done. Door handle grasped, I was caught by the loud ding of the front door bell. I recall Mike standing at the door and me just dropping to the floor. Poor Mike wasn't equipped for this. Who the heck was? I think he called my parents who would sort a taxi, when Colin rang as he always did. He came and drove me to my parents. I had the clothes on my back and my rosary at my neck and that was it.

My parents greeted their broken daughter with such love. Mum sat on my bed and I fell completely to pieces in her arms as she whispered, 'I know sweetheart, I know.' There was a unique bond between us as my mum had been the victim of suicide by her estranged husband. She soothed me and she sat with me as I lay in bed for a few days. The realisation of what had happened now taking a hold of me. Squeezing my heart. So, so tired, I slept, I drank tea, I cried, I bled, Christian's voice soothed as he rang me. With no young ones for me to comfort, it was time for my parents to comfort me.

Both of them worried for me terribly, but also worried for themselves, with Mum taking more of a role over Dad, the three of us didn't know what to do so Colin stepped forward. He said he had cleared his schedule and would be honoured to take care of me. With their other children not offering support to me, Mum and Dad were so terribly embarrassed. Colin assured them he would be there for me. He became such a source of support. He wouldn't take any money. It was as if I had my very own Guardian Angel.

Colin visited every evening the week that I returned from my parents. He had his schedule sorted to spend nights as my carer of sorts at my home, so I didn't have to go home to the silence. I was so afraid to be alone. Then, oddly, two days came and went with no sign of Colin. I tried him at his work, to be told he was on leave. Colin had called me every single day for several weeks and now nothing. I left him text and voice messages and found myself spiralling downward, erratic breathing, panic ensuing. Opening my email for the umpteenth time, finally I saw an email from him. He told me that he had been suspended from his job because someone had called the office saying that he was having a sexual relationship with me. The sadly familiar shock dug into my bones. I shakily called his office and after some time, a man describing himself as Colin's superior came onto the phone. After some initial hesitancy, he advised me that a male person had rung and voiced concerns over an intimate relationship between myself and Colin and said that events at the Gathering had not been handled correctly. Through my shock I found the inner strength to speak up for myself, reminding him that I was the named client on all of the paperwork and asking why he had not contacted me. Of course I knew fundamentally that Colin had gone way above and beyond any call of duty and I had had many conversations with him in reference to this, however he'd insisted to me and my parents that his time was his own to spend however he wanted. When you are in this kind of desperate situation I don't think you really care as to the whys and wherefores. Mum and Dad were so relieved and grateful to him. My guilt at their devastation was incredibly debilitating and Colin was willing to help. Someone was willing to care for me, to be there in my home in the evenings. To be a listening ear. I didn't have anyone else. I was screaming inside my head in agony as realisation took a vice-like grip. I recall a couple of men in suits from the funeral directors, one I believe a VP level person, visiting my home on more than one occasion, and one time a note taker was present. I willingly referred back to all the messages I had received and sent to Colin to show them that there was nothing inappropriate.

After endless conversations about the extra visits Colin had made to my home I was eventually told that the person who'd made the call to them was Jane's son but I felt certain he wouldn't have done it without her say so. It was obvious to those involved this was an attempt to interfere, and discredit me. I learned from my mother that, having been provoked by Jane, she had confessed that it was Colin who had driven my parents to my home for Boxing Day. My mother learned that it was Brad who had asked Jane to intervene, and so as not to get her hands directly dirty, she had delegated this role to her son. My mum was absolutely devastated but she and Dad needed my sister's help, which I understood but I was left facing a lonely, bleak time as a result of her interference.

Not terribly aware at the time of the enormity of what had happened to Colin and the consequences facing the company who employed him, I received another visit from the Director, with news of Colin's dismissal. The services of a counselling group they used were offered to me, and a sum of money that they insisted on terming as a 'refund', which I clearly see now was a way to cover themselves in the event of what would have come of this had I used a solicitor to advise me. I didn't know what to make of all this. I wasn't able to use their counselling service because I was already in treatment and was advised that it would complicate things if I saw more than one person at the same time. Of course, now I see things on many levels from a clearer perspective. I was very upset for Colin, as were my parents, however the Director explained that while knowing Colin as a man with enormous compassion for others, his dismissal was due to calling in sick on a day when he wasn't sick. I think this was a veiled excuse, no one wanting to say what was really on their minds, wanting to avoid a front page news scandal that would have had lasting damage on the large franchise group they were a part of. He did explain to me that my grief recovery would have been hampered by the person who buried my child repeatedly showing up at my door. Continuing to see him would have kept me in that early stage of grief. Hope recently shared with me that during my visit to her Colin had telephoned me multiple times and she had felt there was something untoward about the fact that he kept calling me while I was away, however due to my fragility, she'd decided not to mention it. I don't even recall him calling so I can now, on balance, realise the dire place I was in; clutching to him, another reminder of my child, not wanting to let go of that last memory of Jack's life.

I felt so ashamed and terribly hurt by Colin. I never heard from him again. To have such intense support, albeit a bit fucked up, but let's face it, who the hell knows the best way to manage a suicide of a son, our lives intertwined and now the roots of one of us dying off and the other left with only half the oxygen needed to survive. In spite of his silence, I do feel so very grateful for his support at a time when I so desperately needed it, particularly with my parents, who were also very grateful to Colin for helping them help me.

XV

PURGATORY

The inquest date was approaching and my fear as to who might be there had waned slightly with the knowledge that inquests are a matter of public record. I had called Matt's mother to let her know that he would also be required to be there because he had been in receipt of Jack's final text message. The coroner's clerk had suggested it may be easier if we didn't see each other, as it's always best in these matters to not engage too much, although certainly not a requirement. I felt quite anxious. I didn't really understand it all but the coroner explained to me that the process was an investigation to determine how someone had passed away and not to point fingers or lay blame. He assured me I did not have to sit in on the events and it would be fine for me to just appear for what he needed me for and then to leave. I was petrified to hear anything upsetting in relation to my boy. I didn't know the exact time that it happened, this was one fact I didn't want to know. I didn't know how he was found either, it was too much to remotely even go there in my mind. It had only been two months since he left, which was no time at all. I was told there would be press there and to just avoid the newspapers for a couple of days after, which was easy to do as I hadn't engaged at all in anything news related since Jack's passing. I was and on many levels still am in a time capsule, stuck when the lights in my soul went out and purgatory began.

A few days prior to the inquest I was firming up arrangements with my mum on the phone about how she would travel to the court, and she became very teary and her voice shaky. She told me that Jane was refusing to stay away from the inquest. I don't actually know how to describe my utter disbelief that she would do this. I sobbed my heart out, pleading to Mum to stop her.

There were phone calls back and forth and Mum told me that Dad had tried and that she had screamed at Jane that I was never going to see my son again and to stay away to give me the space without the awful repeat of my child's services and those awful confused feelings that I had in regard to those few family members in attendance. Here she was doing it again, engineering, controlling, and in no way could be told what to do by her younger sister.

I couldn't understand why Jane chose not to respect me as Jack's mother. I didn't want her there, I knew she would be straight on the phone to Brad with all the details, although obviously he could request a copy of testimony anyway, inquests being a matter of public record. I just didn't want any more tension, not on this awful clinical day. I was in pieces, racking my brain trying to think of how to stop her. I was begging and pleading with my mother, who did not know what to do. I blurted out something along the lines of, 'What do I have to do to stop her from going there, take a knife and chop her head off?' The ramblings of desperation. Trying anything I could to make Mum see how terribly upset I was. Nothing resolved, a fitful night's sleep ensued, and I returned to work with Gemma and my tortured mind in tow.

While I was sitting at my desk, two police officers, one male the other female, entered my sweet little haven. 'Are you Tracy Wall?' they asked. 'Yes' I replied, with no thought other than oddly maybe they were neighbourhood police checking on me, maybe they'd been made aware of my loss or something. 'We need you to come with us,' they told me. What happened next is all a bit muddled, as I was completely perplexed. I recall asking several times why and they kept saying, 'Look, just come with us, let's just go get in the car.'

I rang my mum, a bit like a six-year-old wanting my mummy I guess. Mum answered my call already in tears, asking me to give the phone to the police officer. When the phone was handed back to me I cried, 'Mummy, Mummy,' as she tried to reassure me that it would be ok and to just go with them and do as they asked and to call her as soon as I could. I gave Gemma my keys and she said she'd contact her dad for a lift home. I was worried for her, this sweet girl being a party to seeing one of her best friend's mothers being told I had to go with these police but neither of us knowing why? I remember crossing the street to their car and saying, 'I'm the mum whose son just died if you need me for a meeting or something.' But there was no response. Into the back seat I went as the male officer told me they had to do this formal part, and he told me I was being arrested for threats to kill and read me my remainder rights. Still oblivious, I was softly crying, head down during the drive to what I now know to be Waterlooville police station. On the journey there I managed a text to Morgan, telling her what had happened and that I had no idea where I was going. I was told to turn my phone off so I wasn't sure if it had sent. I could hear the police radio and something about mother refusing to speak to them, and the ugly awful realisation that this must be to do with our phone call. I recall saying, 'Oh god, now I know why you are taking me. I was only trying to get my mum to do something to stop her.' To which they told me not to talk as I had been read my rights and for me to just go through this process with them.

Arriving at the police station, I was taken to a small holding cell and I recall tears rolling in disbelief. Fingerprints. Mouth swabbed. All the time muttering over and over, 'When can I go home? I don't understand why I'm here. I was talking to my mum. I was upset over my sister. My son has died.' Churning this over and over during the processing. Then being walked through a cell block and shown to a cell, begging them to please not leave me there on my own. 'I can't be on my own. Please don't leave me on my own.' The police officer sitting in the doorway facing me, my mind questioning why he was doing that? But at least I wasn't alone. I recall he was quite official in his manner but softened as he talked a little to me about his wedding. I was the wedding dress shop lady with the stellar reputation. I laid on the blue plastic cot with no pillow, just laid there asking when could I please go home. He kept saying to let them go through the process. A different police woman arrived for a shift change and I recognised her as one of the community officers from a few years ago, now in a more senior role. She took over from the man sitting in the doorway. She was doing a puzzle book and would ask me questions, I'm guessing to keep me from losing my mind. She knew of Jack and she expressed her condolences and I laid in the little cot telling her about my boy. Reminding her we had met once at my house. She had taken a statement from me as I was a witness in a friend's acrimonious divorce. Jack had come home and she had met him and remembered him. She explained to me that a doctor was coming to visit me and that was why I was having to wait so long and to try to relax and stay as calm as I could and she intimated that all would be OK. I felt so sick inside as she was called away and assured me she would be back. I remember just laying there thinking over and over in my mind that the minute I was out of there I was going straight to the station to die as Jack did. I told myself this over and over silently.

The doctor arrived. She asked me if I ever felt suicidal and I replied that yes, there were many times recently when I'd felt like that but I had been told by my doctor that this was all a normal very early part of the grieving process. I explained that I had returned to my shop and was functioning the best that I could. It seemed she was there to give the OK for me to be interviewed if my mental state was such that I could answer questions. The female police officer returned to ask me if there was someone I would like with me, as I was so fragile, a responsible adult was the term used, so I told them Morgan's number was in my phone. I laid in that cell in a catatonic state. I still didn't really know why I was there. I had heard the charge threat to kill but they hadn't said from who. It seemed it must be about my mum as I'd heard the police on the radio saying something about mother not cooperating but honestly, all that ran through my mind was to get out of there and die the same way as Jack. It's something I've come to understand is some bizarre form of control. The only thing I truly had control over in my life was my life. I had no control over anything at all but that.

I was told that Morgan had arrived and she held me. I was pathetic, pathetically grateful for her to be by my side. I wasn't alone. She told me that Gemma's father had been calling all the police stations trying to find where they had taken me and she had been worried sick and was so thankful to be with me. We were ushered into a small room with the same female police officer, who explained that she had a statement that I was entitled to read and after doing so she would ask me questions and my statement would be recorded and to just get through this. She couldn't say I would be able to go home, but I could tell that was their hope in this.

With Morgan by my side, we learned from the officer that it was Jane who had made the complaint against me. We glanced together at the statement and these sentences leapt off the paper, *"Always been difficult"*, *"doesn't know how to manage money"*, *"was on medication when she was 10"*. This was a full blown attack on me. Why was this written? Why was this even allowed to be part of a statement? My mind reeling back to the police officer who had visited me, asking me to try my very best to leave emotion out and just to stick to the facts of the evening Jack left. Morgan was in tears as I read Jane's scathing assessment of me. Why did she hate me so much? The only reason I could think was that I had stood up to her, I told her off once in my entire life, during the most unbearably painful circumstances, and my goodness the Pandora's box I opened was now shooting out poison darts, in a cruel display of the worst kind of sisterhood.

Jane wrote about how uncomfortable things were in her home after Brad arrived, saying it was me who created the atmosphere. She wrote about her visit to my home with Brad, describing me as immediately being out of control and telling her to fuck off out of my house. There was no mention of why she was there. No mention of the hateful words from Brad. No mention of the bottle of wine and initial thank you I had given her. My god, I knew we were very different people, but being different doesn't give carte blanche to tear me to shreds and attack me. Why, why, why punish me? Again, black comedy is the only way I can place this utter insanity on every imaginable level. To dishonour my son's memory in such a disgusting way, to go to these lengths. I can't to this day imagine picking up the telephone and calling the police on any mother whose child was gone. Morgan strong beside me, the policewoman visibly rattled by these written words. I answered her questions to me with complete truth – the answers you already know. I think I commented, if not then, then certainly since as to her accusations of me being "difficult" "unstable" and "on medication", wait a minute, when she couldn't handle her 15 year old daughter, who did she send her to in America? Me. I had no clue about ever being medicated as a child so Mum thankfully settled my mind by assuring me that at 10 I had tummy aches before school and the doctor had suggested giving me something, which she told me she did for one day, then decided that no, if I was a sensitive girl then that's who I was and never gave me anything again.

Oh boy, was she stonkingly furious with Jane on that. Can't manage money? Wait another fricking minute, when Lisa decided to marry in Thailand, who saved every penny I should have used in my shop to fund that trip? No one else contributed. Who hosted a party for all the wedding guests? Me. In fact, in our early marriage, who hosted a Christmas Eve dinner for her entire family and mine? Me and Brad, we did. Why go to such lengths if worry for my well-being was the reason? Why not call Morgan, call my Doctor? Hell, how about call me? I read that she was afraid for her life, afraid I was going to kill myself and take her down with me. She wanted to go to the inquest because she wanted to hear for herself what had happened and not to hear it from anyone else. This from the same pen who had described our relationship as "never close". Keeping these thoughts to myself out of pure fear and a desire to get out of there, I wondered what kind of police officer thought this type of statement was OK. Did the police officer not advise her, as my parents had done, that she could have a transcript of the inquest, that she wouldn't miss anything? How macabre is it that she could not respect me, this child's mother? Why was she obsessed with being there? There was no relationship between her and Jack ever.

Led to the Sergeant's desk, I shuffled forward with Morgan holding me up and waited to hear my fate. With the police woman standing beside him, tears rolling down her cheeks, the Sergeant announced there would be no further action and I could go home. 'Thank you, thank you,' I repeated, my mind drained of any other response. It was explained to me that sadly in our current climate, if they received a call from anyone saying someone had threatened to kill them, they had to pick up that person, even though firstly I never said I wanted to kill anyone, and secondly it was pure hearsay and my mother had refused to speak with police or give any statement. Mum knew that the chop her head off comment, was the ravings of a bereft mother. It was explained that I could have been running around the village stark naked, screaming and crying, and the reaction of those who care would have been the realisation that I was the mother who had lost her son in an unexpected tragic way, but it was ok, and to just let me be. They advised that Jane wanted police present at my boy's inquest to protect her from me. I was assured that a police presence would be there, as that was the norm at any inquest, and not to feel alarmed and no extra police presence would be dispatched.

My mother took my call as Morgan drove me home. So kind, so gentle to me, furious at Jane, and my Dad in the background then taking the phone telling me, 'Daughter, it will be a cold day in hell before she will ever be welcome in our home.' I knew the reality of that comment but it was something, somebody was acknowledging the wrong that had been done. I did receive advice that I could in fact have reported the false accusations in the statement, and she indeed would have been picked up and questioned, and while those close to me, who were beyond sickened, thought it not such a bad idea, considering, I had no interest in being dragged through the mire again. I could barely manage a few hours a day at my shop, let alone reduce myself any lower than I already felt.

A few days later, I made the trip to my beautiful son's inquest. The clerk greeted me and let me know that Jane and three others he understood to be her husband and children had been placed at the very back of the room and I wouldn't have to see them. I recall being ushered into the courtroom and the coroner asking me to read my statement, the same statement I had given the policeman who had visited me. Morgan was there and she gently took me back out away from the clinical part of the proceedings, although she did share with me later that she noticed all five heads bowed in the back of the room, but Lisa's had risen up to look toward me. I wondered if she still cared for me. Mum had said she wanted to speak out for me, for all the protection and love and devotion I showered on Jack, she wanted the world to know what a lovely mummy I was and those words he had written in text were just not true. However, when asked by the Coroner she relayed to me that she retreated and mumbled something about not understanding why Jack wrote what he did, as I was a lovely mum. It hurt so much that she didn't step forth and follow through. There was this uneasy pattern forming. Mum saying one thing that I would hold onto with every fibre of my being, trusting her but for whatever reason she didn't honour her words to me. This was Mum, always segmenting so as to not have to deal with any situation that might cause a scene or be thought badly about. Her chronic worrying, inherited partly by me. Dad thought of me as much like his departed sister, the risk taker, the free spirit, the one who left Liverpool and worked in London, and 'had a real go at life.'

Within 30 minutes of us leaving such a difficult day my phone rang to request payment for my child's death certificate. Kick me, wind me, what else did I have to endure? It was incredibly insensitive to contact me requesting phone payment within minutes of the verdict. I recall fumbling about in my handbag for my bank card and having to read the numbers over the phone to the bank clerk. Feeling my chest tighten and the push of my back into the seat at having to undergo this surreal experience pure minutes after learning the official outcome, suicide. Mum told me that as she got up to leave, she heard Lisa's brother Curt calling out to her but she chose not to acknowledge him. They were wrong to have attended without asking me, she knew that, she stood strong by me that day. She reminded me of a time that Curt had a court case to attend and the requests that she and Dad not attend and to everyone to respect this request. Dad apparently showed up and was shooed away, we oddly giggled as I drove my darling mumma slowly back to her home, to the comfort of her husband, my Dad, we three again in a painful clinch of love and compassion toward each other. Within minutes of arriving home my phone buzzed with Matt's name. He said how brave I had been and how proud of me he was and that he was anxious to see me. He said that Jane approached him and his parents after the inquest and he had felt so uncomfortable. There she was again. Desperation it surely must be. Not welcome at my son's inquest but determined to feel so by approaching others there.

Sitting with my parents, we three agreed it would be best if they did not talk about me at all with other family. Protect me, keep their desolate daughter safe. I wanted to know nothing of anyone, it was best for me. Keep my circle small and safe was my doctor and therapist's protective advice. This would be easy for my parents. If anyone asked about me they were to reply that they would not talk about Tracy or Jack and to not ask again. This would eliminate the possibility of Mum misquoting or misconstruing me and placing me in a vulnerable position. If Mum didn't acknowledge me then they couldn't twist her words and bring more damage to me. It was the only way we could think of to allow Mum and Dad the freedom to see who they wanted or needed, as the case may be. Those few days I stayed with them were warm and safe. Mum had put the word out that no visitors were allowed without calling first, so I could feel free to visit whenever I needed and a phone call ahead would ensure my emotional safety.

I stayed still and safe in my home and, with the distinct possibility that the local papers may have reported the inquest, I stilled my mind with the mantra 'today's news, tomorrow's fish paper', which Mum had shared with me. Then I received a call from one of Jack's friends. 'Tracy have you seen the paper?' I cried out for him to please not tell me. 'But Tracy you need to know, we are all so upset.' Again I cried, 'No!' and I disconnected the phone. I called Mum, so frightened of what was being said. Later, she told me she had spoken with an editor of AOL in disgust at the inaccurate reporting. She read me a headline: KITCHEN PORTER THREW HIMSELF IN FRONT OF TRAIN. I made calls to the coroner to try and stop this. How could they talk about my beautiful, intelligent, gorgeous son like this? Why not Alton college student, why kitchen porter? We knew how Jack had passed, we had the driver testimony, the only eye witness. But in their desire to sell newspapers it was so much better to print THREW rather than LEANED. I called Joe and instantly he was at my side. He grabbed the laptop and wrote a message to one of the blogs online in complete support and protection of me, of Jack, validating our love as mother and son. Once again Jack's closest held me up, represented their best mate, and stood strong for me.

Mum did share with me that she reached out to her son, my brother, to please look after me, even if just an occasional phone call, but was met with a firm no, and that I was too emotional. This rejection I coped with as I only saw him two or three times in the years Jack was with me in England and my 20 years spent in the USA would naturally have affected any relationship we did have. However, it was devastating to my parents, who lived out the rest of their lives 'faking' their true thoughts for pure survival depending on whoever was with them at the time. Mum so scared all the time it seemed and really sadly, in recent years was removed from England to live out her life in the back bedroom of her son's home in Scotland. She succumbed in less than two months to that climate and passed away, and I felt so relieved for her to now be reunited with her husband and grandson, their three heart beats pressing against mine.

XVI

SOOTHE ME SLAP ME

February came and Mum and Dad went to their familiar hotel in Spain for some warm sun to soothe them. I'd returned to work after Christmas. Erin handled the Saturdays for me and yet another of Jack's pals, who had decided that college wasn't for her, had offered to come with me each weekday. A lovely soft spoken girl, Nicole, girlfriend of Henry who had gifted me an image of myself and Jack, now stretched onto canvas and proudly displayed in my living room. Jack had apparently been instrumental in their meeting, and to this day they remain a happy chilled couple.

In the confines of my shop my mind partially escaped my grief. It resurfaced when a woman came shopping for an evening dress, with her precocious eight-year-old daughter in tow, bouncing around the changing room chanting a memorable line from Psy's Gangnam Style, her voice pounding in my head as I sold her mother a gown. Erin took over the paperwork as I retreated to the changing room and dropped to the floor. Sitting on the changing room floor and leaning against the mirror became my go to place at the end of each appointment. A place where I could remove my mask and release my truth.

My parents rang me from Spain, pleading for me to join them, saying they would arrange a room next to theirs for me. I didn't want to go, I didn't want to do anything, be anywhere, but their pleading voices did bring comfort, so with Erin and Nicole manning the shop, I took quite a giant leap. I don't recall too much about the flight apart from sadly one jarring remark from a departing passenger as we walked through the concourse. She muttered how long her travel day had been and it had all started with, as she put it, 'Some selfish loser jumping in front of a train, delaying my trip.' What the heck were the chances of someone saying that to me on what was quite frankly an extremely brave move on my part – going into an airport, being around people, facing a hectic world I had previously shut out? My response was something along the lines of, 'I don't think they were selfish, spare a thought for that person's family members, receiving this terrible news, as I did less than three months ago.' She hurrumphed but no apology. Maybe she was embarrassed and self-reflected later. It brought into my mind the concept that people will say what they will say and there is nothing I can do to convince others' opinions. All I could do was stay in the moment, get to the hotel and the safety of my parents' loving arms.

I arrived later in the evening, and I recall sitting on my parents' balcony with them both trying to make some kind of small talk. We all three together again, in a four day clinch. We needed each other it seemed. I made a real effort and went down to the beach to lay in the sun. It was so difficult to lay there, feeling the sun on my skin. I didn't care about myself on any level apart from this blinding fear of being left alone. That evening after dinner we said goodnight and I was left to the solitude of my room. Sleeping pills taken, I drifted off but awoke and sat out on my balcony looking at the dark ocean, the moon illuminating, the silence, the stillness. It was too much for me and my deep weeping began. At some point, I don't really know when, my father came into my room. He must have had a spare key or I had forgotten to lock my door, I'm not sure, but there he was, this little man battling his own early dementia. He laid down on my bed and held me in his arms, softly saying over and over that, 'Slowly, slowly, Trace, it will get better, a tiny little bit each day, each month, but it will get better, it will get better.' This became something I relied on from my Daddykins. Right then, right there I needed my parents so desperately.

On my last day we went next door to a very lovely contemporary Italian restaurant and shared a really beautiful meal. It was the first meal that I was able to enjoy – the flavours, the wine, the company of these beautiful parents of mine, who had suffered so at the hands of me and Jack. This is how I thought of it. How else could I? I had brought him into the world, and their world when

I returned home after my marriage ended. This fragile, sensitive little lad with his fragile, sensitive mummy. Spending those days with my parents I became more aware of our similarities. We four were all so sensitive, Mum coping through routine and order, and Dad emoting as I emoted. Jack juggling his acute sensitivity with his Tiggerish nature, aka the dreaded ADHD diagnosis. I felt sure our Jack was with us that evening. My father rose to his feet completely unprompted to sing the Welsh hymn Calon Lan in the restaurant. He sang to me, and to his wife and it was the most intimate, beautiful few minutes I had ever experienced with my parents. Dad took my face in his hands and told me with absolute clarity that there were no two women he would rather have nor ever need in his life than us two. The restaurant bustled back to life as Dad sat down, and from the next table, a group of Germans sang a song in their tongue, then onto another table, Brazilian I think… it was quite an evening. One locked in my heart with the memory of my parents and their love for my Jack and for me.

I learned from my beloved therapist, Jennifer, to think of life as a bus. I was the driver of my bus and the journey I was on was my life. Some people would get on the bus, some would get off, some I would kick off. Some would be on for a good part of the journey and others would hop on and off. I found this a really helpful tool, as those closest to me at times, seemed far away. Dealing with their own lives, their work, their families. It didn't mean they were gone forever, they just had other things to do and I had to try to adjust to that. Always being a sensitive girl, I struggled with hurt feelings and rejection anyway, so the loss of Jack obviously heightened to stratospheric levels every emotion, and oh boy I felt rejection at every turn. But I would focus back on my bus and being the driver of my own life.

I still thought about dying a lot. Searching all over the internet for methods to do it. It was oddly a form of control over something, over my life, or not having my life here any more. Lynn was very supportive during these bouts and it was her efforts that brought Jennifer to me. I was initially so untrusting of this lady arriving at my house every week, who seemed to just sit and nod her head and listen, but didn't seem to be helping me. It's ironic now to think that this same therapist has subsequently opened my mind to the possibility that Jack's incredible sensitivity was probably so painful for him. He probably hated himself inside for just feeling like a teenage lad, a bit ticked off with mum sometimes. The knee jerk reactions of ADHD coupled with incredible sensitivity took him on that walk that night out of this world and into the next. It seemed he had to work himself up to be so cross with me in order to be able to leave, he would never have wanted to have hurt me, just like I would never have sent him out of the house that night if I thought for a second he would leave me permanently. But then the self blame would begin again. The words in his final text to Matt. He blamed me, he blamed me, he blamed me. Of course it was my fault, my best friend, my son, my confidant, my darling beautiful gorgeous son blamed me.

Lynn was such a support to me during this time. I'd first met her shortly before Jack turned eighteen when she popped into my shop with her bouncy little boy Harry, reminding me so much of Jack at that Tiggerish age. I shared as much with her while she tried on gowns. Within thirty minutes I learned of her boy's ADHD diagnosis as well as possible other behaviour related issues as she lamented how exhausting it was for them. Kicked out of the local private school, Lynn had opted for home schooling with several other parents. I shared Jack's ADHD 'status' and I shared tips on how to approach the early teen years and we really connected in a remarkably short space of time. While Lynn decided on her dress, Harry excitedly told me that he was going to be nine in October. October 1st. he exclaimed. Oh really? Well, that is also my son Jack's birthday and he will be eighteen I gleefully exclaimed right back. What a darling coincidence! We all had a little hug and talked of the boys meeting before the holiday season. Then Harry told me that his Mummy's birthday was in October too. Oh wow, so was mine. Looking at Lynn, I asked her what date? 'The 19th,' she replied 'What? Oh my goodness that's my birthday!' I exclaimed. We cupped our hands to our mouths in utter awe. The chances of this was just ridiculous. We chattered on about fate, and no such thing as coincidences, and her complete 'by chance' visit to my shop without an appointment. All the stars were aligned, here I was perched and ready to help this lady with her precious son, wondering if Jack could mentor him possibly. He would understand what Harry was going through. I wanted Lynn to see how Jack had weathered the treacherous waters of senior school and how here he was getting ready to begin his second year of A Levels. All was not lost, I reassured Lynn, we are here to support you both. Unbeknownst at that time how dramatically our roles would reverse.

I recall sitting side by side on the sofa with Jack, recounting my meeting with Lynn and Harry. This young lad weighed on him heavily as he said he didn't want to think about Harry having to go through senior school as it wouldn't be nice for him. I felt a pang of sadness as I saw the angst in his face. Yes, I was on this journey with him, encouraging, supporting, protecting but only as far as the back door. I wasn't able to covet him, to walk next to him at every turn. How many parents haven't felt those feelings at some point raising their younglings?

The few times I was at Lynn's home after Jack passed it seemed that something would happen out of the ordinary. The lights would flicker unexpectedly, and she assured me this had never happened. Lynn believed in life beyond this life. So far, my only experience of this had been Edward who Colin had taken me to, which I now see was far too soon. I was still unsure but wanted guidance from her. On one of the nights I stayed with her Lynn laid three books on my bed. All three introducing spiritualism in some vein. One was about the grief journey, which I felt a bit sick about when I looked at and it didn't sit right with me. Another was a book by a well known medium of sorts from America. Because I had lived there for twenty years I recognised his name but as I flipped through the pages, again I didn't connect. The third book was by someone called Charlie. The image on the cover drew me closer. It was a young man sitting gazing toward the horizon. No shirt on but a tattoo of angel wings upon his back. Low slung jeans, tousled dirty blonde hair. Who was this? Was the book about a young man, I wondered. He looked about Jack's age. I settled into bed among the lovely squishy pillows and began to read. I ended up reading this book every single night. I cherished the two or three pages I could manage before my sleeping pills took over. The book told the true story of this young man Charlie and his realisation of the afterlife. Explaining his thoughts, feelings, emotions, and journey to his place in England as Britain's youngest medium.

This young man told his story so gently. A published author at only nineteen. It wasn't a book filled with aha moments. It was the story of his life so far. Reading, I began to imagine that maybe there was another life after the one here. Maybe, as Charlie talked about in his book, the spirit world or heaven is filled with helping hands. Maybe Lynn was my walking angel.

This young man's book was so important to me. It gave me something to cling onto at night, always sleeping with it under my pillow. All I wanted was to know where Jack was. Mum would say that there must be something else. Look at the beauty of earth, there simply must be. I hoped so much but I questioned in my mind as well. I sat watching endless repeats of Colin Fry's audience show, Theresa Caputo, and recently Tyler Henry. Just watching these people give messages of comfort to grieving loved ones gave me a small amount of hope. I was quick to tear down anything that wasn't a pure validation. Something only those grieving people knew. I wondered if Charlie would see me. I Googled him and emailed. A response came back to message him through Facebook, which I wasn't comfortable doing. All of my information was there plus I didn't want anyone knowing what I was doing and these days with social media nothing seemed sacred. I had explained in my email that I was in desperate grief, and could I speak to him by phone. Charlie supplied his number and we spoke at an agreed time. I was so afraid of tainting the authenticity of a possible meeting by saying too much, so I gave my first name only and booked an appointment for a couple of months' time. Now I had another reason not to go in front of the train, not yet. Always inside of me were the words in the last message Jack sent.

The message had been read out to me in its entirety by the police officer the day he came to take my statement and advise me of the train driver's eye witness account. I was carrying such a heavy, heavy heart, still dragging this weight along with me. Walking through life but not living. I didn't have any success with the larger bereavement organisations, it felt too clinical. I had Jennifer, who came to see me for an hour a week but it wasn't enough for me. I would Google trying to find something, someone to connect to. I wasn't the only mum out there going through this, was I? One day I came across a site dedicated to parents who had lost their children to suicide. No other type of loss, just that one. This little website became my friend. Here I was, part of a group that none of us wanted to be a member of. Reading, posting, sharing, I had such support from parents a little further along the road than me, the newest member. We all understood each other. There was no judgement, just kind, supportive words. Reading posts from other mums describing their children in similar ways to Jack.

The way most of them left was by hanging. I had no idea about this, why would I, why would any of us? Reading the accounts of other wounded mums, and a few dads, I became more aware that I wasn't alone. Often, late into the evening, I would log on and there was usually someone else desperate to push through yet another black night. It was a small group, maybe twenty of us. One awful night I logged on to find a new member who recounted how her teenage daughter had retreated to her bedroom after an argument and tantrum with her siblings. The mother, busy with her other children, then received a visit from the police. They had been called because a neighbour had seen her child hanging from outside her bedroom window. It's so awful to even write let alone begin to process such a scene. A scene played out with more alarming accounts as the site grew. I learned that young lads between the ages of 14 and 25 with ADHD were the highest category. They get mad about something, want it gone from their minds, act impulsively. GONE. Once again, my fault, my fault rained over me. I sent him out the door, It was my fault my fault, my fault.

The online group saved me, we saved each other. Each member spilling forth their grief, whether it be a droplet or a waterfall. All with the same story, different in the telling, but resulting in the same knock at the door, phone call, discovery. I saw images of these youngsters' happy, smiling faces that their parents added. But I couldn't do this. I couldn't bear to look at a recent photo of Jack. The only photos I did look at were ones taken when he was only two or three. These I could just about manage. There was a cute one of the two of us on his second birthday sharing a kiss. It was in Jack's room. I would sit on his bed and talk to this picture. Sit and talk to it every single night. Going to say goodnight to my boy, as I did when he was here. Tears fell, or if they didn't it was only because exhaustion didn't permit. I'd sit there, my heart so heavy, night after night, morning after morning. Imagining my boy maybe there with me. Once again, my fault, my fault rained over me. I sent him out the door. It was my fault my fault, my fault.

The lamp post outside of my house stayed lit 24/7 when the others all timed to turn off as the sun rose. My phone would ring at night, usually after 10pm, always a number unknown and never anyone on the other end. My car dashboard lights would flicker erratically for no reason. These things hadn't happened before Jack left so why now? All could be reasoned away as coincidences of course, but I took comfort in them. Comfort as I awaited for April to arrive and my visit with Charlie.

Jack and I talked about getting a little dog in the weeks leading up to his leaving. He thought a girl would be cute for me. My own little mate. Delilah would be her name. We would know when we found her. With his birthday and trip to Rome I had thought it may be best to get her in the months leading up to Jack leaving college. Of course, it never happened. But now the idea of getting a little dog came back to me.

My nature was and still is very affectionate and loving. Maybe having something to take care of would be healing. The various younglings thought it would be a great idea. As Jack and I had talked so much about getting a dog I felt that by doing so I'd somehow be living our lives. Not my life, not Jack's, but ours. This felt right. I visited a farm who bred all sorts of, shall we say, 'designer dogs'. I entered the farmhouse kitchen to a melee of fluff. I sat on a chair and watched them tearing around the kitchen, jostling for food. I felt a little tug at my leggings and looked down at the dearest little face. Placed in my lap, this little chap sat so still. The connection between us was undeniable. Not a girl, a boy, a sweet, random mix of Yorkshire terrier and Maltese. Coarse and downy, silvery grey with a white face, the profile of a Maltese with his cute little turned up nose, but the gait of a Yorkie. One ear perked up, the other flopped over. A sweet, gorgeous, hot mess of a pup, I belonged to him. He was my charge or was I his. In the next two days I ordered his bed, his little Japanese feeding table and organised the vet visit. A familiar nurturing feeling was reoccurring. I returned to the farm to collect my little boy and on the journey home with this precious face peeking up from the passenger side foot well I drove so carefully, just as I did bringing Jack home from the hospital.

'OK, little one, you must sleep downstairs in your bed,' I told him. I had to ensure he knew his boundaries. That first night he nestled into his bed and never ventured up the stairs to my room. Wow! In the morning there was only one little wee on the wooden floor. We were off to a triumphant start. Vet visit behind us, we settled in for the evening. At only four months old he was really still very much a baby to me. Picking him up he naturally turned onto his back and his little paws flipped forward. I swaddled this little chap in my arms. In that moment I knew his name, it had to be Jackpot. I experienced a swell of love mixed with the most painful guilt as I nestled with Jackpot. To feel an emotion other than the sad emptiness of the past four months was an electric shock of sorts. I thought deeply of Jack. I was doing what we would have done. Sharing Jackpot with Jack was exactly the right thing to do. Jackpot bravely navigated the stairs to my door that second night and, after several attempts to return him to his cosy bed, all good intentions were waived and he nestled up against my neck. This little chap needed me, and oh boy, did I ever need him! This funny, cheeky, random little chap was just adored by all. Jack's mates visited and several commented on how like Jack he was. Not a replacement, but a gift, a treat of a pup. Visiting me now wasn't a completely depressing experience. Jackpot was passed around for cuddles and I think he formed the perfect buffer for these teens. Their mate wasn't here, but this random, quirky little boy was. A source of healing for us all.

I guess the human will to survive works differently for everyone. For me in that first year, in fact still now, in this sixth year, I choose to live my life for Jack, with Jack. It's the only way I know how to cope. During that first year, Jack's friends carried me with their messages and little stories shared about my son. Always a kind word, a hug, an often referred to 'million watt smile'. One boy, Jude, who was going through gender reassignment, told me how the day before Jack left he had stopped him in the hall and asked him what his story was. Jude felt comfortable sharing with Jack, who Jude told me was so kind and supportive to him. Jack told him how proud he was of Jude for being true to who he was, born a female genetically but a boy in every other way. A couple of the college girls, Tia and Ellie, sharing with me how much they loved Jack, one with a secret crush, who was a little put out when Allie stepped into the picture. Tia showed me a photo of her dyed hair with red and purple highlights like Jack. Ellie sharing with me how she had seen Jack on the college bus and been wowed by his personal style, and had told him that very day how cool he was and how she loved his clothing, especially his purple skull belt. It triggered a memory for me as I recounted to her that he had told me about her and the lovely compliment she had given him. She gave me a little treat and she got one back from Jack through a cherished memory. The sweet online messages, their hugs on the street. Words really truly do fail me. I'm in awe and always will be, of these boys and girls who gave their time, their words of comfort to me.

XVII

PURPLE VEIL

The morning of the day I visited Charlie started off like any other, I woke up and walked downstairs in my robe and put the kettle on. Yet today felt different. I felt different. Today was a chance for some of the pain and hurt to go away. Perhaps today the knot that had been embedded in my stomach could be unfastened. Perhaps today would be the day I would be reunited with my son and a day that would again change my life forever. I recall being very distracted on the drive, even though Morgan, George's mum had kindly offered to drive me. My mind felt like it was racing at a hundred miles an hour. I recall feeling so terribly sad and with each passing mile, a little bit more desperate. Up to losing my child, I had never given death much thought. Now death had become all too real and all so morbid. I recall sitting in the car thinking, over and over, that if Jack did not come to me, then I would just go to the train station and die the same way he had. I remember thinking about where Jack was exactly, and worrying so much about him being OK, wondering if I would hear from him or if I was being taken advantage of by some kind of charlatan, who preyed on grief-stricken individuals. These questions would continue spinning round and round in my head until we arrived at the location.

After settling into the room, I was left waiting for what seemed ages, but in truth, was only about fifteen minutes. The woman who had greeted me at the door popped into the room to tell me Charlie would be down soon. He was 'linking in', which having read his book, I sort of understood. I felt myself controlling my breathing as the situation was now feeling utterly surreal. What was I doing there? My child had left me. He had left me, and I was pinning every ounce of hope I had on this young man in the next room.

Just then, Charlie entered looking just as I had imagined. It was a lovely sight. Just like his pictures, he was a handsome young man with tattoos galore, low slung jeans, and tousled hair. I felt instantly more at ease. In some ways, he reminded me of my Jack. Different in ways, but there were undeniable similarities. He began by telling me there were several relatives present, which was nice, but I only wanted to hear from Jack. I told myself sternly not to say anything that might give anything away as I was very, very wary. Charlie had said at the outset he would let me know when I could ask questions, so this worked fine for me. Charlie went on to say there was a younger male there with another older male and a female. He told me that he must have passed very young and he assumed it must be my son. What then followed was a description of Jack's personality and his awareness of Jack's overwhelming remorse and regret over his decision to leave. Charlie explained that this lad was a very emotional boy and highly sensitive, quirky, edgy and different in a good way. When Charlie began to describe these character traits, I knew he had my Jack. As he continued, I tried my hardest to hold back the tears that were ready to burst forth. Not tears of sadness, but tears of relief, tears of a mum hearing from her child, not his voice but his emotion, which felt stronger and more intimate.

There were 101 things that Jack wanted to say to me, and Charlie explained that his mind was all over the place on many things but the strongest emotion and feeling was to let me know that his passing had been very quick, literally he was here one minute, then gone the next, and there was regret with this. The regret stemming from Jack now seeing what he had put me through and that was very much in his mind because he knew how much I needed him to say that today. Charlie then went on to describe the walk Jack took from my home to the station. He took the direct route. This was quite painful to hear with it being me who sent him out of the door, but at least I knew. And I wanted to know. Charlie described Jack's projection to him of his mind being all over the place, all over the place, so many emotions all at once, as Jack took that walk to the station. He sensed that Jack was really, really upset about something and that something had hurt him. It seemed he wasn't connecting with people very well around this time. Then came the acknowledgement that he had seemed to have had a disagreement or a falling out that same evening just prior to his passing, to which I shared that was with me. He immediately asked who Brad or Bradley was, which I disclosed was his father, and Charlie explained there had been a disagreement between the two of them as well. I wasn't aware of that, the last call I had witnessed was the one where he was blanking me while he talked to his Dad which wasn't cross words. However, many cross words had taken place between them and anxiety was in place within their relationship, particularly the last four or five years. Charlie found it interesting that Jack's sensitivity was so heightened and expressed that it was such a shame that he passed over as he was a really good kid and somebody he felt wouldn't have hurt a fly, which he felt was a rare occurrence among their generation, Charlie only being nineteen himself. He sensed Jack to have a selfless quality that would have been ideal in a relationship. He described Jack reflecting on his relationships with his peers, particularly in school and, while he had lots of friends in different groups, he stayed out of the drama and was determined to be who he was and not allow friends to sway him one way or another. Charlie acknowledged with a half laugh that Jack had had his hair cut 'over there', which brought a loving emotion from me. I briefly explained how much that made sense, telling Charlie about Jack's daily morning hair visit with me, along with the hair style changes I had treated him to.

He then went on to tell me that at the very start Jack had mentioned that he visits me at home and he knows that I think of him every day, getting up in the morning, and before bed. Jack wanted to tell me that when I sleep he tries to play with my hair to let me know he's around. Charlie told me to look out for sensations of my hair being played with, as it would be a sure indication of Jack's presence. I felt comforted by that.

Charlie described how the feelings coming through were of the two of us being good mates and even though there was a generation between us, we would both laugh at the same things and we were the very best of friends. He described how we could pretty much say anything to each other and it was just teasing and playful and that we both really enjoyed that part of our relationship.

Charlie referenced the number 17 and Jack being there and seeing me there with someone by the name Jed, a man who I was close to and has remained on the fringe of my life, as close as I can manage these days. Jed had come to my house to see me after learning of the news and the number 17 was our house number and also the date Jack left. Charlie said Jack was bringing this up because I had been asking him in my thoughts to tell me when he had been around me, to give me a validation, and that was what he was now trying to do. He talked of a shirt of Jack's, black with bright colours on the front, that had a significance. Jack had bought that shirt on his eighteenth birthday trip to Camden Market. He said he could see brown to black hairs on the t-shirt and suggested this would have been Jack's hair colour, which is exactly correct. Then he switched back to Brad, saying that Jack was acknowledging further conflict between his father and me and that he was not happy about this because he was very protective of me. He said he saw what was going on, and made references to legal symbols and how unhappy he was about family members not handling things well. He referred to his father trying to point fingers and playing blame games, saying people should have done things differently, and he mentioned that some people had been saying Jack had been made to do what he did but Jack was expressing that no, it was him and nobody made him do anything. For me this was so revealing and important in my healing. To know that my boy who had left such a message behind, was here saying how protective he was of me, which he always had been in his life with me, and to have it acknowledged that he was aware of what I'd had to endure on top of the loss, and that he'd been there with me. I just lost it and tears streamed down my face. My boy was still here, albeit in an altered state, and he was defending and protecting me in the best way that he could by telling me he knew.

Charlie again reinforced the amount of time Jack was around me and said that I'd have trouble getting rid of him as he's with me much, more than most people who cross over as a result of taking their own life. He said that Jack described the intensity of his feelings and that if he was hurt, or felt wronged, or angry he felt it so strongly the people in his life would certainly know how he was feeling. Gently, Charlie said that he couldn't lie and had to say what Jack was expressing. I interjected that I had to know what it was. Charlie relayed to me that Jack had changed his mind but it had been too late, so that would suggest that however he passed, it was too late to react to whatever was going on and he didn't mean to do it in the end. In a split second he changed his mind but it was too late. Jack was aware of my questioning – the 'why, why, why?' over and over and that how he was found and where he was discovered didn't make sense. He was there to let me know that he changed his mind and he was terribly regretful, as he now realised what a life he could have had. With his deep sensitivity he would have had successful relationships, but at the time he felt he tried to let a friend know how he was feeling but his friend, through no fault of his own, didn't realise how serious Jack was and kind of brushed it off, so to speak. Again Charlie came back to Brad and a lack of trust in that area, but the lack of relationship with his dad made him appreciate me more and brought forth an incredible sensitivity uncommon in boys of his age group.

Did he communicate with his friend just before it happened? Charlie asked me, to which I acknowledged that yes, he had. Charlie indicated that the part of that communication that referred to me wasn't meant by Jack, he didn't mean it. While it was incredibly important to me that he acknowledged that he hadn't meant those words, at the time I was in such a state of guilt that while I heard the words, I didn't entirely process it. Others were pleased for me, but I couldn't accept his not meaning it as a means to remove myself from any culpability. There were many references to Jack's friend who had received the message not realising what Jack was saying to him, and while there was no blame being laid for this, it had to be brought forth. I asked for the name of the boy although of course I knew who he was referring to. Charlie mentioned someone called Chris, which threw me. He then brought up a dog and a girl called Christine, and revealed the name Matt. This was astounding to me and I queried how he arrived at Matt's name. Charlie described Jack searching his mind and that in order to get to the name Matt, Jack had to find a memory of Charlie's. He picked a memory of a very close friend of Charlie's called Christine, who had a little dog and was engaged to someone called Matt. It was truly astounding. While my heart was heavy, and my mind in this god awful altered state, I did understand the process when explained to me by this young medium.

Charlie went on to mention someone called Ben, who was in fact a good friend of Jack's, and said that Ben had something that I had given him that had belonged to Jack which he kept on his window ledge. This sounded odd to me as I had given Ben a funky tie of Jack's and felt certain that it would be in a wardrobe or a drawer, but no, Charlie insisted the item was on a window sill. There was a cat that had recently passed over apparently. Somewhere near water, which threw me as I only knew of Joe as having any cats, and I felt sure he would have told me if one of them had recently passed away. Jack was also expressing concerns over a Kyle. This Kyle I could only assume was one of the lads who had visited on Christmas Day. Now Jack was super worried about him. I'd have to find out from them both, I had a little work to do. Checking the validity of this information was just as important to me as hearing it.

Charlie said that one of the females who had been present with Jack at the beginning of the reading was the mother of one of his very good friends, which was a truly beautiful moment. Joe's mum had passed over and to know that she was there with my son, while I was here with hers was so moving. I often make a point of visiting her as she is located a few steps away from Jack, and thank her for looking after my son, promising her that I will do the same for her. A silent agreement between two mothers who had never met, but now through the loss of my son, were forever connected and beholden to each other.

I wanted to hear Jack's Mumsie nickname for me so badly. As far as I was concerned if I heard my nickname that would be absolute validation of his continuing presence around me. Charlie brought up many references that he said were taking him to his own childhood, but sadly not the name. He told me to please just keep asking Jack and over time it would reveal itself. While disappointing, I felt that this first reading had offered so much, truly bringing forth Jack's personality, his sensitive, emotional self.

We talked for a few minutes more and Charlie told me clearly that in his years of doing many, many readings of people who had harmed children, of divorced parents, of very sad, awful things, he had never ever experienced the level of regret and remorse he had felt from Jack. This I found oddly comforting. Not of course Jack having to feel so regretful but more for myself that I wasn't going mad, that I did know my son, that he wouldn't have taken his own life in a planned, thought out way.

Confirmations came the very next day from Ben that yes, the tie I gave him was in fact on his window sill as he had moved recently. The cat death reference was also validated by Ben. At the college both he and Jack attended there had been a sign posted about a cat that had sadly been found dead right next to the pond. I also found out that Kyle had gone through a difficult few weeks and had spent many an evening stretched out on Jack's memorial bench, trying to process his thoughts and feelings. It was quite astonishing to me that my son, from the other side of life, was still worrying and sensitive to his friends. And it made the message I'd had inscribed on the bench all the more poignant: *Hello stranger, come and sit beside me, you're not alone, Jack.*

Obviously Charlie getting Matt's name was a revealing moment, however along with that came nagging thoughts about what else they might possibly have said to each other that night. I wondered if Matt was holding back for fear of hurting me, or maybe hurting himself. Maybe he did have back and forth messages with Jack and as Charlie said, had not taken them seriously and now he was afraid to tell me for fear of the burden of Jack taking his life being his fault, which of course, it certainly is not. I realise now that Jack's leaving wasn't down to one thing, it was several, and as Charlie explained to me, people do not take their own lives over one thing, they just don't, and I do believe him. Of course, I still regularly doubt this, that stick of self blame still slaps me.

XVIII

FOOTSTEPS IN THE SAND?
CONVERSE, SLIPPERS, SANDALS

Jack's nineteenth birthday was approaching, which gave me something else to focus on. Friends gathered at 'Jack's Place' and we sent nineteen purple lanterns skyward. Drinks and cupcakes and dance music blaring. Candles trailing around his little piece of England. This has since become an annual event, and has allowed me the opportunity to celebrate Jack's birthday, letting go as many purple lanterns as his age would dictate.

With early November upon me Jack's stone would soon be in place and Christian suggested I plan a memorial. We chose the sweetest little chapel, with just room enough for sixteen, where I'd spent many an afternoon in silent reflection and prayer with Christian. I was still confused about God but becoming aware that God, at least to me, was a word encompassing heaven, the other side of life. While one of God's disciples, Christian understood my predicament and when questioned by me as to where Jack was, would refer to him being with God and God was always with me, protecting me, to which I blurted back on one occasion 'Where was God when Jack was walking to the station?' The very next day he posted a copy of the book The Shack through my letterbox. It took me until the next year before I could bring myself to read it, but when I did it helped me so, so much. Christian was just about the most beautiful man inside and out that I had ever met. Finding a way to blend the teachings of the church with today's questioning and varied points of view, he was and in fact still is, a true disciple.

I continued with the planning of the memorial event marking the date Jack left. If a task involved Jack I felt like my waking up had some sense of purpose. With little Jackpot providing so much physical comfort, I could do this. With my lovely Nicole's help, we invited those younglings who meant the most to Jack before he left to his memorial, and those who continued to stay close to me, his Mumsie.

When I was told that Jack's stone was in place I visited ahead of time to face whatever emotion may come at seeing his name, at seeing the reality. I left my beloved pup at home as I had to do this alone. I had to give Jack my full and complete attention. I approached the bench, diverting my eyes from the marked place. Sitting on Jack's bench clutching my rosary to my chest I bravely faced this permanent marker, this epitaph of a life, that will one day be two lives, and eventually three, when Mum completes our reunion of souls. As I took in this permanent marker, a myriad of thoughts swirled through my head. Beautiful, ugly, stunning, tragic, what to think, what not to think, feel, don't feel, wonderment, deep, deep sadness. When going through the application process for the stone, I simply could not imagine Jack being represented by the required 6" by 6" image and a couple of basic lines with dates etc as the rules stated. Christian kindly offered to request permission for something different and said that the church would cover the application costs involved. He understood how I felt. I was asked why I had chosen what I did so, putting pen to paper, I poured out my feelings about Jack. This village was his home, he was his happiest here. I spoke of his friends, the teenagers of the village, of the legacy of my son and how many young peoples' lives he'd had a positive lasting effect on. How, as years would pass, these teens would become parents themselves and maybe need to call on Jack to guide them as they faced challenges raising their own families. Of me wanting us both represented on this piece of ceremonial art as it too would be my resting place. Thankfully, after some months, permission was granted.

And now here I was, in sight of where I too would lie. I always thought I'd be with Jack long before my mother. Grieving, wanting to get in the dirt, to comfort him, but now unsure and fighting thoughts of what seemed to be the reality of the other side of life. Confusion washed over me. The words

Jack Wall, McGrath for my Nana and Papa, (Jack had told his Papa that when he joined the navy he wanted to change his name to theirs, to my given one), *18 years. To be joined here by my Mumsie when God calls her home* (a space left to add my name and age). The plinth with '*Two hearts beating as one*', reverse plinth, '*Jammie Dodger and Mumsie*', and lastly, centred on the back, '*Let me lay down beside you, let me always be with you*' (lines from my baby boy's lullaby *Annie's Song*).

The image was so representative of us, a mother's face gazing downward with long sweeping hair like mine, and a boy's face gazing up to her. His Mumsie, her Jammie. It represented us both so reverently. I sat on Jack's bench as the tears began to flood my face. Time passed and Christian was at my side. We had agreed to meet at this spot to firm up the plans for the memorial. Prayerful words were shared in the stillness of the early evening.

The anniversary of my son's passing dawned and knowing friends were gathering helped so very much. For those closest I had commissioned necklaces of gold with a dove and two sweet hearts, each heart containing a J and the first initial of the recipient's name. All received with respectful warmth. Purple crocuses and ivory roses tied in ribbon laid upon each chair and a cherished image of my boy during his time in Rome, with little birds perched upon his shoulder and a winning smile across his face, stood upon an easel. It was small, intimate, peaceful. Contemporary etchings adorned the glass walls, the Dove of Peace centre stage. It was all so right for this day of remembrance.

Jamie sang with guitar in hand, a beautiful song composed for his friend, I recall the refrain:

And the world is black without our friend Jack
A hundred candles light up the sky
Just like he did in life
A hundred memories burn bright
He holds our hand tonight

Kyle read a poem, again written himself. I had asked this of him as Jack had expressed concern for him.

My lovely Erin, grasping my hand, sat with me alongside Mum and Dad. Then I released her comforting hand and she stood to sing, an emotion filled rendition of 'See You Again' by Carrie Underwood. Everyone sat in such wonderment, the words reaching all of them.

I spoke of a quilt of love I had made in memory of Jack in a piece I titled, MY CHILD'S CLOTHES. Here is the transcript…

We are now here at the one year anniversary since losing my beautiful son Jack. I simply cannot believe a year has come and gone, and quite frankly that I am still here. Those gathered here you know my life has been all about my Jack. Just the two of us, always and forever. The empty void is incredibly painful, however as the weeks and months have passed, I have gained acceptance now of what took place on November 17th 2012. I sit in Jack's room a little less often now, and have been able to gift to you, his closest friends, a few items that belonged to Jack. However, I have sat bewildered about his clothing, his shoes, what am I to do with these items? Everyone has their own timeline to make these kinds of decisions. I remember speaking to a bereaved mother who said ten years had passed before she did anything to her son's bedroom, and other parents who immediately removed all memories. It is different for all of us and it seems that the natural course of time works wonders.

A few days ago I entered my Jack's room and carefully and lovingly folded his skinny jeans, his Criminal Damage Jacket, his bountiful designer t shirt collection, his funky boxers, his school blazer, his PE shorts, his prized Vivienne Westwood tie. My son's clothing packed into two medium sized suitcases, his life, the closest things to his body, his clothing. What to do with these wonderful memories? Jack was such a fashionisto, he loved being edgy and different. I remember him clipping a red paisley bow tie onto his green t shirt in nursery school. His boxers, the funkier the better, were always showing, the funniest being his Sponge Bob eyes and nose peeking out behind his low slung red and black pinstriped skinny jeans.

The memories, the chilly evenings rolling in, the reminder of the knock on the door at gone midnight by two police officers telling me my son was found on the platform at the local train station, where he was pronounced deceased. The shock, the chill that came over me, how do I comfort myself these days? How do I bathe myself in warmth and security? Decision made. My beloved son's amazing wardrobe of clothes are being taken tomorrow to a seamstress friend, who will lovingly cut and sew Jack's belongings into a warm quilt. A quilt of love. A quilt of memories. A quilt to keep him close to me. He protected and defended me, he was and still is and will remain always a warm blanket of love around me. I can think of no greater fitting tribute to my edgy, amazing, loving, sweet, sensitive, beautiful son.

Then Christian spoke on a level that reached each of us. No clichéd preaching, just warm words of comfort and remembrance of my son. Lastly, Dad was ushered forward by Mum, so smart in his hounds' tooth blazer, every inch the country gentleman, wearing his dolphin pin from his Royal Navy days, and carrying in his pocket the miniature replica that Jack had given him for Father's Day, of the Tally Ho submarine that his beloved Papa would recount stories of, his happiest days below the seas. 'Eileen,' he whispered to Mum, 'what should I say?' His mind was stalling, as was becoming more frequent. Mum stepping forward with a cupped whisper. The room stilled as Jack's beloved Papa, standing shoulder to shoulder with his Grandson's image sang to utter perfection in Welsh, the hymn Calon Lân, the same hymn he had sung during my visit to Spain that bonded the four of us in a way only we could possibly truly understand.

Calon Lân

I'd not ask a life that's easy
Gold and pearls so little mean
Rather seek a heart that's joyful

Heart that's honest, heart that's clean
Heart that's clean and filled with virtue
Fairer far than lilies white
Only pure hearts praise God truly
Praise him all the day and night.
Why should I seek earthly treasures
On swift wings they fly away
Pure clean hearts bring greater riches
That for life eternal stay
Heart that's clean and filled with virtue
Fairer far than lilies white
Only pure hearts praise God truly
Praise him all the day and night.
Dawn and sunset still I'm searching
Reaching on a wing of song
Give me Lord, through Christ my Saviour
That clean heart for which I long.
Heart that's clean and filled with virtue
Fairer far than lilies white
Only pure hearts praise God truly
Praise him all the day and night

Gentle, beautiful, touching every one of us, I turned to see the wash of tears across the faces of Jack's loyal band of brothers. United right there on this most spiritual of days.

Delivered to Jack's Place, we gathered as the light dimmed and Nicole stepped forward to read Sonnet 73 from my beloved Sonnets, that she had selected. Her emotions overtaking her, she bravely spoke up and out for her dear friend. There were prayers from Christian, then Erin stepped forward, this time to sing my lullaby, Annie's Song, as we each placed our flowers from our seat upon the earth that blanketed our boy.

It's actually so comforting for me to recount this day. Mum and Dad were speechless upon viewing the stone and the rightful acknowledgement of their name. Those sixteen of us gathered, drinking in the beauty and the solemnity. The intimacy of this time captured my heart truly.

The conversations shared with many of Jack's friends later that evening and the following day began to make me realise that the stick I was slapping myself with so very much I really had to work toward lessening. They shared with me times when they had been difficult with their parents and several had spent more than one night out of the house, crashing at the skate park or a local bench. They recounted how hurtful words had been said, one lad showing me on his mobile phone a rant he had spat out to his mother. Jamie in particular stands out, as we both sat at Jack's Place the day after the one year anniversary. Jamie and Jack became close during college, they both had this beautiful exterior with an inner sensitivity that Jamie expressed through music as Jack did through his dance and edgy style. Jamie shared with me the many times his father had referred to him with the dreaded 'loser, you won't amount to anything' rants, and he had felt this anger and disconnect. Knowing how sensitive Jamie was and that he was still here, and hadn't chosen Jack's path, I did begin to think more of why someone chooses to end their life, there always seems to be several reasons why. I'm so happy to report that the sensitive Jamie is now preparing for life in the Royal Marines, after 5 years in the Infantry, is a husband and father and so happy, and of course he and his father are way beyond those difficult teen years. Such is the course for most parents and their children as they navigate the treacherous waters of teen to young adult.

XIX

IT'S A PURPLE LIFE

I journeyed with less trepidation to my second reading with Charlie. Meeting in the same, now familiar room and Charlie stepping in, glass of water to hand, as he began relating again the layers of sensitivity and emotion that were emanating from Jack. He explained that there was a marked difference between the first reading and now, as Jack's natural progression over there was strengthening. Charlie told me that Jack continued to visit me daily and acknowledged the interactions between the two of us as I spoke to Jack out loud, and within myself every day. Charlie reflected on the months of October and November as being particularly difficult for me, these months having included both our birthdays and Jack's leaving date. He said Jack was describing me as spiralling downward and how he was using what energy he could to reverse the spiral back upward. He was still very much aware of how my feelings and emotions were, which he described as very different to others in the grieving process. I can only really take from that the intense grief I was still in. Jack was my entire world and I only knew how to cope by staying close to him in my thoughts and by talking to him. I spent so much of my time without any human contact so I guess I could see why my mind, apart from being his mother and confidant, would be more focused on my son.

Charlie mentioned Wiltshire, specifically Salisbury, and Jack indicating that he had been visiting a couple of people there. Wow, I thought excitedly, this had to be my parents. Charlie referred to a picture that the lady would talk to often, while the male was less present. This I understood as my father's early dementia, which meant that he spent a lot of time lost in his own thoughts.

Mum had told me many times that she would talk to Jack's picture every night before she went to bed, so to hear that my son was aware of this was a lovely validation that I could share with my parents. Charlie brought up both their names, which was astounding. He talked of Jack communicating with his papa, my father, while in a REM state of sleep and that my father was probably talking in his sleep a lot. Mum had recently told me exactly that, telling me that Dad had been chattering away at night for a few weeks, keeping her awake. It was so lovely to think that my boy was concerned for his nana and papa.

Charlie told me that Jack had skipped on to Matt and he said that Matt would be making a move soon and that Jack was happy for him to be doing this. He stressed that Jack wished that Matt would get out of his own way. Jack was often around him but while Matt sensed something he would push it away with his logic and not develop the notion that his friend was there. Jack felt that if only Matt could relax his mind and try to have more of an open point of view it would afford more opportunity for Jack to get a closer connection. I offered that I knew Matt wished that he received some kind of validation from Jack. Sunglasses were brought up to do with Matt. I had bought Matt Armani sunglasses on his eighteenth birthday. Charlie giggled slightly at a reference to Gangnam. Of course this dance and song had featured at Jack's services, maybe Matt had been out clubbing and danced to it. This was something I would ask him when I next saw him. There was another validation through the mention of 'Manor hotel', as Charlie put it. This was where Jack and Matt had worked.

Then he went on to a phone ringing and stopping, which was what had been happening to my phone at home. It still rang in the evenings, usually around 10:30, past the normal sales call time, and the display would read UNKNOWN. I would answer the phone and it would disconnect.

'OK, we are skipping along here at a rapid pace,' Charlie said with a grin. Then there was an awkward, 'Um, Jack seems to visit you when you are in the bath.' I understood this completely. I bathed pretty much every day and laid in the warm soothing water thinking so very much of my boy, recounting the countless times he sat atop the toilet seat with his snack, chatting to me about his day at school, and now thinking of him and sending him as much love as I could muster as I tried my best to soothe him, to still parent him. To know that Jack visited me there in the bathroom of all places, was so very special as we had some of our best talks there. One of us in the bath and the other atop the seat. This warmed my heart and truly did soothe my broken spirit, as I was sure now that my love for Jack was reaching his soul also.

Then Jack apparently revealed himself surrounded by masses of species of birds. Of course, Jack loved birds so very much so it was brilliant to hear that he was able to surround himself with these sweet little creatures. A loving acknowledgement that he still had Teddy and always would comforted me, Teddy and Jack were together in their new normal. Again October and November time was mentioned but this time in relation to birds and my use of birds. Had I had a tattoo, he asked. Coyly, I asked that he tell me more. I was still sceptical, and it was fairly good odds that these days someone would have had a tattoo in remembrance of a loved one. Charlie described my tattoo including a word and a bird in flight. I have the word LOVE and flying from the E is a bird, the Dove of Peace. It was so amazing that he knew. I'd never had a tattoo before but was determined to do this for Jack and for me. Matt had taken me and kept a protective eye on me as I had the tattoo done, on Jack's birthday October 1st, a pinchy ouchy way to spend my boy's birthday. Charlie interjected that Jack also had a tattoo, on his lower arm, inner wrist area, which is precisely where mine is. He described it as also a bird but his was in flight leaving the feathers trailing behind. Charlie explained to me that if I buy Jack something over here he can have that item made over there. I really love that idea. I buy him a birthday and Christmas gift and I give myself something from him for Mother's Day. Knowing he is with me helping me choose gives me a lovely warm feeling.

At home I have this little white painter's style step stool where I keep items that remind me of Jack. A beautiful purple flower made of hand blown glass. A baseball cap with the purple words 'Purple Haze' across the front. An Egyptian glass bottle in purple that Jack and I had selected as a keepsake on our visit there. A sweet purple glass candle holder that lives sometimes at his resting place and sometimes on the step stool. Most recently our rosaries, mine and my boy's. They will be gifted to him and to me when I visit this Christmas and sit with him. Last year it was my beloved Mumsie necklace that I never take off. Always something fitting seems to come to mind. We struggled again at this reading to bring my nickname forward. Once again there were references to Charlie's childhood but no revelation of Mumsie. But I couldn't be disappointed. The plethora of lovely reminders of my son's continual presence in my life was so incredibly warming and Charlie again reminded me that somehow they would figure out over there how to get the reference I wanted.

The next time I saw Matt I played him the recording of the reading and he confirmed that literally a week or two earlier he had been in a club and Gangnam had come on and he had danced and thought so much about Jack. He was so happy and relieved to know that his mate was with him and hadn't really left him at all.

I began to find living in the village more and more difficult, seeing the students passing the house and life moving forward for Jack's friends, as it should. But my life was only about Jack and living my life with him. I was fully aware of the reality, my son had left, but in order for me to try my best to stay here I had to live with the thought that my son was near me, looking after me. I continued to talk to him out loud in his room, letting him know that I was here for him also. Telling him I could try to keep going in this altered state if I knew he was helping guide me.

On Sundays when I wasn't working I'd load Jackpot up and we would go out driving, looking for somewhere else to live. It was pure survival. We visited many surrounding communities but nothing grabbed me. On one overnight stay with 'fringe man' Jed, which was a welcome distraction, we were in Warwickshire as his work had brought him there. We were looking at the map in the morning for a spot to visit when I spied Bourton on the Water. This was such a lovely place filled with such happy memories of a long weekend I'd taken with Jack there. I felt strong enough to go. Parking and wandering towards the hotel I had stayed at with my boy, Jed and I settled on the deck area. Sitting enjoying an unusually bright and warm September day I felt a calmness, an inner peace that was so unfamiliar to me but so, so lovely. And I knew right then that this was where I would be moving to. I would make the commute to my shop, all eighty-six miles, a few days a week, and Erin, who was taking a gap year between college and University, was available to cover a day during the week. My search for a new home was officially on.

I'll never forget the complete relief and stillness I felt as I drove into the small village of Bibury to view a barn conversion I had seen online. The sweet cottages in the Cotswold stone, the gorgeous bright red leaves festooning the local hotel, the gentle river walk. It was truly the most perfect place to grieve. Tears rolled, however this time they were survival tears. Tears of relief, of hope. I was going to live a ten minute drive away from the sweetest memories ever.

I oddly did not feel upset at leaving Jack's Place behind. He wasn't there. He was with me inside my heart. He was walking next to me. If I chose to visit Jack's Place he would be visiting with me. And anyway, I could still visit when I was at my shop. While emptying the house I found letters that I had written only five weeks after he left. There was one to the coroner, one to my doctor, one to my parents, and one to the funeral director, Colin, outlining my plans to end my life. My God, I had forgotten completely that I had even written them. I opened each envelope and read them and it was shocking to see the place I was in. I sounded so matter of fact, no emotion, just like those who do leave, with blinkers on. I felt so sorry for the woman who had written these notes. There in my writing, were my goodbye messages, preparing for my life to end by my own hand, and now I couldn't even remember that I'd actually written them. I cried and I laughed at the things I said. The handwriting was perfect. I'd laid out my entire wishes for my funeral, right down to the minute details of laying me on my right side so my face could be closest to Jack, the music to be played, the colour of my casket, pink, why? The letter to the Coroner explaining it was my choice and no one had helped me, thanking my doctor for all she had done to help me. And the letter to my parents, my goodness, telling them this was exactly what I wanted. So matter of fact, so clinical, so much like the tunnel that suicide takes us to, the tunnel to the end. It was insanity, temporary insanity.

Letter to my parents dated 24th December 2012

To my beautiful Mum and Dad,

Please I beg of you both to forgive me and not think of me as being selfish for choosing to end my life. You both did EVERYTHING you could for me and Jack. I just cannot bear the pain of living without him. I miss him all the time. My son is my entire world. I have nothing to live for now. I can't bear the pain of knowing he is alone in the ground. I just want to get in the earth and be as close to him as I can. Spiritually, I hope and pray I will be reunited with my Jack. I need to be with him, but if I am punished by those beyond for suicide then I am at peace with that. What I cannot bear is LIVING WITHOUT HIM.

Jack gave me my voice to be stronger in life against those who hurt him. Oh the hope I have to fall asleep and not awake is on my mind ALL THE TIME. I don't want to leave you both but I cannot bear the thought of burying either of you. My siblings really don't understand me at all. There will be clashes and lots of horrible drama to deal with and I would rather not have to face her again, especially when it comes to you Mum.

I love you too much to see you put in a nursing home, as she did Roy's Aunty against her wishes, who bolted back to her home within a few short weeks, and I think you should be able to stay right where you are. You love your garden, you deep down are filled with emotion that you have suppressed since your first husband's passing, you really are much like me, as is Dad. I really hope you won't be PRACTICAL and SENSIBLE about how you spend your final years. Live your lives surrounded by your memories of each other, your lovely home, your garden, your memories of Jack. Mum you are in many ways the STRONGEST woman I have ever known so draw from that strength and don't be bullied into doing something you feel in your heart is not right, and arrive at your decision based purely on how YOU feel. You have money left in your house, and I beg of you to please use whatever share would have been my inheritance to fund your lifestyle.

Dad, my lovely Daddykins, peacefully look forward to the day you come to be with

me and Jack where you belong, after you leave Mum one day. Me and Jack will be there to
greet you and keep you safe with us until Mum joins us. We are four true kindred spirits, all
artistic, all emotional, all loving, all future Angels who will bathe together in a gentle calm.
I'm not taking anything away from my siblings, your son is so much like us, but his Scottish
roots through his marriage may have a strong spiritual influence when his time comes.

I love you both more than you could ever imagine. I'm not afraid to leave you,
I know you both want me to be happy and my happiness can only come from leaving this
excruciating pain and going to be with my perfect beautiful son.

I have left everything in order. A letter to Colin explains my funeral requests and I
have left a detailed will. I have nothing much but at the very least my business has value after
debts are paid, and I have instructed how any remaining monies should be divided - hopefully
there will be something for me to give back to those who truly knew and loved us both.

So sorry to waffle on so much. When you put me in the ground with my Jack, I
beg of you to understand that this is what I truly want. I am happy with this choice, my life
was pre-ordained to be Jack's Mumsie and going to be with him is a beautiful thing.

I love you both desperately,

love Tracy xx

I had made progress indeed. It is stunning to me to reread my written word. I hit my rock bottom the night Mike, Joe's Dad arrived as I was about to go out of the back door. To think that the letters I had written, and left in my dresser drawer, would probably have been read at my inquest. The newspaper headline would probably have been something as undignified as Jack's, *"Mother died in same place as kitchen porter son...selected a pink coffin"*. Dad had been right that time when he comforted me in Spain. Little by little, hour by hour, day by day, I was coping. The day I left for the Cotswolds I lit a candle in my Jack's room and sung him his lullaby *Annie's Song*.

I cosied up in my pretty little barn, and comfort came from my Jack, by way of my Quilt of Love. Comfort during the difficult Christmas season. Spending Christmas day by myself was a choice I made. I spent the day with my Jack, my extraordinary Quilt of Love wrapped around me all day long. I am absolutely in awe of the beautiful work that went into making this gift to myself. My son's clothes lovingly sewn together into a stunning work of art. I have beautiful memories of each and every piece of clothing. I have the front section of his pea coat, two rows of buttons, and when I open the buttons I find two of Jack's ties sewn in that I can pull out and gaze at. A five pence coin was found in his jacket and this has been sewn into the quilt. The top of his joggers with the pull string are there. I can tie and untie to my heart's desire. The front right section of his school blazer is there, with his school tie peeking out from the pocket. Purple, bright blue, red and black striped skinny jeans are represented. A sweet little patch from his PE shorts. A strip of checked PJs. Tie-dye thermals. T-shirts from various holidays. Two pairs of swimming trunks, a belt loop here, a collar there. This Quilt of Love and its memories has brought me immense comfort. The reverse side is a lovely soft fleece.

This gift has brought my Jack to me in the most intimate, heart wrenching, soul lifting way. I still feel the most intense need to be able to parent Jack and this Quilt of Love has made it possible. Straightening his tie, doing up his top button, zipping and poppering his lovely warm college jacket, smiling at his little row of boxer waistbands, finding 5p in his pocket, oh gosh, it's so intense. I miss him with every ounce of my being but now when those dark days appear, I can sleep with my son keeping me warm, protecting me, as he always did.

Mum and Dad provided me with the funds needed to cover my petrol to and from Hampshire. This helped me so much, allowing me the wondrous opportunity to live in an idyllic, memory-filled part of England and continue to run my shop. The almost two hour drive each way, particularly the drive home, was a great time-filler. The difficult early evening period was spent in the car. Sundays and days I didn't go to the shop were spent exploring the beautiful villages of the area, mostly in Bourton. Remembering my boy darting along the riverbed chasing the ducks, so happy, so free. My sadness was still there; I learned from my therapist, Jennifer, that the black hole inside me would never get smaller or go away but she assured me that I would begin to build a new different kind of life around the grief hole. Jed would visit me every couple of weeks and Joe and Matt came to stay at various times. I didn't have to be someone's wife or live in partner, I could cry when I wanted to, step outside when I wanted to and live my life on my terms.

A cherished, happy moment occurred at my shop a few months after my second reading. It was the middle of the day and Erin and I were quietly working on a marketing plan when we were interrupted by the ding of a message on my phone. It was from Charlie: 'Hey hun, bit of a random question here, but did anyone ever call you Mumsie?' Oh my, oh my, oh my. The phone slid from my hand and happy tears welled up. Not wanting to tarnish the validity of this message, I was due to see Charlie the very next day as I was a contributor to a second book he was developing, I replied that I would discuss his message when I saw him. When I left the shop that evening my car dashboard literally took off like a firework display. I never suspected any car mechanical issue that day that's for sure. I had a fitful, anxious night's sleep and the next day, upon arriving at Charlie's, his text message was the first topic of conversation. Charlie told me that he had been sitting on The Common, a large, lovely park area very close to where he lived. He said he was just chilling in the sunshine when he observed a little girl, maybe six or seven years old, who had done a bolt on her bicycle, with her mum running behind trying to catch her. The girl was hurtling along one of the paths that cut through the common when she spilled forward and landed in a heap on the path, crying out 'Mumsie', as her mum eventually caught up to her. Not really giving it much thought, apart from the obvious, glad she's ok, Charlie went about the rest of his day. That evening when he was meditating he sensed Jack's presence. He described Jack as being super hyper and within that hyperactivity an image of me was being shown, along with an image of the little girl falling off her bike. He described it as there was me, then there was the girl falling, with the images flashing back and forth and Jack's hyper energy fuelling it. Hence his quizzical text message. I was beside myself with so much happiness. I disclosed to Charlie that 'Mumsie' was Jack's nickname for me. He was taken aback for a minute, a bemused grin across his face as I leapt up hugging him and giggling with delight. This lad of mine, along with I'm sure, help from my relatives and maybe even Charlie's guides, had been able to place Charlie at the right time in the park in order to experience seeing this child fall and call out 'Mumsie'. This word and image now imprinted in Charlie's memory, they were able to find it and present to him the word I desperately wanted to hear. It was soul-lifting stuff. Returning to my car after our meeting I was met with the same fizzing and twinkling of lights on my dashboard. I drove home in such a heady, happy state of mind. I got 'Mumsie.' Jack did this. It was literally the moment that exposed for me the unquestionable reality of the other side of life; a parallel universe of sorts, where my son now resided. I really, truly would see him again, hold him, care for him, feel his arms around me. He never, ever gave up. He knew I needed to hear 'Mumsie' and he made it happen. I sent massive love and a gazillion kisses skyward, I was so happy. And while it was shit to have to live here without my son's physical presence, I didn't have to live without him. He really truly was still living.

XX

FEATHERS IN EVERY SHADE
OF PURPLE AND PINK!

By the time of my third annual reading Charlie and I had become friends and, while keeping my life to myself in order to maintain the authenticity of the readings, I knew this young man was a sensitive, thoughtful person. He was also newly married but always had time for me, including an invitation to his wedding and wedding gown selection from my shop. We had lunch maybe once or twice a year, and Charlie would not accept any money from me for readings. On this particular visit I was gifted two bunches of pink roses, one from Jack and one also from Charlie. It was such a lovely gesture.

During that reading Charlie brought up a bear that I had. I reminded him that we had already talked about Jack's teddy in a prior reading but he insisted that there was another bear and I was thinking of doing something with the audio in it and that Jack was telling me to 'do it'. This was another beautiful validation for me. Jack had given me a bear when he was just eight years old. My friend Carol had taken him shopping to buy me something for my birthday, a difficult time on the heels of his father leaving. Jack presented me with a beautiful squishy bear and encouraged me to, 'Press the paw, Mum, press the paw.' I did as I was told and heard Jack's little voice coming from the bear saying, 'Heyyyy, Mum, you're the best Mum in the woooooorld, are you gonna give me a hug? I love yoouuu!' For any Mum that was just the sweetest gift and for me so incredibly meaningful.

For a month or two I had been thinking about having Jack's voice turned into a sound wave design and putting myself through the pinchy pain of another tattoo. Well now there was no more thinking about it, I had Jack's ringing endorsement, so a tattoo appointment was booked. A strange series of coincidences went along with that visit. I took the bear with me and the tattoo artist printed out the sound wave and I decided I wanted it as a bracelet style around my wrist and to join with a Jammie Dodger biscuit, in reference to my nickname for Jack. The amount of time the tattoo artist used on printing and reprinting the image to correctly fit my wrist meant that he felt he would not have the time to complete the tattoo that day. I was heartsick, and I exclaimed that no, no, he had to finish that day and I could withstand the pain and to just go for it. He was a really nice man, and wanted to make sure this permanent mark in honour of my son was done properly so rushing it was not an option. He said he would do what he could and I could revisit to complete the following week. He stressed that his next appointment was a regular who never cancelled and then he had a couple booked in for the last slot of the day. Why was I surprised when his phone rang twice within thirty minutes as both these appointments cancelled? Then inexplicably, the lights dimmed in the shop several times. I can't help feeling Jack had something to do with it. There's no such thing as a coincidence, it was a lovely moment. Wrist tattoo complete, I was so in love with it. To have my son's words in a sound wave circling my right wrist truly was the best gift I gave myself ever. Made all the more special because my son had endorsed it with his, 'Do it, Mum, do it' message.

Next, Charlie picked up on a birthday cake. He said it was a recent birthday but it was funny as it was to do with a dog. Oh, I giggled at that one. I had just had Jackpot's birthday and shared a Victoria sponge cake with him and friends. Charlie told me that Jack saw many similarities between Jackpot and himself and he found my interactions with the little dog quite funny because it's how he and I had been together. That cheered me immensely, especially when Charlie asked whether Jack wore glasses, as he was seeing Jack placing glasses on Jackpot. This was Jack's way of representing a mini version of what he looked like, and that I treated the dog in many ways as I did Jack. Apparently, he thought it was hilarious. And it's so true, this pup of mine has hoodies and jackets and a temperament so like Jack, playful and fun, but also sensitive, spending many an evening licking away my tears. It was such a lovely comparison for Jack to have brought up.

I learned of a girl he had met there who was apparently more than a friend. They were very close and had much in common. Aaaw I just loved this for Jack. Oooh I wanted more. Her name Charlie felt was Em or Emily, and she was around 15 or so at the time she passed, and possibly from the United States. She had left by her own hand around a year after Jack, and it seemed their sensitive similarities had brought them together, along with as Charlie explained Jack's time now spent partly in greeting and helping those who did take their own lives to settle in to their new reality. Such a lovely feeling in my heart that my boy had a friend there, and was experiencing maybe deep affection again, for another girl, this time one it seemed in his own image on many levels. This revelation has helped remove much of the worry over my boy being lonely and I find myself often thanking Emily for the comfort and affection she is able to bestow on him for me.

My beloved son came full circle with this reading by going back to the crux of the message that he wants me to be happy. Charlie explained that Jack wanted me to have a real think about the things that will make me happy in life and to go out and make them happen and not to hold back. He said that the biggest present I could ever give him would be for him to visit me one day and see and feel me being really, really happy. He acknowledged that it wouldn't be all sunshine and roses all the time, but as long as I was happy and content at the base level and talking to him about things that I'm excited about, that would make him happy. He told me to relax into this and not to expect him to perform magic tricks and to accept his presence.

With a heavy heart I made the decision to move back to Hampshire and closer to my shop. I loved the Cotswolds so very much but with another cold winter coming and insufficient heat and no hope of any central heating, I knew I had to move. I could have moved to another home in the area, however the inclement weather pattern precluded me from visiting the shop sometimes for a week at a time, and I knew that at least when I was there my mind was occupied. Also the need to improve my financial situation and reduce the monies my parents helped me with was beginning to press on me. Not by them but by me. Besides, the Cotswolds would still be there, if I felt I needed to hide away from life again, to bathe in the charm and idyllic surroundings of a weekend long memory of my pre-teen son, a snippet of a beautiful cherished time.

I realised that my shop needed my full attention. With Erin heading to university I needed to be fully back at the helm. While I could hire Saturday staff, there was no one who knew the reins of the business as she did, so I moved back into the area. My goodness, it was a yin and yang time. Being at the shop more, sales were up, way up, the reputation had spread and brides were visiting from all over. While being busy did occupy my thoughts, I began to realise that it was probably time I stepped away from this line of work. I desperately wanted to write this book, and had made a valiant attempt but never seemed to be able to get past the first 30,000 words. The shop consumed me and when I would try to write I found myself too distracted with running what was now a successful business. I looked at the remainder of my lease, which had 3 years left, and decided that in the next year I would attempt to sell and focus fully on my writing. Going out at the top of my game felt right, and the prospect of writing and getting lost in my life with Jack beckoned.

With my shop so demanding on my time my next annual reading with Charlie was happily upon me. I spoke with Charlie about coming to see him with a view to hearing from the young girl that had befriended Jack, if that was at all in fact possible. I had participated in Charlie's 2nd book, so this request while of course, (who am I kidding!), gave me the opportunity to hear from Jack, was for my book, so with that as the end goal in place, Charlie agreed. He encouraged me to as always talk to Jack, ask him to bring her with him and see if she was in any way willing to share any of her story. This time he would not be able to record as this was a delicate area, it wasn't her family asking. I was someone unknown to them, but this young girl was known to me through my Jack, and if I was going to tell his story, maybe this would also include Emily, and in my wildest dreams, possibly her family. I thought of this situation as if it applied to me. If there was a mother who had lost her child, and had found out that their child had a friend on the other side would I want to know? Knowing the sceptic that I was 5 years ago I did wonder how I would have reacted but thought it would certainly not harm anyone to at least visit this possibility. I prepared questions ahead of time, and Charlie said that he would certainly speak to his peeps on the other side and try to gather as much information as he possibly could. By now the sceptic in me was long gone, I had no fear of being taken advantage of. I knew that Jack was invested in Charlie, that was evident, as Charlie would tell me Jack would sometimes make a comment about his new hair style, as Charlie was prone to changing his look as young adults do! He also, while Charlie was visiting South Africa had made contact with a message to pass to me of his love for me, and had brought a few newly made friends with him to introduce to Charlie, one being Emily.

Settling in the usual space, chairs opposite, Charlie relayed, Jack and a younger female energy were already here together. Charlie divulged that upon their arrival that Jack had stepped into the room to give me a lovely big hug, and then settling next to Emily he revealed, helping her with energy to bring forward whatever she could. I learned that she was indeed from the USA, the north west around Washington, particularly he felt Seattle. Her father was involved in the the Coast Guard and she had a privileged upbringing, although did move around as her father's career determined. How did he know this I queried and Charlie explained Emily had brought an image to him of the badge of the Puget Sound coast guard although his prononciation was 'pugget!' She described her home with the porch across the front and family life involving the church. She was concerned that her parents may not accept my communication with them, due to their religion however it appeared their beliefs were more mainstream. This girl Emily, Charlie described as blonde, very sensitive, quite sporty. She shared she had been feeling out of sorts for quite some time with bouts of depression, and had left by asphyxiation, which usually would mean hanging. Her family she described as 'All American' with emphasis on success, which was in no way meant as a detriment, for this as I knew myself from 20 years in the USA, is how many families thrive. Charlie mentioned a male who was on the other side in a grandfatherly role to her and gave his name, Andrew. He brought up the name that he felt was her school, and also the name of a sports club that he felt she was a part of. He described her personality as sweet and wholesome, and someone who wouldn't hurt anyone intentionally, in fact many similarities to Jack. He explained that it was very important to her that I relay a message to her Mother. The message being that she had not passed over on the day they thought but the day before. I didn't really know what that meant, but Charlie went on to explain she had left her physical body around a certain date in January but it wasn't the date the family had as her leaving date. Possibly she had been on life support or not found until the next day. He wasn't wholly sure on that. She was pressing and really wanted her family to know this and how important it was to her. She shared as I questioned again if it was ok for me to try to find them, and the feeling back was a resounding yes and that she felt that while initially they may feel unsettled by this news, that over time they would adjust. I thought of myself in the role of her parents, and how my scepticism got in the way in the first year or two of losing Jack. I asked for a validation of sorts that maybe was something she knew that other people maybe would not, and her response was she had a pink butterfly pillow case, and the family had kept it. Both she and Jack wanted her parents and me to know that they were working and caring very much in the area of helping those who had crossed over by their own hand, and there was much to learn, as Jack had seemingly done for her. How to communicate without a physical body, not how to read and write and speak, but how to communicate with their minds. They spoke together of how someone who may have passed over and not been able to walk would now be able to, or if they had a physical ailment such as cancer, that would all be gone in their new existence. The same did not apply for emotion and depression, which involved more help and guidance which was where they were aiding others through the distressing time, of crossing over after taking their own lives, and having to learn acceptance of their choice.

Having made copious amounts of notes I travelled home straight to my laptop to begin investigating the possibility of finding Emily's family, and one brother and one sister that Charlie relayed to me. Every single question I had asked Charlie at the reading, I received a version of an answer for. A last name, and back came Williams or Williamson. The coast guard references to her father. The words North West. Her leaving day not being what they thought. I held such a responsibility to treat this exploration with respect and completely privately. Obviously these days with the internet, information could be found, and armed with a first name of Em or Emily, and the USA as a home connection from a prior reading, I had googled various websites in the USA coming across the name Emily, as someone passed away by her own hand but never a correct age or time frame. Here in the UK we can search for Inquests on line and find information fairly easily but I was unsure how this process would work with information available through the USA system.

I made myself a calming cup of tea and part of me thought better than to start looking this very evening, but my curiosity was overwhelming, so I thought a little opening piece of research would be enough to wrap up what had been an emotional day. Having Emily's name and city I googled her. There right in front of my eyes was her name! The next post was what appeared to be an obituary so I clicked on it and read. Pretty much everything Charlie had told me was in print right in front of my eyes. Confusion flooded my mind as so much of what had been shared was right here in print. While tears rolled from reading her story, and knowing this sweet girl, had made this tragic choice that so many teenagers make, my thoughts were swirling. Everything from joy that I had found these references to her, deep sorrow for her parents, a heart swelling as I turned to Facebook to Google further, only to see her beautiful, innocent open face. This girl who was smitten with my son, who I begged for in the silence of my mind would be looking after him, as I knew he would be her. At the same time, a frustration that I had found her so quickly. If I did ever choose to approach her mother how on earth would I get around this very fact. One search and found. An uncomfortable panicked feeling layering everything, that maybe Charlie had done this to maybe try to help me in some now thwarted attempt to give me what I wanted. No of course not, I felt irrational thinking permeating my thoughts. But why was it that pretty much word for word he had nailed where she lived, her father's coast guard background, her physical description, her sporty side as the website revealed her track and field accomplishments at a club in North West Washington! Her grandfather mentioned as being deceased, the vibrant pink colour awash over her obituary. I messaged Charlie right away and we spoke by phone. Such an uncomfortable conversation for me to have. I trusted this young man, he had already brought me Emily's name, her approximate age, her passing, and type of passing in earlier readings before I had asked to visit. Why why why was I questioning this. I guess I was putting myself in her parents role, imagining being contacted over this and their answer being well that's all found on line. Shit, crap, ugh, this was the best and the worst all on the same day. Speaking to Charlie telling him what I had found, he was his usual calm self. I related how I felt that it looked as though he had made everything up, I wasn't accusing him, I was letting him know how things looked, and truthfully inside a teeny part of me questioned. Oh god I hated feeling that way. This young man had brought my son to me on many occasions, and now had done as I had asked of him and brought forth this young lady, lovely sweet Emily. He referred to the internet as in some ways being problematic for mediums and psychics because of how easy information could be found, but at the same time if this Emily was not found people could interpret the polar opposite thinking that it was all made up and I should be able to find her on line!! I knew logically how this would appear, and here I am writing it just as it happened, holding nothing back. Pouring out everything here in this cathartic life review in many ways, before I too am passed over, I'm facing my fears, sharing absolutely everything here in print. No other way to do it. The rose coloured dreamy idea that I would become some kind of extended family member to this young girl's family, a bond that our children were together on the other side of life, and we would all cry and sing bloody kumbaya together was looking dodgy at best.

Allowing things to settle for a week or two, I discovered Facebook pages for Emily, her parents, and siblings. Beginning to see the faces of this very real family, viewing photographs of Emily at different ages, seeing her as part of this beautiful family, and how they appeared to be coping with their loss and through the timeline that is Facebook, to view little changes as she was less often mentioned, just as it was with Jack, just as it is in life, with everyone. Emily's older sister, a mirror image of her littler one, a permanent reminder of their Emily looking at them, looking at all of us. I knew Charlie, and more importantly I knew myself, and their daughter was with my son. Yes I would attempt in some way to reach out but I had accepted that a rejection could come, and while that pained me, would not in fact change what I knew. My son had a sweet love in his life, and this was such a comfort to me. A little sad at not being able to meet her, but no wait, I had met her, Jack had brought her to me. To reject this notion would be to reject him, and the work they both would of done in order to be there and have such a strong connection to me through Charlie.

I decided I would initially send a friend request to Emily's mother. As she appeared to have friends listed who were bereft parents, I summised that she probably received requests from random people, so worth a try. After not being accepted as a friend, I realised probably as my Facebook profile was an animated picture that represented Jack and me, and the page actually under the name Jack Tracy as I had merged our two pages into one, that maybe it looked like a boy contacting her. I then decided a brief e mail just gently saying that I was a mother in similar circumstances as herself, and was sorry she had to go through that experience etc. From there she did accept my friend request and we exchanged some emails of comfort to each other. I felt that if at least she could view my Facebook page, she would see who I was, as a grieving mother, not really using the page as much of an outlet but the odd random post was there, usually around Jack's birthday and leaving day, and other symbolic dates. I could see myself from her posts that there was plenty of activity that gradually lessened as those supporting her returned to their lives. Oh how I relate to that passage of time being the best healer and applying this thought to myself, but not to others. Of course life was moving as it should, but leaving behind those of us in grief at the level of a suicide of a child.

I'm not exactly sure how long, possibly 8 months or so of the odd message here and there before I plucked up the courage and asked if I may speak with her by phone. I thought if I tried to message what I wanted to say it wouldn't resonate the way it needed to by phone. I was carrying this welcome burden of responsibility to share with this lady, this brave mother, what her daughter had shared with me. She replied to say she wasn't quite ready to talk and of course I completely understood and told her I was here and understood how she felt. She was a year behind me on this awful grief journey, and I knew myself that I kept my circle so small and safe. It seemed to me that maybe having her other children and husband keeping her busy that this was her coping mechanism, as mine was to live somehow through Jack's friends, treating them, visiting them, and living my life by somehow retracing our footsteps together. One thing I learned in this god awful hell on earth experience is to never ever judge the actions of a parent who had lost their child in this manner. Grief is unique to each person. I backed off, and began to settle in my mind that I knew our children were together, and I had tried in as gentle a way that I could think of to open the door a chink in the dearest hope to reveal this astounding news.

A month or two later, it was a Monday, out of the clear blue she messaged me saying that she was ready to talk. Monday was my day off and I thankfully was at home. Being caught somewhat off guard I stilled myself and agreed to call and she sent me her phone number. I felt panicked, I wasn't prepared, but then neither was she! This is so random, I'm anxious to possibly offend this family. For all I knew they had visited mediums themselves, or were cross with God as I had become in the earlier part of my loss. I decided the best way was to ask her to bear with me as I gave her a full recounting of my son, our lives in America, and losing Jack, and how I coped. I couldn't lead with 'uh guess what you don't know me from Adam but our children's souls are united on the other flipping side of life!' I dialled the number and heard her lovely warm accent, telling me she was home by herself sitting on her front porch, and that it was I think labour day there and no one was home. Her initial words were of concern for me and what could she do to help me. It seemed she assumed it was I who needed her. I explained to her that no in fact I had wanted for some time to speak to her about our children and if she wouldn't mind listening to me before forming any opinion. She welcomed the conversation so I carefully went through my life with Jack in America and our return to England. I talked of his personality traits and eventual choice to leave. I spoke of my confusion with God and wanted desperately to know where my son was, and my eventual visit to Charlie. I shared details of visits, of my scepticism, and eventually landed on the day Charlie brought up Emily. I continued with my curiosity about this young girl who my son was so close to, and wanting to know more and shared with her the details of the reading where Emily was in fact present. I found myself, not justifying, but reiterating that I was a smart woman, not one hanging onto just anything to help me feel better, and that I had received unequivocal proof of Jack's eternal connection with me.

Her initial response, her voice crackled with emotion was that everything I had said could be found on the internet. There it was, the feedback that was just about impossible to disprove as of course this is how I researched finding her daughter, although only because of Charlie and Jack bringing her to me. I asked if it was ok to talk more on this subject which she agreed and we talked for 3 plus hours. She acknowledged to me that her beliefs, although she did express feeling separated somewhat emotionally from the church these days, but that seeing and being reconnected with loved ones after passing away was a belief, and the struggle was that those beyond the veil could communicate through another person she found troubling. I shared with her Emily's question about the pillowcase, and told her this was her daughter asking me to ask her about this, and she did acknowledge that yes they did still have the pillowcase, infact Emily loved drawing pink butterflies and they had an abstract painting they had kept. There were tears on both sides as we shared loving memories of our children. I learned that Emily had been found by her father in her bedroom, and she had been on life support before the decision was made as a family to turn off the equipment. As gently, and with as much respect as I could I asked her if I could share with her something that her daughter very much wanted her and the family to know, and with her agreement, went on to tell her about Emily's soul having already left and that they hadn't made that decision, she had already departed and how important it was that they knew this in case of any guilt, but at the same time I stressed that I in no way wanted to take away their memory of that day, of that decision made together, but I felt I had to pass this message to her from her girl. Just writing this I carry such a plethora of emotion as to when is enough and that would this information help this family, or cause unnecessary angst. I recall her quiet tears, how she, just like the rest of us parents of children who take their own lives, struggle faking it through life the best that we can. She a mother with other children to support, and a husband, plus I learned that day battling her own ailments. How brave is this woman. I admire her so very much. We haven't spoken by phone since that day however do exchange email messages. I have the sense that maybe she has not shared this information with anyone, I'm not entirely sure. I must try not to suppose, it's not a healthy option to make assumptions about others, all I can do is be here at the end of the computer. I sent an image of a purple angel candle that I had lit for her daughter on her leaving day, and a sweet pink heart shaped tree ornament that appeared outside of my bedroom window during the holiday season.

I also recounted part of a visit I made to a female medium in the days after learning of my mother's passing. I had been out of town in Somerset at a lodge I visited a couple of times a year to in part write this book, when I received the news of my mother's unexpected passing, but felt a need to see a medium before I faced my mother's services, as her request was to be buried next to Jack and this meant standing among what I knew would be a chilly reception, both physically and metaphorically. A source of some comfort if I was able to receive a message as I was going to have to bury my mother next to my son one day before the anniversary of his passing. What she did reveal was a female, blonde, bubbly young and so joyous about me, said how very fond she was of me and exuded much love. Not a relative of mine but connected to my son, and brought also the name Emily. She enquired if I was in some kind of communication with her mother! Well that for me was not something I necessarily needed, but it did make me feel that at least in the writing of this book, another medium had brought through this young girl. Interestingly she also brought up my brother and sister, referring to the latter as having 'no flies on her' and cleverly manipulating my brother who was the executor of my mother's estate, and for me to let him know to watch out for her! Considering I was leaving right then to head back home for Mum's services the next day, it all made sense. Soooo at least by letting Emily's mother know meant I was keeping my promise to Emily to stay close to her mum. I really do still hope that maybe over time a meeting with Emily's mother would be so very special. Both our children would certainly be present, and the joy I know they would feel at such a meeting is why I would want to do it, however I don't need to rush, and if it never materialises then I'm ok with that truly I am. I love so much still feeling a part of Jack's life on the other side.

XXI

CONVERSE AND HEELS ... WALKING TOGETHER

Living my life as if Jack is with me is my truth. It's the only way for me and revisiting places we visited is part of that process. Having experienced the comforting feeling of visiting the Cotswolds, and the subsequent couple of years living there, I decided to return to Tobago. Just me, and a feeling of hope that Jack would come along with me. I contacted the hotel that Jack and I had stayed at. Over the years I had stayed in touch with a staff member called Rachel who, knowing my situation, kindly booked me into a room next door to the room Jack and I had stayed in. In the weeks leading up to the trip I contacted Charlie, asking him to please assure me that Jack would be there with me as I was feeling anxious about revisiting such a beautiful memory. Charlie told me that I needed to accept Jack's continued presence in my life and that I shouldn't need to be reminded of it by a medium. It was painful to hear but Charlie stood his ground with me, and I left for Tobago without the extra layer of reassurance that I always seemed to need. Although I'd had so many validations through my readings with Charlie I still struggled internally with the concept of not actually hearing from Jack directly.

Walking through the tall glass doors into the beautiful boutique hotel in Tobago was like stepping back in time. I had worried that I'd be punishing myself by returning to such a memory-filled place. Would there be tears and sadness, possibly too much, even for me? But when I arrived I felt an inner strength and peace. I ask myself to this day where this inner stillness and incredible strength came from. Do I hand it all over to Jack? It feels right to, but I gave myself a gentle pat on the back on that arrival day for making the trip.

I spent my week on Tobago as I had done with Jack. Walking down the treadmill staircase to the beach cove. I opted to sit in the same spot we had. Just me on the beach with my bag hanging from a low branch, I allowed the ocean breezes and eventual incoming tide to cleanse me. My imagination allowed me to see my Jack jumping in the waves, zooming along the shore line on his boogie board. So free, so playful, so beautiful. I had brought with me a therapeutic colouring book filled with tropical scenes. I selected one to shade in that was filled with tropical birds. Every day I sat for an hour or so shading this page, agreeing to frame it and include Jack's photograph from our first trip. It's a photo I can only glance at. His innocence is completely hypnotic. The gorgeous open smile, board in hand, soaked from top to toe. Truly encapsulating for his Mumsie the spirit of our holiday. It was very therapeutic indeed to feel the warm sun on my skin, and colour these birds. I took dinner in my room sitting on the terrace as we two had done. A symbolic purchase of a dish of chocolate ice cream placed next to me. Playing Seal and the Black Eyed Peas as we had done. Remembering, reliving, it was just the most healing time.

I realised on that trip that I did know what was best for me. On this trip I found myself, the self Jack tried to make me reveal. My fear of what others might think of me was no longer a hindrance. Living with Jack symbolically with me would be how I would navigate life. A couple of the nights I was there Rachel joined me for drinks in the restaurant. It was a wonderful Caribbean windowless bar, allowing the ocean breezes to fill the space, high ceilings and paddle fans, and sweet unexpected little birds swooping in, just as before. Just because I couldn't see Jack it didn't mean he wasn't there and during my next reading with Charlie he announced that Jack had forgotten he was in spirit form and had attempted to buy me a drink at the bar in Tobago. I love that.

Returning to England I knew that preserving memories, walking tall and proud and speaking out, as I am in this memoir for my son, is how I must live the remainder of my journey here. With this book on my mind more and more and an offer to purchase my shop I had the financial freedom to spend the next year writing.

When Charlie decided to retire from doing readings to spend more time on his university degree he obliged me with all his love and kindness one last reading.

I had one question on my mind, only one, my nickname for Jack. On the drive down I had been chattering away to Jack excitedly, as this was a somewhat unexpected reading, and I told him how much it would thrill me to hear his nickname, Jammie Dodger. Having learned a little about how these souls communicated with a medium ie; to search their mind and memories for information and details, I was pressing the point that if he was able to bring with him a packet of Jammie Dodger biscuits that would bring me what I needed. Charlie surely must have known what they were. He must have some kind of memory of them stored away in his mind. Most English kids were familiar with this yummy treat. It's not that I didn't appreciate and value all that Jack had already brought me, through Charlie, it was just so comforting to receive each new validation.

After we'd got settled and Charlie was 'linked in' I told him that I had one question only and of course, being such a fantastic human, he indulged me. After my initial, 'Hi son, how's my boy'? and the reply that he was very chilled out indeed, more so than at any other visit, which was comforting, Charlie described Jack talking about cooking with Emily, a little begrudging on his part but if that's what she wanted he went along with it. He described baking trays and lots of different kinds of biscuits but of a retro style. I sat there poker-faced but inside my hope was bountiful. He described the custard cream variety then the long chocolate sandwich Bourbons, then he became animated in his description of an enormous pile of *Jammie Dodgers*, which was interesting to him as when Jack had initially come through, he had been holding a pack that he had brought to share with us. *What???* I leapt out of my seat, hugging Charlie with joyful tears streaming. Jackpot was with me that day and he kicked off barking. A melee of hugs, tears, thanks to Jack and calming my nutty little dog ensued. 'Well now, that really was random!' piped up Charlie, shaking his head and grinning with delight for me and for Jack.

I recounted that Joe and I had left a pack of Jammie Dodgers at Jack's Place on his birthday and Charlie instantly responded that Jack had sent him an image of his actual resting place. He was indicating writing as the main part of the stone and there was a feeling of intense love and a sentimental connection that I had really captured the two of us on the headstone. This was so beautiful to hear. 'There were cans of drinks there, quite a few,' Charlie continued, 'but tall cans not coke cans. Were they Monster or Relentless or something?' Yes, oh yes, this was just great to hear, as I could share with his mates who dropped the odd can off from time to time that Jack knew what they were doing. Charlie went on, referring quizzically to a small box of about five inches or so. I was initially stumped then remembered something I had placed there during the first year of my grief. I asked if he could tell me more and he said he felt it was a game, the Battleship game. That was exactly what it was. I was just beaming. Jack and I would play the travel Battleship game when we took trips away, and also during the odd bath time visit. I had kept one set and laid the other with him. I was so joyful that day, to have Jammie Dodger, the headstone reference, the cans of Monster, and Battleships, it was just the absolute best feeling that Charlie had managed to interpret for Jack and for me such beautiful, fantastic memories.

Charlie finished asking me from Jack to pass a message to Joe, as he could see him struggling with some anxiety. Jack wanted to help in some way, and asked me to tell Joe to please visit his bench. He said that if Joe would sit there Jack would come and Joe could talk out loud to him and they could just talk as they used to. He wanted Joe to know that whenever he went to that bench Jack would come. He was always caring and loving for others. I drove away that evening feeling so much love from my boy and a rare feeling of complete happiness within myself.

I have received signs of Jack's continuing presence around me. I remember Charlie telling me that if Jack was still here in the physical world by this stage in his life he probably wouldn't be at home anymore and would be busy with work, friends, girls etc. Like most parents, I would probably have felt a sense of rejection as my son moved forward with his life. In that sense I guess I'm oddly lucky. Jack is still with me, and although I can't see him he leaves signs of his love and presence. Here are just a few...

In the run-up to selling the shop anxiety was at a high and I had received a call to visit my doctor the next day to receive some blood test results. Before bed, I always stopped to kiss Jack's picture, sometimes have a chat, sometimes just a quick 'love you Jammie'. That night I stood and asked Jack if he could possibly come with me to the doctor's appointment the next day. Having always been a sensitive person and now with the trauma of losing Jack, my emotions were even more heightened when something felt out of my control. In the morning I left for the doctor's with a kiss to my boy and drove the five miles along country roads to the surgery. Turning onto the longer stretch of road before the last turn to the doctors, I slowed as a car pulled out in front of me and turned to continue in the same direction. I immediately noticed the license plate on the car that read JL42 JAM. Wow, there he was, showing me his presence. Such a lovely moment. What are the chances of a license plate, obviously personalised, with letters clearly representing his Jammie nick name. It's not like I was on the M25 with hundreds of cars passing, eventually recognising one that was similar, this was completely random and perfectly perfect as Jack was. I felt warmed that he was showing me that I wasn't alone. The results were OK, high blood pressure, but no real surprise there, given my circumstances.

The next day, a bride who had become a friend visited the shop on the hunt for a wedding dress. She was getting married again and had come back to me to help her. Terribly flattered by this, I invited her for lunch after her appointment. Of course, I excitedly shared the car license plate treat from the day before. We had a great girly lunch and I decided to close up and head home. It turned out we were both parked in the same car park right by the shop. Approaching our cars we discovered that she had only parked one car away from me and she pointed to the car that was parked in between us. The license place read JAM616E. It was such a lovely moment as we hugged and giggled right there in front of the car. I had parked there first and she said that when she had parked this JAM616E car was not there because she had to wriggle to get out as the previous vehicle was a van. It had to have parked there during our lunch. I can't help smiling as I type this. There is no such thing as a coincidence. What a lovely moment.

Lovely playful Hannah who had joined me in Rome, popped into my shop with her usual excitable personality, 'I've been meaning to tell you but I keep forgetting!' She recounted how Jack had been present in a dream. He was inside a house waving her in to look around, and she described our home in Florida. She described a picket fence a long front porch and the house roofline sloping on the right side. She described lots of glass doors and exposed bricks in the kitchen and breakfast room with white island or table that led out to the garden, all the while with Jack's face beaming his incredible smile. Jaw dropping as Hannah had no idea of the style or layout of our home where the happiest of family times took place. She never personally met Jack, only through memories I had shared with her, however she feels and expresses often how she thinks of him as her brother, most recently gifting me at the holiday season with a beautiful pair of purple twinkly angel wings with the card signed from them both.

A couple of months ago I decided to go down to London. I had only made this trip a couple of times since Jack left. London was our place. We loved going there and it was only the year before that I had made my first trip there since he left with Erin for my birthday. We had visited one of the Gaucho Grills, not the one Jack and I frequented, but at the time it was a really good step for me to even entertain the idea of a meal there. On this second visit to the city I decided to brave it and go to the actual restaurant in Piccadilly that was filled with heady, loving memories. I had Jackpot with me and with the weather being unseasonably lovely for a September in England I knew he would be welcome in their outdoor dining area. It felt really right to go there. Just me and the pup. I ordered Jack's fave drink, a Strawberry Mojito, and a humitas, which is an Argentinian tapas of mashed corn with cream and cheese, wrapped up in the husk and then oven baked. They're delish and Jack and I loved them, so it was a sort of ceremonial thing to do. I snapped an image of the table for one, but I wasnt alone, how could I be on this most intimate of moments. I spoke to my boy as I toasted him with his drink and enjoyed the sweet humitas, sharing with Jackpot. It was a lovely, lovely evening and I returned home feeling so much love for my son, and not sad at all about enjoying the food and ambience at our spot. I spent the next day with Erin and we talked about what we had been up to. I of course, began to share about my visit to Gaucho, to which she stepped in, telling me that the night before she'd had a dream about the two of us trying to make a humitas and giving up and ending up at Gaucho having one. Why, oh why would Erin be dreaming about a humitas at Gaucho? I feel certain it was my boy, entering Erin's dream in order to find a way to let me know that he was there at Gaucho when I toasted him. I love that validation so much.

The last sign that Jack was with me came about six months ago. I had sold a dress and the bride, Amy, was paying for it in instalments so I saw her for several weeks when she would pop in. We would invariably end up having a coffee and a chat, sitting outside the shop on the little courtyard wall. On her final visit to make her last payment she told me that she was going to a medium that evening with a friend. Amy had sadly lost her mother two months prior. She was aware of my situation, so possibly felt comfortable sharing this news with me. Always a little anxious for those who first visit a medium, particularly when there are so many calling themselves mediums when their ability to relate information is not as well honed as others. I asked her for her mother's name, which was Sara. I looked up to the sky and asked Jack if he was aware of Sara and to please help her with the energy needed to be able to come through for Amy. With Sara's passing only having been a couple of months previously, and me having more than a grasp on how information is gently given, I knew that it may be a struggle for Sara that early in the process.

Amy rang me later that evening and excitedly told me about the reading and the mention of her relatives and her recently passed over mother. She talked about her mother repeating, 'Shut up, shut up, shut up,' which had Amy reeling, as she and her mother often did the whole 'Shut up, no you shut up, no you shut up,' joke with each other. She told me that the medium, a woman, had asked if she was aware or knew of a younger male passed over by the name of Jack. She thought of me instantly as we had just spoken of him earlier that day, and with no other Jack she was aware of, shared that she had never met him but it could be the son of a friend of hers. The lady went on to describe what Jack was wearing the night he passed over, and how important fashion and cool clothes were to him. She described him as 'a bit of a mummy's boy' which I guess to a degree he was, in terms of how close we were, however I'm not sure he would have liked that description! This is a medium interpreting the information she is receiving. Someone else may have said how close he was to his mum. She also imparted that he had not given his mother any notice. Still doing his best to comfort me, it turns out that Jack had hijacked the reading! If Charlie was not available to connect my son to me then my goodness, this lad of mine was hell bent on finding a way to let me know of his continuing presence around me. Love, love, love my Jammie Dodger.

XXII

ROME

In September 2018 I made the decision to walk in my son's footsteps and visit Rome. It had been in my thoughts for quite some time, to revisit his birthday trip to the eternal city. Matt had shared as much as I think his mind would allow but it wasn't enough for me. Knowing that Jack would walk beside me, I arranged for a guide to take me on a tour following in my son's footsteps. Footsteps retraced through the photographs he took. These photographs tell me everything I already know about Jack. To revisit those feelings through his photographs is just the most beautiful way to see and feel him. I felt inside that I might rejoice on this trip. Rejoice in his sensitivity and rejoice in his personal style with a little retail therapy. I was sure he would guide me to Valentino, Prada, Gucci, or all three. I would rejoice in leaving purple amethyst hearts at locations that felt right. I bought eighteen of them, one for each year of his life here.

I guess it was a pilgrimage of sorts, with the last couple of days set aside for a dear friend Hannah, who would join me for an attempt at frivolity. The trip began with a three hour delay at the airport, which included being booted off one plane and on to another, however I kept really chilled. Eventually passing through passport control, I was selected for a search. After clearing customs I met with the driver arranged by my hotel to transport me, a journey which took place in stony silence but was oddly fine. I was in my own head. It was all a vacuum of sorts. This was to be a date in Rome, a date with my son.

The welcome from the staff was warm, and I settled into my lovely room with a wrap-around stone terrace, on the lovely Via Veneto. I had initially wanted to stay at Jack's hotel, however it had been sold and turned into a completely different style venue. All unpacked, I rested for an hour before my guide was due to arrive for the first part of my photographic tour. There was a stillness inside me as I chose to walk the five flights of marble stairs down to reception. I had been told via email that the owner of the company, Jerry, would be my guide, however after greeting me, he then introduced a female guide from his firm called Rosanna who would be taking care of me. A driver was also provided at my disposal. A rush of emotion flooded over me. It wasn't as I expected, they knew the purpose of my trip, I felt instantly protective of Jack, and horribly emotional. I had asked for the guide to be male. For me I felt I could be more authentic with a man than a woman. Jerry had been thinking the opposite, and expressed that he felt in my circumstances a female would be a better choice. Mars vs Venus, that old chestnut. Assured I was in good hands I was ushered to a sleek black Mercedes and greeted by Peter, my softly spoken driver. Sitting in the back the tears came flooding as I whispered my apologies. They both were chattering in Italian looking at the print-out of images I had sent on ahead of my visit, obviously planning the four hour tour. They handed me tissue packets, showing me such kindness and acceptance of why I was their charge for these few days. I breathed through my emotion, not annoyed with myself but not liking this wave of sadness that was enveloping me, and I resolved to accept this minor change. Jack would be there, I didn't want to hurt him. I steadied my breathing and focused on why I was there. To walk in my boy's footsteps, to stand where he stood, to feel his energy, to leave my imprint with him.

The bridge where the two boys had stood for hours chatting and people watching was our first stop. I felt oddly vulnerable standing there and my emotions were on the surface. This was where they had lived my entire life though, so I guess I wasn't surprised, just more disappointed in myself. Comparing Jack's photo with the scene and knowing I was in the correct place, I chose to drop the first amethyst heart into the river below. Peter circled and transported me safely from this location to the Castel Sant'Angelo. Jack had taken a couple of images there as it sits in close proximity to the Vatican City. I realised from looking past the Castel I could see the dome of St Peter's. I was standing in the same place my boy had stood with little birds upon his shoulder and the most beautiful smile upon his face. This image, I have enlarged and framed. It's the image that sends me out into the world and greets me when I get home, with me bestowing a kiss and often a silent cheek to cheek moment. There wasn't a bird in sight, which initially felt disappointing, however Rosanna explained that they were brought into the area by local gypsies and not a part of the natural habitat. I placed another amethyst heart on the cobbled approach with the Vatican in the distance. Placed exactly where Jack had stood beaming so brightly. It didn't matter to me that some hearts were left in the open to be possibly trod into the cement or picked up by a curious passerby. What mattered was the imprint of his energy that would go with them. Both our energies. For me, leaving the hearts was leaving a little piece of my son behind, so those who may have picked one up were incredibly lucky. I stood and took in the scene. There was a street performer sitting with the illusion that he had no face. Glasses on, pork pie hat, purple checked shirt sleeves, oh how Jack would have loved him. How like Jack this character was. He was sitting as Jack often sat. One knee bent, the other leg stretched out. Head tilted forward slightly. The feeling I had was, while knowing this performer wasn't Jack, the essence of Jack was there. As I approached, the colour purple popped and I realised his glasses were in this emotion-filled colour. I popped a heart onto the white gloved hand and snapped a photo. While I was taking these images another performer, a busker of sorts, was singing a familiar song. As I took in the performance I realised he was singing a John Denver song, Country Roads. It was by the same artist whose Annie's Song was my nightly gift to Jack to aid in his slumber. Why would this street performer be singing John Denver in the middle of Rome, Italy? There's no such thing as a coincidence. I felt really warm inside, so in love with my child. Representing himself with the rectangle glasses just like his, the purple checked shirt, the energy of this edgy, funky street performer, and adding a sprinkle of a music infused with a mother and son memory. A very happy, intimate memory. I felt better, joyous in fact. It was a perfect beginning to my date with my son.

The Castel image was next, just thirty or so paces on from the street artists. Taking an image I wondered where I could leave Jack's next heart as the building walls were high and the stonework smooth at the lower section. Plan of action in place, Rosanna and I braved the climb up onto the ledge of the lower wall and snuck a heart into the brickwork. I'm sure the wind or rain will eventually release it but placing it there was mischievous and funny, not unlike Jack hopping over the school fence.

Next we went to see the Coliseum even though, oddly, Jack took no photos there but he'd told me that he'd visited. Peter kindly took me there and I stood on a little bridge and snapped a couple of shots of the arena, this gathering place, that Jack had said was good to see but didn't have the same effect on him as Vatican City.

Interestingly, Peter also gave me the opportunity to photograph the actual tracked land where the chariot race from *Ben Hur*, with the great Charlton Heston was shot. Jack would have loved that, so here he was, walking with me, seeing something new. It felt great to be able to show my son a piece of Rome he had probably not seen. *Ben Hur* was a film we had watched together on one of our many Sundays. It was a soaring feeling to think we had sat side by side, snuggled on the sofa watching one of the most epic races in movie history, and now here we were in Rome experiencing that memory.

Later that day we had cocktails and antipasti at a charming local cafe, kindly provided by Jerry. We chatted for an hour or two and I felt so very welcome into his family-run business. He did care, this I could see, but he was a very busy man, with his phone constantly interrupting the flow of conversation. With a dinner offering for the following evening arranged, I was carefully transported back to my hotel by Peter, who throughout the day had opened and closed my door countless times. Always, as I positioned myself, gently scooping up my dress, I felt protected.

Rosanna and Peter arrived the next day to take me to my four hour tour of the Vatican. Jack had taken many photos of various pieces in the Vatican museums. I had the Pieta on my mind. Of course this famous image of a mother and child would bring a reaction, and I steeled myself, telling myself to go with the flow of the day and not make any assumptions. I just had to let the day unfold and drink in the moment.

I had visited St Peter's Basilica as a twenty-one-year-old but not the museums, being so young and with limited funds on an au pair's income. It was a faded memory, now being relived with my son at my side. A lovely young man called Antonio was there to greet us and arrange our entry tickets. He was like an adorable puppy and Jerry had shared with me the evening before, upon seeing Jack's images, how he felt they resembled each other. Antonio approached with a lovely cuddle for me and I immediately noticed the print on his shirt was identical to a set of Jack's bedding. A blue grey camouflage print. I felt overwhelmingly emotional again and lowered my head as he ushered me to a bench to sit for a moment. The sea of people everywhere I hadn't expected. Why? It's so odd, I was prepared for seeing each piece of art Jack had taken, and the variety of reactions that may come, however I hadn't processed on any level the multitude of people queuing and jockeying for position. Being with a guide offered some release as we were able to bypass the crowd and move at a less frenetic pace. Coming across what was at the time the Pope's private garden, now open to visitors, was particularly memorable. Jack had told me of his deep pleasure at being shown this particular garden so I spent the time I needed there. Leaving one of his hearts on the manicured lawn and another atop the ledge from where he had photographed this beautiful garden. During his visit the gardens were private but now he was walking with me and able come in, a lovely feeling. A group of young priests in training walked by. They were all under twenty-five and I felt a wave of sadness. This trip was pulling every emotion from my body and they were changeable within a split second, depending on so many variables. Not unlike my day to day life as it is for me and for all of us who have outlived our children. How on earth do I manage this, it's such crap, I thought, watching these young lads, robes on, chattering, moving toward their classroom. If Jack was indeed present then he would be sensing my feelings, so my sadness was instantly replaced with guilt. My mind was so tormented and conflicted. If I'd never sought out a medium I wondered how I would be. I wondered if knowing of my son's presence actually made things harder because it made me worry about what he might feel about how I was feeling? Would it have been better to think that the lights had just gone out and there was no heaven, no afterlife? How did other parents in my circumstances cope? How often do we hear the words, 'they are at peace'? What the fuck does that mean?

Trying to ground myself, I returned to the present moment. Here I was sitting in what was the Pope's private garden, in the centre of Christianity, seeing so many nationalities, so many faiths experiencing this beautiful city. It had been Jack's favourite part of Rome he'd told me, which had been evident in his photographs. My son had brought me here. I don't think I would have revisited if he hadn't left. The vibrancy of this holiest of places felt charged and mini electric shocks ran through me. I needed to accept what I could not change, accept who I was. Sensitivity always my core. Jack had described me once as a Gerbera Daisy; 'a really pretty, very delicate, fragile, bright flower, being held up on such a strong stem'. I resolved to continue this day and the rest of my trip how Jack would have wanted me to, and actually how I would also. I would drink in his energy, revel in his experiences here, maybe take a trip out of the city, do some crazy fun retail therapy, experience this beautiful country. That was what we always did together anyway. Bit of culture, some fun shopping, a yummy meal or two. I looked around at this incredible garden and knelt down and placed one of Jack's hearts on the manicured grass.

The visit was beginning to feel epic. But then I had to face the Pieta. My son had stood there, he had photographed this heralded statue and he told Matt to give me the miniature figurine they'd brought back. As much as I feared my reaction I also could barely wait to be there. Rosanna explained there were two Pietas and we would first visit the one Jack had been able to photograph. She explained that someone not in their right mind had attacked the original statue and caused damage so a second was made for people to approach, while the original, now restored, sat behind glass in St Peter's Basilica and would be the final stop in our tour.

As we approached the Pieta there was a throng of people blocking a clear view. I waited, my heart beating quickly and I took some breaths to calm myself. Then I stepped forward and took in this saddest of scenes. Mary seated and holding her son in her arms. One hand supporting him, the other hand gesturing as if she was giving him to me, to all. As I glanced at her son my initial reaction was the lean physique was so similar to my Jack's. A small stubbly beard, his hand drooping. I leaned forward and gently stroked each finger as I had with Jack. I was lost in my own thoughts, completely unaware of anyone else near me, near us. Rosanna captured some images so I can now see my hand to my face in initial shock, head lowered in deference to this moment, my arm outstretched reaching to this young man's hand. Of course the statue is of Mary and Jesus but as I stood there I could only feel and see a mother and her child. We were two mothers grieving. Backing away slowly I couldn't turn my back until I was outside again. The significance of this moment was deeply personal.

Upon seeing the original Pieta later that day a realisation occurred to me. When going through the selection process for my son's headstone I had unwittingly selected a modern interpretation of The Pieta. Placed in a cabinet not 6 feet from me was the little miniature Pieta that Matt had given to me, without me even recalling it was there. A symbolic gift that I couldn't bear to look at was now where I received the deepest most spiritual comfort. This realisation was utterly surreal, utterly beautiful, utterly perfect. A deeply moving end to this day, a day Jack had experienced five years earlier as he bore witness to the beauty and the rich history of the Vatican.

During a dinner I had been invited to by Jerry and a few members of his core team, Peter told me that he had researched and found the café that Jack and Matt spent time at. It was in Piazza Babberini, only a ten minute walk from my hotel. Plans were in place for a visit to Tuscany the next day, so we agreed for Peter to pick me up from the cafe at eleven in the morning. Upon arriving at the piazza I spied what we in the UK might call a builders' cafe, and ordered a cappuccino and took it upstairs. There were only two tables downstairs so I surmised that Jack and Matt must have been sitting on the upper level. The cappuccino was only one euro so it made sense that they would have come here on their limited budget. I gazed out of the broken window, wondering what they had chatted about. Weirdly, Peter was late turning up to meet me, but

I finally spied him standing in the square so I hastened to leave, with a quick stop to snap a photo of the super friendly staff, who I had recounted Jack's visit to, and I left them with one of his amethyst hearts. One of the girls was quite emotional, it was very lovely. Dashing over to Peter, I excitedly told him of my experience at 'Jack's cafe'. 'No, no, no, Signora, that's not the cafe this is!' He gestured toward a lovely indoor/outdoor cafe spilling with atmosphere. It turned out that this was why he was 'late' – he'd gone there to meet me. Oops! I giggled as I turned to see the young girl waving to me from the door of the 'builders' cafe'. Oh my! I couldn't tell her the terrible truth, so I cheerily waved back and Peter ushered me off to the car. Fits of giggles ensued as he realised my error. He thoughtfully offered for us to go to the right café but I thought it best to leave with that memory. I decided I'd visit the next morning for coffee. Jack was definitely going to be a dinner table conversation for that sweet girl's family!

The two hour journey to Orvieto, a hill town, and further on to Tuscany for some wine tasting was a delight. A couple of months previously I had put together a play list of songs all memorable to me and Peter kindly played them, so the drive there was a fun, chatty time as I explained the relevance of each song to my life. Luckily it seemed we had the same taste in music, so when my last song, Barry White's, *My First, My Last, My Everything* concluded, he revealed that Barry was his fave and would I mind if we continued the journey with his collection of the soul man's music. How amusing, driving through the luscious Italian countryside with the milky tones of Mr White accompanying us.

Orvieto was a very pretty 'city' due to its magnificent cathedral but it seemed more like a quaint hill town to me. The cathedral was built to honour the Virgin Mary and while quietly exploring its interior, I again came face to face with a peachy marble version of the Pieta. I lit a candle for my boy as Peter stood at a respectful distance. How do I get through each day, I wondered as I stood there in silence, feeling so much love for Jack pouring out of me. I left one of his hearts next to a precious white feather that was lodged into a corniche. Lovely.

The Montepulciano Vineyard beckoned and some wine tasting and anti pasti was a delight. Having Peter with me I felt quietly looked after. I didn't need anyone, I had Jack, but to not have to think about anything at all other than drinking in the essence of the day was incredibly calming. Delicious wine tasted, six bottles were purchased with delivery arranged for ten days later to my home. This was an added pleasure I could look forward to somehow. Leaving Tuscany with plentiful photos taken of the beautiful region, I had my son very much on my mind. Back in the car I requested Andrea Bocelli's *Time To Say Goodbye* to be played and settled back, finding myself swept away literally on a wing and a prayer as I recalled my little four-year-old curled up on my lap on Christmas morning, with a fire crackling and this beautiful song gifted to myself playing. As it ended, Jack said, 'Again Mummy' and I rose to repeat the track. Then, with him sitting on my hip and our hands grasped in the sweetest embrace, we swayed and danced to the magnificent tones of this master opera singer and the sweet notes of Sarah Brightman. What an utterly epic moment. Tears trickling down my cheeks, I embraced this *Splendour in the Grass, Glory in the Flower* moment. How about that, I did dance with my son. It was a truly incredible moment, bringing me such a connection to my precious child. In fact, on that car journey back to Rome with Barry White keeping us company a darling memory revealed itself to me. Jack would have been around 14 and we were both at home, me having a glass or two of wine and playing my Barry White CD. There I was having a little cheeky mummy dance when I spied Jack in the doorway, with a bemused grin. Come on son, I beckoned, and after a little cajoling my darling gorgeous boy cranked up the volume and the two of us bopped around the living room to *My First, My Last, My Everything*....We had it goin' on, thanks Barry.

With Hannah arriving the next day my shopping spirit was lifted. I booked a hair appointment with the legendary Giancarlo Baldestein for a blow dry that morning with plans to visit the real 'Jack's Café' for coffee. Three hours later with a cut, colour and restyle, I emerged feeling light of heart and wallet. This new look really suited me and I trotted down the road to Pepe's wondering how often I may need to visit for maintenance. With my cappuccino and heart shaped cookies at Pepe's after calling Matt to determine exactly where the two of them sat, the exquisite feeling of love overpowered me as a small table became available in the precise location Matt had described. I was inside my own head, lost in cherished thoughts of my son, as I imagined him next to me, an overwhelming feeling of the most exquisite love, you know the the kind, painful, but soul encompassing all at once.

The highlight of my last couple of days was the incredible shopping. I'm not one to go shopping, this was something Jack and I did together maybe two or three times a year, so I decided why not, be indulgent. He would be right with me anyway. It was a nice tonic having Hannah there. She's young, full of life and funny, so it made for a lighter heart. We revisited Pepe's, which was special. Repeating the cappuccino and the little heart-shaped cookies. I loved sitting there, chattering away this time about the two lads, eating for free as long as they were drinking wine!

I had yet to drop my last three hearts into the Trevi Fountain. I'd been waiting so that Hannah could experience this final gesture. But when we got there the fountain was drained of water so the moment I'd planned in my mind as my goodbye to Rome and an end to my pilgrimage was usurped. Sadly, once again my emotions got the better of me and I slumped forward in a sea of tourists, feeling that familiar wet trickle of tears begin to roll. Why did it have to be drained today? The words 'no coincidences' had become a running message in my brain, like the ticker tape at the stock market and Hannah's reassuring words that I was clearly meant to return, can be the only explanation. Such wisdom, out of the mouth of one so young. I still have my three amethyst hearts remaining. Once again a reason to stay alive, to stay connected, my coping mechanism lifting me out of this horrid disappointment. Come on Trace, I told myself, it doesn't have to be the end, I will return soon. My love affair with my son Jack continues ad infinitum.

REFLECTION

Writing this with my boy has been such a cathartic experience. Feeling so close to Jack, sensing his presence close by. Having messages and validations from across our purple veil has brought me such solace. To know that my son is able to use his emotions to project his true feelings to me, and my boy has and continues to help to heal my tortured mind. I want to help heal his as well, and I worry so much that if I did choose to leave too soon then Jack would carry the burden of responsibility for my actions and I just can't bear to think that I would have caused him more angst over his decision, which I now know he regretted. I do have some bright days, it's not always black. The heavy boulder I dragged along reharnesses itself every once in a while, however no longer a daily burden.

Ultimately, living for Jack is how I personally cope. Knowing how proud he would be of me. It's a bit like a rebirth really. I've been a wife, a Mumsie (still am), a career woman, and now I'm figuring out this next chapter in my life, as I realise I won't be a grandmother and I won't retire with a husband somewhere sunny. I treat myself these days and it feels nice to go shopping just for me, which is a very foreign concept. Having said that, I have in a fairy godmother type way taken two young ladies Erin and Hannah under my wing, who I spoil and chatter to, as I did with Jack. I help them and they help me by allowing me to sprinkle glitter on them!

I have rediscovered my relationship with God. I reread The Shack that Christian gave me and discovered there was a film made, and have watched it a handful of times. I recall Christian saying that while he understood how I felt, with my desire for that instant knowledge that my boy was safe, and I would see him again, he also gently explained that God, or as I think of God....the Father, the Son and the Holy Spirit, does love me and loves all of us, those in Heaven and those here. Receiving snippets once a year Christian explained would probably not sustain me, whereas God would always be with me and I could hand over to God my thoughts and feelings. Understanding through watching The Shack that God isn't here to stop us from making the wrong choices, God is here to clean up the mess that we as humans create for ourselves has had a profound affect on me. I feel comforted that Jack is also with God, he is so safe, and so loved, and so protected.

I'm jostling along through life in the only way I can. Sharing my warrior child and his quirky, cheeky, sweet, deeply sensitive soul with the world at pretty much every juncture. As a mother I am so proud of my son. His exquisite love for me has allowed me to be true to my own sensitivity and to live proudly. Thank you my Jack, for allowing me to embrace my true self, sensitive, emotional, scatty, bright, intuitive, a reflection of you. Truly, I cannot wait to wrap my arms around you again, my first, my last, my everything. When I listen closely, I hear your footsteps dancing across my heart.

FOOTNOTE

It was the night before Jack's first birthday since he left. I was questioning, as I often had, why his first girlfriend Leila had never contacted me, or posted anything online about Jack's leaving. It felt hurtful. This girl who really was a large part of my last proper conversation with my son, had not seemingly cared as much as maybe Jack or I had hoped she had. I decided to write to her, and in order to do that I would need to write from Jack's Facebook page and continue the thread of messages between them. I was reaching out, I knew that. Reaching out to the girl his delicate heart had cherished. Connecting to her on the anniversary of his birthday. I had just written the first five or six words when DING a message arrived for Jack. How odd. I had been through his page and shut down all the messages from various gaming companies so who was this? There truly is no such thing as a coincidence, and everything in this world we live in really does happen for a reason. Our natural human response when our footing does not feel steady, is to blame those we love the most, and become insular in our thinking of others when we are protecting our young. A lesson for us all, to never make assumptions about anyone. I'll leave you with the message overleaf, dated 30 September, 2013, to Jack from Leila.

LEILA

This has taken a few days to put into some order, I tried writing but ended up making it almost story like. I guess it's hard for me to express all my thoughts and feelings. ♥ *The nights are drawing in, the air begins to cool, and the leaves on the trees begin to turn golden brown, the colours of warmth, fire, yet the wind is just so cold it's whipping my face, it's that time of year, a stark reminder that you're gone. Lately it hurts particularly bad.*

Every day is the same, head resting against the window whilst the world becomes a blur. My eyes see nothing but the memories you left behind, they swell up, salty tears roll down my cheeks. I remember where I am, eyes watching, the question on their lips. Pulling the sleeves over my hands to wipe my watery eyes, I shake my head and try to busy my mind.

I stand, and drag my feet to the doors, press the button, I have a headache. Strangers barge past me, pushing and shoving before I notice the doors open. Lazily, I drop my feet to the platform and out of habit look the opposite way I'm going. Turning my head to look at the faces, I look ahead, begin my lonely walk to college, trying to notice any differences in my surroundings to yesterday but I always seem to end up thinking of you, of what would happen if. What if I had...? The ifs and buts. I write letters to you in my head, but never finish them. My thoughts seem to be so fragmented, it's so easy to think you're listening to my thoughts, I hope you can.

I guess a lot of people feel a sense of guilt that maybe something could have been done. I could never regret that we had been together. I have some of the best memories with you but I wish that we could have communicated more. I guess neither of us wanted to hurt each other, we're both so sensitive. But we both ended up hurting one another in the end. I was heartbroken that you gave up on us and ended it over the internet without talking about it. And you were upset that I moved on a few months down the line. The fact is, you couldn't look at me and I couldn't look at you, it hurt so bad.

I wish I could have been quicker forgiving you with our ending and that we could have been on better terms faster. I wish that you knew I still cared for you, even after moving on. However, we began to talk and I particularly remember the time we were all sat down on the sofas in the shop. I was messing about with Lizzie and the voice predictive text controller on my phone, telling it silly messages and the predictive text getting it wrong. You came over and sat on the corner of the sofa next to me, we all sat there laughing together, that's when things got better, you joined in and we were talking normally. I have so many great memories with you, the first time I saw you, our trip to Guildford, and when you asked me out on the train, our first kiss, your incredible dancing, your smile, laugh, your warmth, I will never forget those.

The last day I saw you was Friday, I think after lunch in the shop. I was sat drawing for art at a table with Seb, you sat next to him and leant over. You were all smiles, I felt awful, I can't remember why, but you made me smile. You asked if I was OK. I nodded and asked you in return and you said you were fine, with a gleaming smile. You turned away. If only I knew, I would have held you so tight one more time.

Pointing to what would be the ring finger but on my right hand, I asked the tattoo artist for a string bow tattoo last week. I had entered a tattoo shop with Eric because I'm not brave enough to go by myself. We booked ourselves in this Thursday, the only time available. Although now it has been moved a week back. We decided we wanted to see what it was like before getting something big. On the internet I searched what my new tattoo would symbolise, it is the remembrance of someone who has passed. From the second I read it, I thought of you, and the colour purple. So I am determined to get this next week.

I feel I need some closure, I need to know what happened, your thoughts, but I'm not sure I'll ever know. Just typing this to you after planning to for months is making this a little, thoughts clearer, easier. I never wrote on your Facebook page when you passed. Gill thought it was rude of me, but it was far too hard to even… my eyes are watering… I must have jinxed myself. It was so hard to even put words together. I cried myself to sleep countless times. I felt your presence at that time though. Now I have put thoughts, although in a bit of a mess, in writing, maybe it's better for you, I know it's a bit better for me. I hope you know I care so much. I'm so grateful I was a part of your life and so happy you were a part of mine.

Anyway, I didn't mean this to be negative at all. It's your birthday tomorrow. I can't believe it's been a year. You're a beautiful person Jack, I hope that wherever you may be that you're flying high and free as a bird. I know that your presence is here with us all. I miss you so much. Happy Birthday you lovely, happy person. I feel at ease knowing that your spirit is free. I'll imagine us having a tea party tomorrow just for you.

I never stop thinking of you
Take Care Jack xxxx

My Jackaroo, my best friend. I will miss you forever xx

A smile to replace the moon.

Gone but I'll never forget you.

Contagiously smiley, and heart warmingly kind x

Whenever life gets me down, Jack reminds me to just keep dancing through it.

The coolest look, the warmest heart, wrapped up in purple.

Your bench keeps me company.

Jack's star will always shine bright in my heart

So quirky, flirty, kind, funny and absolutely 100% unique ♥ xxx

Sharing my thoughts with Jack keeps me going.

Such a fun loving, entertaining and caring friend

Jack I shine because of you.

Never change who you are.

A kind funny and true friend who I miss dearly.

Forever dancing across the stars.

Never will I retire your PS account, PurpleVine4 lives on forever.

A world so dark, you are our light, our Jack xxx